Blitzscaling security

Diary of a security engineer

Copyright © 2023 Sparc FLOW

To our little Danny boy

Important disclaimer

This book contains information about hacking techniques and is intended for educational purposes only. The examples and names used in this book are entirely fictitious and any resemblance to real individuals or organizations is purely coincidental. For instance, the company called Mirage in this book does not exist, nor do the links and URLs referring to its assets.

The tools and techniques presented are open source, and thus available to everyone. Investigators and pentesters use them regularly in assignments, but so do attackers. If you recently suffered a breach and found a technique or tool illustrated in this book, this neither incriminates the author of this book in any way, nor implies any connection between the author and the perpetrators.

Any actions and/or activities related to the material contained within this book are solely your responsibility. Misuse of the information in this book can result in criminal charges being brought against the persons in question. The author will not be held responsible in the event that any criminal charges are brought against any individuals using the information in this book to break the law.

Th is book does not promote hacking, software cracking, and/or piracy. All the information provided in this book is for educational purposes only. It will help companies secure their networks against the attacks presented, and it will help investigators assess the evidence collected during an incident.

Performing any hack attempts or tests without written permission from the owner of the computer system is illegal.

Content table

Prologue

When should a startup really invest in information security? Ask any seasoned consultant and their eyes will gleam at the opportunity of whipping out slides showing how the cost of fixing a vulnerability exponentially grows over time. *"Of course, you should strive to build security right from the start,"* they claim.

Alright. Allow me to elaborate then. Our startup is composed of three people. Two programmers who call themselves the CTO and VP of engineering, and a CEO who is actually closer to a product manager, accountant and office manager. When she is not dialing for dollars or thinking about customer experience, she is testing every line of code feverishly pushed to production by her two colleagues. The product is a mumble jumble of half-baked features, all once hailed as the "next big breakthrough". They don't know if their company will survive the next six months. Their runway cash surely won't. Product-market fit is still an elusive concept they only hear about in TED talks. Every hour they don't spend developing basic features is another missed opportunity to crack the puzzle of business growth before the competition. A missed opportunity to secure a roof over their heads. A missed opportunity to cast away the ever-looming feeling of failure.

Now, when should this startup invest in their first security engineer?

Maybe our consultant friend will shrug away any feeling of uneasiness and stick to their guns. Security is, after all, paramount to a company's success. But I want to argue a different stance that some security experts would dismiss as pure heresy: Forget about security. First, make it work.

However well-thought-out some online infosec preaching may appear, the truth is that many accepted security practices will latch your product to the ground while the competition acquires precious market share. Can you imagine talking about dynamic code analysis and network segmentation when the team is really just free-throwing ideas labelled as features to see what sticks to the wall? These are hard problems in computer security. The only people who refer to them as "the basics" never had the exquisite pleasure of implementing and maintaining them. Of course, it's easy to write tight firewall rules that only allow trusted protocols in the network, but can you deploy them safely without breaking the product or slowing down the dev team? How will you test new changes in a safe and controlled way? Should every new feature that makes a network call entail a request to update firewall rules? What's the impact on the feature's delivery time? Is it really worth it given your threat profile at this stage?

But I digress. We will get back to these particular problems later on in this book.

So, how should our typical startup handle its security at such a young age? I find it easier to make the analogy with performance. You don't buy a 3Tb-memory machine to host the alpha version of a product. An optimist who expects virality in the first 30 days may get a machine with 4Gb of RAM instead of 2Gb, but that's about it. It's much more sensible—and cheaper—to follow well-defined metrics and progressively increase the capacity of machines to match the projected user activity. In the early stages of a startup, it's a bad investment to spend days refactoring code to save a few milliseconds of execution. It would make more sense to just throw money at the problem: upscale the machine's capacity with the click of a button on the cloud console, and then focus on growth.

The same holds true for security. The threat of product failure dwarfs every other security risk one can imagine. It's the only risk that matters. Every vulnerability that does not directly contribute to this risk is fair game to accept *for now*. If using generic accounts speeds up publishing code, so be it. If figuring out AWS permissions is too darn hard, go with default policies. They're okay for now. Upgrading dependencies every week is a waste of time when you have 0 paying customers. Whatever helps you iterate faster is probably okay so long as it does not immediately threaten the livelihood of the product, i.e., publishing the admin panel on the Internet with test/test credentials is taking it a tad too far.

Reid Hoffmann, founder of LinkedIn, when talking about hyper growth in the startup world, refers to this early phase as the "Family" phase: less than 10 employees and a few would-be customers are trying out the product. Barely any revenue is coming in. The biggest goal of the Family phase is to reel in those early adopters. Understand what drives them to use the product, and quickly morph key characteristics of the product into features most customers actually want.

A company that succeeds in this phase slowly lifts off the ground by the sheer force of product-market fit. Investors, once a scarce breed, suddenly appear at every corner trying to get in on the action. The company raises its first or second round of funding around one core idea: scaling. They have the right formula, they've proved it at a tiny scale, now it's time to expand it to a larger audience, double down on the core features that fit their customer profile and hire a hundred people to make it happen. The company enters what Reid refers to as the "Tribe" phase, and *that's when you should start really caring about security*.

In this book, we will follow the journey of the first security engineer, Alex, hired by a scale-up to design and implement its first real security practices. You and I will dive into Alex's mind and embody their intellectual experience, from the first encounter with the company during the interview process all the way to their first months on the job.

We will follow their day-to-day interactions with other teams, the difficult but oh so important exercise of prioritizing vulnerabilities, the hard limits of technology and, most importantly, the phenomenal clash between common security wisdom and the hard reality of the field.

Such a position is not usually for entry-level engineers who have just started to tame their first exploits. It may happen, but it's not common, so our protagonist will have a background of a few years in penetration testing, which will color some of their reflexes and endeavors. Does that mean that it's the only path to break into the startup world and design secure systems? Absolutely not. I had to settle on an experience trait that I was familiar with and that was in continuity with my other books, so it made sense to go with this one.

One of the main goals of this book is to give you a peek at what it takes to implement practical security in a scale-up, so you can extrapolate the skills required and work on them. If you have a different background, great, you'll get to appreciate the world through a new lens, which will empower you in your day-to-day life. If you have no security background, don't worry, relax and enjoy the adventure. We'll take it step by step and explain everything from first principles with links for further reading. If you have a thriving career in penetration testing and designing secure systems, prepare for some controversial statements that will make you wince and hopefully rethink and challenge how you usually approach certain issues.

This book will swing between deep technical content and high-level overviews of both the security and the tech worlds. At first, I tried to avoid constraining the scenario to specific vendors and their shortcomings, but the narrative quickly acquired a bland and generic taste, so far away from the complexities of real-world issues. Security is easy on paper but very hard in real life. Therefore, we will dare to name some tech solutions, such as AWS, Kubernetes and GitLab. We will suffer their limitations and leverage their capabilities to build a secure environment. That being said, the principles that we will follow apply to any other technological environment, from Active Directory to Mainframes. Don't let the technological specificity fool you. My goal is to convey a thought pattern and structure to approach security, not nitpick tools and vendors.

I am shooting for timeless.

Little talks

"If you wish to make an apple pie from scratch, you must first invent the universe."

Carl Sagan

Hot pursuit

Our journey starts with the sound of a phone ringing on a cloudy Thursday afternoon...

We had been in the penetration industry for quite a few years now. Our team performed offensive attack simulations for companies, ranging from a small regional bank with three IT specialists stashed in the basement to a big Fortune 500 company with a fully staffed security team, compliance decks and state-of-the art detection engines. Yet, all of our summary meetings with clients started with the same slide: *"We successfully breached every machine in your company"*.

By the fifth pentest or red team engagement, it was bewildering how easy it could be to shatter a company to pieces because of a single mistake they made when configuring their Active Directory[1]. After a year or so of engagements, our colleagues stopped asking whether we successfully rooted the company. The question quickly became *how* we did it and in how many hours.

It's easy to reach new levels of nihilism when we have the unfortunate pleasure of auditing a client a second and a third time. We were so concise in our recommendations, yet the same vulnerabilities still welcomed us with wide-open arms inside the infrastructure. We could simply copy and paste the previous report, change the dates, and save our client 20 days' worth of work. We just cannot understand why they take these issues so lightly. Don't they see everyone around getting ransomed through the exact same vulnerabilities? Plus, they're easy to fix. Who can't upgrade a Java library? If only we had access to the machine, we'd be done in a day.

If only...

We slowly start picturing ourselves organizing the effort to patch a few thousand servers, scripting the whole thing using a dirty Python script.

---

[1] In many companies, almost all resources from user accounts to machines are bound together by Microsoft Active Directory, a configuration database orchestrated by a few select servers called "domain controllers". Read my book *How to Hack Like a Pornstar* (http://bit.ly/3VagyoV) to learn how to hack Active Directory environments.

No, that would never sit well with the compliance team. Their only concern is the average score according to the ISO 27001[2] norm enforced by clueless big auditing firms. We imagine reporting to the group Chief Information Security Officer (CISO), whose last technical prowess was racking Solaris machines in 1999. Not much fun either. No, that cannot possibly be what security looks like inside all corporations. Maybe if we were to join a scale-up free of bureaucracy and inertia, we could do things on our terms, like building a scalable and technical security team free of the shackles of norms and compliance requirements.

While browsing through security job offers, we spot a few companies that look gorgeous on paper: less than five years old, which means no untouchable legacy SAP with arcane technical constraints, and cloud-native, so it's easy to leverage the innovation of cloud providers in terms of security and scalability. Some of these companies even tout a working product with existing customers, so we'd have some job security for the next year or so.

We chat with a few of them and go as far as scheduling phone calls, but only one really stands out: a small expense management firm that allows their customers to easily handle invoicing and customer payments. They are looking for their first head of security. Today is the day we have a phone call with their talent manager and…

The phone is still ringing

Shit.

"Hello, I am Sarah, the talent manager for Mirage. We received your online application for a position of head of security. Do you have a few minutes to go over it?" says the joyful voice on the phone.

She starts the conversation with a couple of questions about Mirage, but apart from the initial job posting, we did not have time to check much information about the company. We politely ask for a quick presentation.

---

[2] The ISO 27001 is one of the most common security standards. It lists close to 149 controls that companies should enforce in order to protect their assets. It is often implemented by companies to prove their security maturity.

"No problem! Our story begins with Nate and Gabrielle," replies Sarah. "They started the company four years ago to revolutionize the way companies handle their expenses. They took on the challenge of simplifying invoicing, customer payments, team budgets, and other manual and tedious financial obligations. Our main customers are companies with a small finance team crumbling under the load of an ever-growing organization. They love the product and the attention to detail because it makes their lives so much easier. We doubled our number of employees to 120 and just recently raised a new round of funding from large venture capital firms to scale our business even more. The security of our clients is obviously important, so we are looking for a head of security to help us scale in a safe way."

"Can you tell me a bit more about yourself?" she adds as a follow-up.

The most natural way to answer this question is in a chronological fashion, faithful to the resume they certainly hold in their hands: *I graduated from this school, had my first job in this company, did this and that project and so on.* But here's a fact that few people care to admit: except for you, nobody really cares about your life story that much.

At this stage, a recruiter or a future boss is essentially looking to determine a few precious points: what can this person bring to the table? Do they have the skills to solve the issues at hand, and will they fit the company's culture? Any presentation of oneself should strive to answer these questions, not narrate one's life events as a Homerian novel.

In a lecture at MIT, available on YouTube *(http://bit.ly/3Ek6ZwZ)*, Patrick Winston beautifully synthesized it as presenting our vision and contributions. What problem can we solve for this company, and what interesting and innovative approach will we take to solve it? Patrick advocates for demonstrating this in under five minutes. My personal preference is three minutes. So, a candidate who spends ten minutes recounting their life's achievements, starting with their first internship, is not making the awesome impression they think they are.

Like many pentesters, we developed a plethora of skills during these few years of service, but there are really three that we want to highlight for this position, so we'll go with:

"I usually think of my skills as belonging to three segments. The first is technical expertise in offensive security. I conducted several penetration tests with my current employer where we simulated attacks and successfully breached many Fortune 500 companies, no matter what technology they were relying on. The second set of skills is helping companies build multi-year security programs, from securing workstations to rethinking their network architectures. Finally, the last skill relates to communication and flexibility. A vulnerability that is not properly communicated and understood by stakeholders is never fixed. I presented our findings to many board meetings where we had to translate complex attack scenarios into business-oriented risks to illustrate the importance of the ordeal."

This type of answer is guaranteed to stand out from the regular chronological trips down memory lane. Instead of passively narrating our life events, we demonstrate that we are the kind of person who reflects on their life, extracts value from their assignments and molds it into a new skill that serves a definite purpose. These are the attributes of a conscious learner. And that's the persona we're conveying.

The delivery is equally important, of course. First, we announce the three points we are going to make. This is not a random monologue that haphazardly finds its purpose along the way. No, the ideas are already clearly formulated in our mind. There will be three points. Not two, not four. Three. The punch line of each point is stated at the beginning as an easy-to-understand summary followed by a concrete example. We move from generic abstract principles to narrow and specific details. Picture a funnel that draws in large quantities of water to guide it to a specific destination. It's much easier for the brain of the listener to follow along as they're always anchored by that summary we provided beforehand.

Next, we highlight our vision and how these skills will help us achieve it and solve Mirage's problem:

"While working for my current employer, we tested the security of many financial institutions. A lot of them fail at security, either through impractical measures that never get truly enforced or useless processes that slow down the business and do not improve security. I like to take an innovative approach to security—one rooted in pragmatism and based on real-life attacks. Efficient security that promotes the business, acts as a competitive advantage and helps people get things done."

And that's our promise, the vision, the problem we will solve for Mirage that no one can.

Sarah continues with a few specific questions about challenging assignments, team collaboration and other points straight from the recruitment playbook. The pentesting world is rife with challenging assignments, so it's really the dealer's choice as to what particular example to take. The trap to avoid is losing the recruiter in the midst of explaining an NTLM relay attack just for the sake of accuracy. The real purpose of these questions is assessing how you approach a problem, test multiple solutions, get feedback and improve until you get satisfying results. The NTLM relay is just an excuse to demonstrate that thought pattern, so we're not going to get too hung up on implementation details.

After answering a few questions and helping the recruiter check off a few boxes, it's now our turn to quiz her. Interviews are a two-way street after all. We have a pretty clear idea about the kind of organization we want to join, so let's see if this one passes the test:

"From what I can see, Mirage is clearly growing fast. What is the current organization, and who will I report to should I accept the job?"

"Great question. The CTO currently relies on three engineering directors and a VP of engineering to manage the 60 people in the tech team. We have a Chief Risk Officer who holds internal control and compliance. Finally, the IT department, which handles workstations and the corporate platform, like Google Workspace and Salesforce, is attached to the CFO. To whom you would report is still an open question. Do you have an opinion on that?" Sarah asks candidly.

In the infosec industry? Yes, almost everyone does...

It is a tricky subject to bring up in the first few pages of a book but this question is likely to come up in almost every interview with a small company, so it is worth spending some time on.

The answer highly depends on the organization, established political power balance, culture and, of course, the affinities of the stakeholders involved. Large organizations of more than tens of thousands of employees tend to have multiple security teams. There may be one team in charge of building and supervising security solutions, a second team performing audits and penetration tests to make sure systems are indeed secure, and a third team dedicated to supporting developers, producing secure coding standards, reviewing product specifications, and so on. All or part of these teams could report to a single CISO, who is usually directly under the CEO. There is hardly any standard as each organization is subject to its own skill constraints, legacy organization, mergers, executive affinities and so forth.

Smaller organizations that do not have the luxury of resources often have no choice but to opt for a centralized team responsible for conducting the security symphony for the company. Now, much ink was wasted on the right placement of the CISO and her team. Should they be attached to the risk officer because security is a second-line team that only controls what has been implemented by other teams? Should they directly report to the founder or CEO? How about the board of directors to avoid conflict of interest? Should they be placed under the IT function because that's where the servers are? What if the IT function is under the Chief Financial Officer (CFO)? Is it wise then to lump security with finance to unlock budgets more easily? But hold on, security is largely a technical subject, isn't the chief technical/information officer (CTO or CIO) the most logical choice?

I would resolve these questions by saying that you can't go wrong with tying the security team to the executive function that has the largest sway over the company. Security is not only about infrastructure and code. It's about reviewing contractual clauses and hiring processes, product decisions and physical security in many cases. We can argue that it does not matter to whom the head of security or the CISO reports, what matters is that they have the proper latitude and credibility to reach out, and, most importantly, collaborate in a hands-on way with almost every other team in the company. A central security team that comfortably stays in the silos of its organizational unit, whether tech or internal controls or general audit, is doomed to fail. They need to reach out to other teams, gain credibility by performing hands-on tasks and lead by example. If they advise the legal department to add security clauses to the standard contract, they should schedule a meeting to talk it over and work together on a draft, not dump the work on the legal team's lap and revisit the issue three months later expecting it to be done. Whichever reporting line grants this freedom is probably the right move.

I have seen way too many security directors sigh in exasperation about some patch that was neglected for far too long by the IT team. "*I don't understand,*" they say, "*we sent them the report last month, it was clear as day that we were vulnerable to CVE-2021-34535.*" Should you ask if they followed up with them or if they thought about performing the upgrade together, you would get a resounding "*No, that's not our job. We're part of the audit team that reports to the CEO. We find vulnerabilities. It's their job to fix them.*"

And then people wonder why infosec is such a dumpster fire.

Now to circle back to the original question from our dear Sara about hierarchical position. I would reframe it as the following: *Which hierarchical attachment is likely to empower us the most in a scale-up?* Given that fintech scale-ups are mostly tech and product-driven, it makes sense to either report to the CTO or the Chief Product Officer (CPO). I would not advise reporting to lower management spheres like director of development or director of IT. We need someone with executive power to sign off on the most strategic decisions and support some difficult changes that will probably impact the whole company. You cannot count on an intermediary to explain the nuances of the risk tradeoffs behind complex decisions. Much will be lost in translation.

"Sarah, I would like to report to the CTO if possible. However, keep in mind that it is a transverse topic that will probably touch many teams. Whoever my boss is, I want to have a large scope of action, ranging from legal to tech. In essence I want *carte blanche* to poke my nose anywhere and propose fixes that we implement together with each team. What do you say?"

"That's great," she replies. "I will provide this feedback to the hiring team. I think we're all set for this interview. I just need to know your current salary and expectations for this position."

That's a trap.

There's no other way of putting it. Give them your real actual salary and they will wield it as a weapon to slash down your future compensation. Even the friendliest and most well-intentioned recruiter will subconsciously base the new offer on your current package in what psychologists have dubbed the "priming" or "suggestion effect" *(https://thedecisionlab.com/biases/priming).*

"We are barely in the getting to know each other phase. Plus, I am sure you have an internal grid for handling the compensation package for this type of position. I would like to make sure we are the right fit for each other before discussing compensation. It's pointless otherwise." We respond.

Sarah politely understands and wraps up the conversation with a promise to send us an email with the next steps should Mirage decide to go forward with the process.

Stubborn recruiters in a feat of craftiness will rephrase the question in some shape or form later in the discussion. *"We're a small company without a fixed compensation grid"* or *"this a new skillset that we don't know how to properly price."* Some will even boldly state *"we need this number to move the process forward."* The reality underlying this charade is a form of power game. Plain and simple.

I had many recruiters appeal to a sort of moral authority to rebuke the salary I requested after I faltered and disclosed my current salary. *"You cannot possibly request a 25% increase on your current compensation,"* they denounced in outrage. In what world is it anyone's concern how much money another person makes changing jobs? Maybe you are underpaid in your current job. Will you carry that malus with you to your next job? I hope not.

If one is really hard pressed to answer the salary question, the most elegant form of answer is to hijack the frame and the narrative. The recruiter sees us as this potential candidate transitioning from job A to job B and so they cannot help but establish a line of comparison between the two jobs. We need to seize this frame, throw it away and make them see the situation through our lens.

"You're looking for a head of security who reports to a C-level, probably the CTO. This person has to build the entire security of Mirage, which is vital for its growth and success. You need a technical expert who can cut through the noise of security and actually implement decent measures that do not slow down production and development. This person also needs to build and structure a team, coach them and help on legal and risk assessment questions. I demonstrated that experience in my previous assignments and find that a proper compensation for these duties is X."

The discussion is no longer about comparing salaries. Our new frame includes a vision of what we want to achieve together. It highlights the unique qualities required to achieve that vision and states a price for achieving it. It's not a negotiation. It's a statement. We don't give a salary range; we give the exact amount we deem reasonable for these duties. People don't negotiate the price on Amazon. They read the description and choose whether to hit the buy button or continue shopping.

I will not go into the actual amount one should ask because the answer highly depends on the market, geography and so many other factors. Instead, ask people who occupy similar jobs, go through many interviews and get a feeling of the current market price for your skills. What I will insist on, though, is that you ask for equity in a scale-up. Equity is an ownership of the company in the form of shares or options.

Salary is great. But equity rules. I wish someone told me that back in the day. Successful[3] scale-ups will easily double their revenue every year for the first five years, which means that their valuation—and therefore the price of their stock—will likely follow a similar trend. I can assure you that your base salary won't. So, ask for equity from the get-go. That's the real end game for joining a scale-up: stock options, restricted stock options, free shares, whatever their policy is. If you're not familiar with the topic, take a look at the article titled Equity 101 by Gergely Orosz *https://blog.pragmaticengineer.com/equity-for-software-engineers/.*

Salary discussion and negotiation are deep topics in their own right. There are countless articles about achieving the best possible deal, from negotiation tactics detailed in the book *Influence* by Robert Cialdini to Patrick McKenzie's blog post *https://www.kalzumeus.com/2012/01/23/salary-negotiation.* I just wanted to brush over some key points that can greatly help you land a better deal.

---

[3] "Successful" is the key word in that sentence. The crushing majority of startups fail miserably for any number of reasons. Furthermore, equity won't immediately pay your rent, food and other expenses. So, find the proper balance between cash and equity that fits your lifestyle and investment strategies.

Messy tech

No sooner than the evening, we get an invitation to our first interview with the tech team at Mirage.

We research the two people copied in the email: Marc and Tony. Marc is the director of infrastructure. According to his business profile, he joined Mirage six months ago. He held the same position at another scale-up for about a year, managing a team of 10 people and administering a cloud platform. Though he has dipped his toes into the cloud environment in his previous companies, he has solely held a management position lately.

Tony is a whole other specimen. He is a backend staff engineer who has been with Mirage for three years now, almost since the official launch of the company. His public GitHub repo has many samples of cryptographic methods and random number generators written in Golang and C++. Pretty decent work.

The invitation sent by Sarah lays out the interview process. We'll talk to Marc and Tony for about an hour and a half, which includes a technical skill.

Wait—what?

More and more startups and scale-ups are borrowing the entire hiring textbook of big tech companies like Google and Facebook. Somewhere in this unholy tome must be a dedicated chapter about technical interviews and whiteboard brain-fuck exercises. Never mind the sheer stupidity of basing your hiring strategy on a company whose head count is three orders of magnitude bigger than your barely surviving enterprise, in most cases, the technical test has no relevance whatsoever to the actual day-to-day job. It's uncanny!

Some companies are famous for their eccentric hiring strategies. Peter Thiel at PayPal reportedly liked to throw math puzzles at people to assess their cognitive abilities[4]. He wanted to recruit problem solvers and analytical people who could reason from first principles and not simply replicate what they did in their previous jobs. Fair enough. He liked math puzzles and chess, so he quizzed people about math puzzles. It's one thing to define a set of traits that would fit the culture of the company and then test for these traits. It's quite another to blindly copy the process of your previously successful and bigger employer and start asking people to implement a sorting algorithm on a whiteboard.

---

[4] As reported in the book *The Founders: The Story of Paypal and the Entrepreneurs Who Shaped Silicon Valley.*

Google may need people who can achieve a tiny bit of edge in their already established computing platform, but a startup most likely does not. It's even more fallacious to use these tests and exercises as proxies for the skills required day to day to achieve success. It's gotten so bad that people spend days studying linked lists, reversing binary trees and other frivolities just for the purpose of passing interviews. Interviews that land them jobs writing web apps in high-level frameworks. What a waste of time.

I once interviewed for a tech startup in San Francisco for a lead security engineer position. They wanted someone to build the security strategy of this company of 40 people. Exciting job, for sure. Twenty minutes after my meeting with the VP of engineering, he sends me a skill test to—*wait for it*—recursively flatten an array and extract the largest 10 numbers from a very large file.

This company figured it out alright! The crux of security, the cure to all vulnerabilities and the elixir of life is, of course, algorithmic complexity! How mind-numbingly clueless do you have to be to copycat dubious recruitment strategies that have no bearing whatsoever on the actual skills required for the job?

Not that I undervalue algorithmic topics, far from it, but if I wanted to probe the skills of the person in charge of designing the security of my company, I would explore 50 other technical skills before bringing up a top-K algorithm: AWS quirky S3 permissions, Linux capabilities, container hardening, web application vulnerabilities and so many more topics. And those are only the tech skills. One should also probe relational skills, communication and prioritization. You don't have to take my word for it; we will get to live it later on this book with concrete scenarios.

So, what did I respond to this array-flattening company? A cold email commanding them to shove the exercise somewhere ugly? A sanctimonious reminder of what security really is about? Sadly, no. I decided to give them the benefit of the doubt: "*oh well, it must be a classic HR process. I'll just write the damn thing quickly and send it.*" I sent over my code and got greeted with a congratulatory message asking me to book an additional hour to debrief about the code…

Hell no. When are we going to talk about security, for fuck's sake?! I kindly thanked them for their reply and stopped the process right there. It felt good.

I understand that this reply comes from a position of comfort and stability. If you are desperate to land a job, you will jump through any hoop they throw at you. Beggars can't be choosers. My only advice to prospective candidates in this case is to work hard and smart to build a set of skills that will grant you that bargaining power and therefore maximum freedom of choice. Call it a diploma, a certification, open-source projects, conference talks, blog posts, rants on social media... These are all valid levers you wield in front of recruiters, future colleagues and bosses to adamantly stick to your position.

So, what do we do about Mirage? We visit their online product and it really looks great. The technical stack is full-on cloud-native, in line with what we want to do. What's an hour and half of interview? In the worst-case scenario, if they bring out that dreadful whiteboard and quiz us about the merge-sort algorithm, we'll reply back with a question about the Feistel diagram used in some encryption block-ciphers. After all, anyone can play the who's-got-the-biggest-spiel contest. The interviewer just has the privilege and advantage of going first.

**

Fast forward to the day of the meeting. We're greeted on site by Tony, who gives us the classic we-have-a-fun-office tour: beer tap, foosball table and a kitchen full of top of the shelf, bottom of the flavor organic candy. It's understandable for startups to create the best environment to foster employee relationships, help them forget the long hours and create a sense of camaraderie to push the boundaries of hard work. I admire the sentiment, but I adamantly believe that if companies really want people bending over backward to deliver the best product possible, it's often wiser and more efficient to give them equity. Equity and a mission. I like to foosball as much as the next hacker, but I'd rather bust my ass for equity that will multiply ten or twenty times in a few years. Then I'll get my own foosball table.

After a rather brief tour of the office, we join Marc in a small meeting room to start the interview. We start with the classic round of introductions. Each of them takes their turn, detailing their previous experiences working for various companies, building platforms, deploying software and so on. We're tempted to follow their lead, but we know better than to spew our resume in a chronological fashion. We deliver our rehearsed presentation about our three main skills—technical expertise in penetration testing, designing security programs for companies and communication skills—and how they are going to help the company achieve better security.

"Very clear, thank you. Could you tell us more about your penetration testing engagements?" asks Marc.

See what happened? Marc did not go probing into some obscure skill we developed seven years ago in a faded internship. He naturally chose one of the three cards we presented to him: penetration testing, security programs and communication. That's a powerful way to steer the interview to your advantage right from the start.

"We usually work in teams of two, where I act as the project lead and organize the audit test cases, from collecting requirements to scheduling the assessment dates. We agree on the threats they want to model and play them out. Say they want to test whether an employee's workstation has been compromised. They hand us the credentials to access a computer and we start our exploration phase: We discover machines on the network, the services they are hosting, whether they have default credentials and so on. Most of our clients run a Windows environment so we try a combination of attacks: NTLM relay[5], where we position ourselves between a client and a server to grab password hashes. We bruteforce the local administrator account across all Windows machines, and we comb through Active Directory shares looking for hardcoded secrets in admin commands, such as `psexec` (a tool for remote command execution) or `mssql` (a tool for interacting with SQL servers) commands.

In 90% of the cases, at least one of these methods yields a valid admin account. We then propagate laterally using pass the hash and dumping clear text passwords until we get full control of all the machines. From then on, we target the most valuable business data, often the CEO's email inbox, HR files, and so on. Sometimes we run into some form of fancy detection box, but it never really makes a difference for several reasons that we can get into if you want."

"Very interesting," replies Marc. "I don't think we have Windows machines here, do we Tony? Maybe a couple of accounting servers. But 90% of our employees are on MacOS. Our production platform is running on AWS. Our emails are on Google workspace. Are you comfortable with this technical environment? How would you tackle a cloud-native environment based on AWS?"

---

[5] Intro to NTLM relay: http://bit.ly/3Xg01le by hackndo. Also check out practical NTLM relay by byt3bl33d3r http://bit.ly/3EhakNg.

The only reason we're even considering this job is because the company is fully cloud-native. No money in the world could ever persuade us to take on the responsibility of securing an on-premises Windows Active Directory platform. As I am writing this, it's easy to imagine people shaking their fists in the air in protest. I was once called a technology racist for stating that opinion in a gathering of security professionals. True story. But hear me out. I am not saying that Mac or even AWS are more secure than Windows. All I am saying is that every week I see Windows admins clench their butts to weather yet another massively exploited vulnerability that propagates like wildfire between workstations and servers. I do not like butt clenching.

"I did a few assignments on AWS, and I have a personal account where I simulate some common faulty configurations. I've dabbled in S3's twisted security policies, AWS IAM roles and the flexibility they provide in avoiding hardcoded permanent credentials, but I am not an AWS-certified expert. Not yet anyway. But I will learn. I will investigate how we can abuse each and every setting of the AWS services used by Mirage and help you tweak them to get the best protection against a given threat scenario. Penetration tests are all about rapidly adapting to new contexts and technologies. I had to quickly acquire knowledge about SAP and z/OS mainframes and their inner workings for an audit…I am more than excited to explore AWS and find its darkest secrets."

"Oh, you worked on mainframes? My first internship was on an AS/400 writing COBOL," Marc exclaims.

The discussion takes a weird turn as we compare notes about the quirks of the mainframe world. A sense of camaraderie almost started to blossom as we recounted our common struggle with obscure JCL syntax, which is the scripting language on mainframes. Tony lets the show go on for a minute or two before forcefully steering the conversation to the present and bringing up what seems to be a sore subject for the team:

"We recently had a penetration test on our web application. The results were rather dire. We don't know what to do about some CORS and CSRF issues they highlighted. How do you plan to resolve them?" asks Tony.

Cross-Origin Resource Sharing (CORS) is browser mechanism that allows website A to use JavaScript to make a call to website B and retrieve the response, in direct violation of the famous Same-Origin Policy protection. Mozilla showcases this security setting rather well *(http://bit.ly/3EMjNO4)*. When severely misconfigured, it can be abused by malicious or hacked websites to scrape information from other websites you're logged in on, such as your bank's website. Cross-Site Request Forgery (CSRF) *(http://bit.ly/3Ve7saC)* appears when actions on a website are performed through simple, predictable HTTP requests. In which case, any website can send unsolicited requests through JavaScript to these HTTP endpoints to make wire transfers or password resets, unbeknownst to the user currently visiting them.

"Are they affecting critical actions and resources such as password renewal forms, payment initiation and so on?"

"I don't think so. We require SMS OTP for most of these actions," Tony blurts out.

"I don't mean to be too blunt, but honestly, unless CORS settings are severely misconfigured and allow the whole Internet to query banking endpoint, I don't think CORS issues and CSRF will likely crack the top 10 technical issues we will start working on. They don't present a fair enough gain/difficulty-to-exploit ratio and have a hard time scaling for small unknown targets like Mirage. I bet there are more direct attack scenarios that we should first look into: Do you require multi-factor authentication at log in? Are permissions properly set up on all S3 buckets[6]? Do you have tight user right segregation in the app? Are all public endpoints accounted for? How about container hardening? I think we're better off talking about these subjects and many others rather than CORS and CSRF."

They genuinely look stunned. We just dismissed their question and bombarded them with several rhetorical questions to which they certainly have no answer. It may seem like a cocky response in an interview, but remember that this company is looking to build its security practice from the ground up. They need someone who can assert an opinion and prioritize issues based on their expertise and knowledge of the field. What better way to demonstrate it than to drive the conversation away from what could be trivial bugs and focus on actual vulnerabilities exploited in the wild by countless attackers.

---

[6] AWS S3 is a highly redundant and cheap storage service offered by Amazon. Objects are organized into buckets. Each bucket has a unique name (and URL) across all AWS accounts: *https://aws.amazon.com/s3/.*

We continue chatting about web vulnerabilities, from SQL injections to remote code execution[7]. Tony, who's much more familiar with coding practices, throws in a few short questions about mitigating each vulnerability. We recall the hundreds of reports written about prepared statements and special character encoding in almost every programming language and answer in a straightforward fashion. After a few minutes, Marc declares:

"It's time for the technical challenge. Are you ready?"

Huh, no? But I doubt that qualifies as an answer, so we politely reply back, "Yes, of course."

"Alright. Well, we don't really have a security expert with us so we did not really know what kind of technical skill is most appropriate in your field. We managed to compile a list of questions about programming and infrastructure. We'll go through it now if that's okay with you."

"We'll start with a little bit of cryptography," says Tony.

Hu-ho...They proceed to write down the following string on the whiteboard and turn to us expectantly:

ECDHE-ECDSA-AES128-GCM-SHA256

"That's a cipher suite used when configuring SSL connections," we reply confidently. "It instructs the server to propose to the client the following algorithms: Elliptic curve Diffie-Hellman Ephemeral (ECDHE) for key exchange, Elliptic curve Digital Signature Algorithm (ECDSA) for signing payloads, AES with 128 bits key in GCM mode for encryption traffic and SHA-256 for hashing."

They follow up with a question about the internal working of AES. We manage to recall some old cryptography lessons and cook a half-baked response:

"My crypto is really rusty. I think AES is based on S-boxes, multiple rounds each with their own derived keys, but I cannot recall how many rounds—maybe 16?"

"10, actually, for 128 bits," corrects Tony

Ouch...

---

[7] SQL injection *(http://bit.ly/3UPnYhz)* and remote code *(http://bit.ly/3Xe8Qfo)* execution according to OWASP.

"Let's move on. How does GCM mode work? And is it better than ECB?"

They're quite insistent on cryptography. We explain how GCM adds authentication to the encryption process, that it's based on encrypting a counter and XORing it with the plaintext[8]. We give examples of ECB shortcomings, such as replaying or rearranging ciphertext, all of which are due to the fact that ECB has no feedback loop when encrypting more than one block of bytes.

They seem satisfied with the answer, but then Marc takes the interview to awkward town:

"Alright. Let's talk about infrastructure. Do you know how Cassandra and Kafka work? How would you secure them?" he asks.

"I've never had the opportunity to work on these components," we reply after a moment's hesitation, "but I would follow the same approach I've used countless times: install them on my lab, tweak their configurations to mimic commonly deployed settings, and find ways to abuse what they're supposed to do. Do they accept input through common protocols such as HTTP or do they use a custom protocol? How do they handle authentication? Authorization? Can I spoof an existing session? How do they handle malformed packets? And so on? I wish I had the actual answer for Kafka and Cassandra, but I'd have to dig into them."

It's a shame we don't have an immediate answer. We don't even know what Kafka is, but that's the best we can muster in the moment.

"Ok, let's step back then and talk about AWS a little bit," says Marc.

This goes on for a few more minutes, but we manage to get every AWS question down: AWS trust policies, resource policies and so on. Their technical questions are very focused on the exact setup they seem to have deployed. All those years pwning Windows seem frustratingly useless in this interview. But one has to see the silver lining, at least nobody is making us write a merge sort algorithm on a whiteboard.

Toward the end of the technical test, they invite us to ask questions about the company's technical stack...*oh, it's payback time.*

"Yes, actually your questions did make me curious about your AWS setup. What does the global architecture look like?"

---

[8] If you are interested in cryptography, the book *Serious Cryptography* by Jean-Philippe Aumasson *(https://nostarch.com/seriouscrypto)* breaks it down in a fascinating way.

Marc proceeds to explain that they only have one AWS account hosting everything from the core banking applications to the GitLab code repository. They have around 50 microservices that gravitate around a single historical monolith. A number of apps share the same AWS IAM user[9]. Tony interjects candidly that some passwords are even written in clear text in the code.

"We would like to use state-of-the-art secret management solutions, but we have no bandwidth to work on that," admits Marc almost apologetically. "We embrace the DevOps philosophy where we empower developers to take control of the infrastructure, so all 60 tech people have access to AWS and can interact with the services. We're thinking of transitioning to a multi-account configuration but it's challenging." says Marc.

Clear-text passwords, staging resources mixed with production workloads, mixed IAM users, and yet they wanted to talk about CORS and CSRF…

They did mention, however, an interesting concept that is worth pursuing further in this interview:

"I like the concept of DevOps, and that's how I imagine us working together. I am not interested in opening tickets and asking developers or the infrastructure engineers to deploy a secret management solution. I would like us to work closely together, agree on a technical solution and implement it together, either through a joint project involving both of our teams, or through a project led by the security team with async feedback and regular check points with other teams. Or vice-versa. This sense of strong ownership is, I believe, the only way we can get things done."

Both of them cheer up: "Perfect, this way of working suits us as well."

We continue chatting for a while and then conclude the interview.

As we exit the meeting, we cannot help but feel a sense of accomplishment. There were some hits and misses but, overall, it went alright, no? It's true that our heavy Windows background did not score any meaningful points. Busting the question about AES encryption rounds and the weak response to GCM mode did not really help either. Kafka was a disaster…As we ride the tube back home, we cannot think of a worse interview.

The phone rings the same evening.

---

[9] IAM is the identity access management service of AWS. A user represents an elementary unit that can have permissions to interact with other AWS services: S3, RDS (databases), EC2 (virtual machines), etc.

"Hey, Alex. It's Sarah, do you have a minute? I wanted to get your feedback on the interview you had today. How did it go?"

You know exactly how it went. Why should we go first?

We tell her about our missed technical questions, but stress the quality of the exchange and the well-rounded conversation we had with Marc and Tony.

"Great to hear that! Well, I am delighted to share that both Marc and Tony gave us great feedback about your performance. They loved your practical approach to security, your technical knowledge and willingness to learn and evolve. This is fully in line with our company values," Sarah says gleefully.

"Well, that's good news!" we cheerfully reply.

"It is! So, I understand from your tone that you want to continue the recruitment process with us," she says, "Your next and final interview would be with our CTO, Henry."

We set up the details of the meeting, gracefully finish the call and crash on the sofa with a sigh of relief...

When you think about it, the skills you utilize in your daily work are so vastly different from the academic teachings and requirements of most interviews that it's really crazy to nitpick on this or that technical question. So what if we don't know that AES relies on 10 rounds to encrypt data? First of all, a simple Google search would give us the information, and second, how is that relevant to hacking or even securing a company? I understand the need to make sure that the candidate has a minimum level of technical knowledge, but the ability to recall facts or numbers should not be the only proxy to that end.

A lot of recruiters and managers look for experience: they want someone who has already secured an AWS environment. They want someone who has already worked in a tech scale-up, and so on. This rigidity unfortunately excludes so many bright, new, talented people who may well forge the future of the company. Eric Schmidt said it best in an interview: *"The industry overvalues experience and undervalues intellectual flexibility and strategic thinking."*[10] Experience is not necessarily the sacred stamp that everyone takes it to be. It is hard to distinguish a ten-year experience from one year of experience repeated ten times. If anything, those ten years of experience should trigger a deeper inspection into the innovation that was produced during such a large timeframe and how it shaped the candidate's way of thinking.

---

[10] *http://bit.ly/3EmsBc3.*

The final stage

How do you prepare for a C-level interview? It's not like they are going to quiz us on Linux hardening techniques...are they? We look up Henry's profile, searching for potential clues: he was the CTO of an e-commerce company for about two years, chained a couple gigs as VP of engineering before that...and he has an active GitHub account full of unfinished projects to optimize this or that library in Golang, Python and other languages. Odd for a CTO to be this hands-on. He very well might take us down a rabbit hole during the interview. This will be fun!

We come to the dreaded interview day. Henry welcomes us at the lobby and takes us to a meeting room on the first floor. He sits down and immediately takes control of the room:

"Tony and Marc already briefed me about your technical background. I went through your online resume. It's very clear and detailed. I think I have a pretty clear picture of your work experience so far. The first question that comes to my mind is what are you going to do when you join us?"

He is not fucking about. A very direct question that cuts through the small talk and unnecessary details.

This type of vague, all-encompassing question is not an invitation to recount your most heroic hacking experience. This is a question that requires a step back from the everyday tasks to explain the operating model one follows to perform their duties. In essence, how do we tackle the problem of security in a company, and how do we prioritize one task over another? This is the underlying meaning behind such a question.

"Every discussion about security involves two key questions: what are we trying to protect, and who are we protecting against? Mirage is a payment institution, so I guess we're protecting customer balances and transactions, payment means, employee information and so on. The company is still small enough to stay under the radar of nation state attacks, so let's cap our threat level at organized crimes with under $300k resources, about the price of a couple of zero-days, okay? It's just an arbitrary threshold that we can later adjust."

"The best way to approach this, in my opinion, is to build an attack graph with, on the far-left, attackers with different resources and access: simple robot scanner, a lonely hacker, an advanced hacking team, a compromised employee and so on. And on the far-right: the customer database, servers, S3 buckets holding data, etc. I will leverage my experience as a penetration tester to identify every possible direct or indirect link between the two extremities of this graph. To give an example, say I could find a web vulnerability in the app that allows me to download a file, and that file includes a hardcoded password that I can use to connect to the database because of unfiltered firewall rules. This database runs on a server that has AWS credentials with overly permissive access that grant me access to all S3 objects and therefore all customer data. That's a multi-hop link that can be followed by any hacker with an account on your platform, for instance."

We pause for a second, and then continue: "After we assemble this graph, we can assign weight to edges (vulnerabilities) depending on the complexity of the attack and its impact. That way, we get a helicopter view of all the potential weaknesses and confidently identify the most pressing issues to remediate. We're not just fixing the first issues that we stumble upon, stuck in an improvisation loop. No, we're consciously choosing this or that flaw to fix because it can be more easily exploited by attackers, as demonstrated by our attack graph. We continuously update this graph as we add new features, discover new vulnerabilities and so on."

Henry does not seem impressed at all. He casually retorts back: "Alright, you build a list of all vulnerabilities, but how do you objectively know which item deserves this or that score?"

"I am sorry to insist but it's not a list. It's a graph of vulnerabilities and assets that yields a list of actions. When considered as an entry in a list, a given weakness may not seem that important, but when placed in its context along with other vulnerabilities, suddenly a previously concealed exploit path emerges that can be deadly to an organization."

We pause for five seconds to let that sink in. We then continue:

"Attackers chain vulnerabilities and misconfigurations. We must see the world through their eyes to understand what to prioritize. I spent years exploiting vulnerabilities and hacking companies. I have seen so many teams waste their time hunting for TLSv1.0 configurations while they have vulnerable, out-of-date VPN appliances exposed on the web. I can think as an attacker. I acted as an attacker so I know how to weigh attack paths based on probability, ease of exploitation, signal-to-noise ratio, and so on. And that's what I am bringing to the table," we reply.

"Thank you for the clear articulation of your vision. Now, say you join us and you successfully follow your ambitious plan of patching up one vulnerability after the other. How do you know that you're succeeding in your mission in making Mirage more secure? I know it's a tough and abstract question, especially in security where it's hard to tangibly assess results, but I am curious to have your take on it."

He landed a valid point. It's much easier to refute the security of a system than to prove it. We may find and even fix a vulnerability in a point in time, but preventing it from popping up somewhere else is an entirely different problem. A harder one.

We think about it for a few seconds: "I find that the NIST cybersecurity framework *(http://bit.ly/3AspDS0)* is the best way to model this problem. It proposes to tackle security issues through a set of five actions: identify, protect, detect, respond and recover. For each critical asset that we have identified, we need a set of protective measures. These measures will drastically reduce the attack surface but will surely suffer from blind spots: new vulnerabilities and technical limitations among other things. So, we supplement these protections with a set of detection rules. Should any of these rules get triggered we must be able to quickly respond and investigate the issue. That means a proper incident response procedure, team members with the necessary skills and so on. Finally, should the investigation reveal a compromised asset, we must remediate efficiently.

Just like in a whack a mole game, a company with little security maturity will mostly juggle between the identify and protect steps. It's a rat race where most companies get trapped for years. You secure the fifteenth app just in time for the sixteenth app to show its nose, full of vulnerabilities that you thought were gone for good. As we gain more security maturity, the challenge will slowly shift from identifying assets to generalizing protection and detection measures. Our threat models will also evolve. We'll no longer be struggling to protect against robots scanning the Internet or opportunistic attackers. We'll be debating how to protect against organized crime and hackers with meaningful resources. New vulnerabilities will no longer be caused by design flaws or systemic issues in our systems. They would be localized, proactively detected and quickly remediated. That's the trend I expect us to be on when we're succeeding in security."

Henry responds back: "Let me rephrase then. Your key performance indicators are the number of vulnerabilities we report, when they are introduced in the production cycle—design phase versus development versus release—and the type of actions the security team is focusing on according the NIST framework. That's an interesting way to put it."

We feel like we've cleared the first check box as Henry pauses the relentless questioning for a second and spontaneously starts describing the development cycle of a new feature at Mirage.

First, the product managers aggregate customer needs, tear down the competition and write a specification document for a given feature. This document is then handed over to a team of developers to produce a technical analysis and an implementation proposal, i.e., what are the key technical components required to ship this feature given the success goals of the specification document? Only when this document is validated does the coding actually begin, which is followed by the traditional peer reviews and quality assurance.

"Mainstream tech companies popularized the iterative approach to coding: move fast and break things, as Facebook famously preached. However, not all iterations are equal. Iterations used to validate a feature idea or a customer behavior leads to business learning. We want more of those. Iterations because the previously delivered component—specification document, technical document, feature—is faulty and cannot move to the next phase are a waste of time. We'd rather spend more time on sound design that guarantees fewer defects, more focus, and a faster production pace. We do prototype, of course, but we prototype to support a design or business hypothesis, not to luckily stumble onto the best design through blind iteration. That's, in a nutshell, how our engineering team works. Your challenge, I presume, would be to fit into that model and define the principles of a secure design," says Henry.

That's interesting way to approach software development but is certainly not innovative. Back in the fifties and sixties, when code was punched into cardboards and manually inserted into a machine for compilations that lasted hours, one certainly could not so easily iterate their way out of a problem. Programmers would spend days designing and writing their code so that it would work on the first try because compilation time was a matter of hours. There was simply no other way. Here is a company more than half a century later that embraces those same ancestral concepts and bets its entire future on them.

We continue listening to Henry talk about production cycles and constraints. It is refreshing for a pentester, whose only concern has been about breaking systems, to discover the hidden facet of designing systems and factories to produce something in this world. After a long monologue, Henry asks us the following question: "Alright, Alex, imagine you decide to join us at Mirage. How can I help you succeed in your mission?"

"I have seen, time and time again, security being relegated to the deepest corners of the corporate attic. Simple spectators of a business of which they're no longer a part. To be fair, I also have seen the extreme opposite: a security department so rigid and risk-averse that it almost destroys any business initiative. I want neither. I want to build a security system that gives Mirage a competitive advantage. A system that allows it to take measured and calculated risks to achieve its full market potential. For that, we need a good deal of creativity and innovation. I want *carte blanche* over the security roadmap: what to prioritize, how to work on it and how to deliver it. I want the security team to actively work with other teams. That entails permission to submit code changes, infrastructure upgrades and so on. I will, of course, justify any measure we put in place and any budget request, and I will follow standard practices, but I want your honest and full support in this endeavor."

Henry locks his gaze on us for a brief second, as if evaluating the hidden implications of this bold request, then replies sternly:

"Understood. Our goal is to build the most intuitive and simple payment platform on the market. Our whole business rests on the trust of our customers. Without it, we're done. The security of our platform is, therefore, critical to me. We're not a big company with rigid process and meaningless bureaucracy. You can and should take on any project that boosts the business and its security. I am expecting you to get things done. Whether you use the keyboard to do it or arrange a deal with other teams is up to you. In any case, I will support you to make it happen. About budgets, if you make a rational case for a tool or a solution, I will approve it. We're not at the stage of cutting costs. Between spending two weeks developing a custom solution and spending $10k on a ready-to-use product that does the same thing, I am expecting you to choose the latter if everything else is equal."

One cannot hope for a better answer.

"Awesome," we reply. "I cannot wait to join the team of 60 engineers!"

"70 engineers," he corrects. "By the time you'll be joining us, we will probably be 100 in the tech department alone. Get ready to work at scale."

We finish the meeting by discussing the desired salary and equity allocation and part ways.

The next day, Sarah calls us with a job offer. We got the position!

Shellshock

"The first principle is that you must not fool yourself, and you are the easiest person to fool."

Richard P. Feynman

Today is our first day at Mirage. There is excitement in the air as we step inside the four-floor building hosting the company's staff. There are a dozen people waiting at the reception, each of them projecting that characteristic nervousness of first-day starters. We receive a tag name that we proudly stick on our chest like the rest of the cohort, a bag full of company branded can openers, socks and what have you. And, of course, a computer.

Rough start

We sit through the first presentation led by Nate, co-founder of the company. He starts with the founding story, a paramount piece of the company's identity and culture, but also probably the most well-rehearsed pitch in his repertoire. He depicts his struggle as an e-commerce entrepreneur to accept payments, manage revenue, handle their finances and so on. When meeting long-term acolyte Gabrielle one fateful night, they rejoiced in each other's war stories about handling payments. All this built-up frustration and angst that each harbored fueled the genesis of what now became Mirage.

A beautiful story that left everyone in the room hanging between a feeling of awe and deep disappointment: everyone knew that banking was a horrible experience. That was hardly the idea of the century. Yet, somehow, only these two people who had the temerity to do something about it.

Nate went on to describe the business model of the company. As a payment provider, they receive a few percentage points of every card transaction on the merchants' websites. Merchants can also subscribe to cutting-edge features, such as automatic invoicing and other fancy accounting features that help boost Mirage's revenue.

A new joiner in the audience raised his hand and asked the question on everyone's mind:

"Is the company profitable yet?"

Nate chuckles and gleefully responds: "Of course not. We could be profitable if we dialed down our growth investments, but our goal is not to be profitable. We want to conquer the two markets we penetrated and expand worldwide. Profitability will naturally follow."

The presentation ended on a slide with four bold-printed values: Curiosity, User obsession, Mastery and Courage. Nate went on to explain:

"Values are usually cute and inspiring terms coined by big companies to please HR and only prove useful to nag candidates in interviews. That's not the case here. We truly use our values as decision-making tools. When we have doubts about a feature, we go back to the customer and see the world through their lens. When someone does not agree with a decision, we expect them to have the courage to speak up and change things, instead of loudly complaining on a message board. We are in it together and these values represent the way we do things," concludes Nate.

This is going to be interesting!

Next up in the onboarding journey is John, the lead IT person who will help set up our laptops and corporate accounts.

"Ok, folks, you can turn on your laptops. We've already configured your personal accounts. The password to log in is *test*: t-e-s-t."

Wait what?

Is this a practical joke to rattle the new security guy? Maybe a test to see if we have the courage to say something reflecting the fourth and last value of the company?

We reluctantly type in the password and lo and behold, the lock screen gives way to the desktop. The password is really the four-character word "test". We look around hoping that people will spontaneously change it to something less ridiculous, but that fleeting speck of hope evaporates when John jumps to the next item on the agenda.

At this point, there are probably 150 current employees at Mirage. 150 people likely onboarded with the infamous "test" password configured, but there is no way we're going to add the current batch of users to that lot. This ends now.

"I am sorry, but can we take the time to change this password? We'll each have a good deal of confidential information on these laptops, both personal and professional. It would be a shame to lose it all for a password so trivial. John, would you mind walking us through it, please?"

John quickly apologizes: "Oh yes, I am sorry. I forgot to tell you that you should update your password. Of course! Also, please add at least two numbers and special characters."

The 20 people in the onboarding session gently comply and update their passwords. Yay, our first win! Who said security was hard?! There are probably many broken computers in the wild, but at least this cohort will get a decent start.

We log into the computer, change the password, and our pentester brain goes into auto mode. We open the security settings: disk encryption and the local firewall are not activated. Automatic updates are disabled. Team viewer is installed on the computer. No third-party antivirus. We have root privileges on the machine. We find no hint of a device management solution running in the background. An IT account seems to be installed on the machine. We really hope its password is not set to "test"...

Meanwhile, the onboarding slides are quickly streaming by, so we put a pin in the workstation issues for now. We catch up with John and set up Gmail, Slack and other corporate tools. Of course, no second factor is required on any of these applications. At this point, we're just counting the number of passwords people had to enter and memorize. They're probably going reuse the same password everywhere, or write all of them down in an Excel sheet—what other choice do they have?

We move on to configure the OpenVPN client. This time the dance is different. We download certificates, choose a six-digit pin code and set up a one-time password. A total of three factors. Interesting. We wonder which zealous security maniac configured this.

The little green circle indicates that we've successfully mounted the VPN tunnel. *Is it too early to scan the internal network for open ports and unauthenticated applications?* we wonder as we near the end of the onboarding session. We head to lunch in the midst of a cacophony of random chatter.

The first session of the afternoon slides by rather quickly. The head of product, Melissa, presents the core features of the payment platform and the lifecycle of a typical feature from conception to implementation. Just like Airbnb, Netflix and so many other tech companies, Mirage follows the lean startup principles[11]. She explains how they don't spend months blindly planning the perfect feature and writing the perfect code. They formulate a hypothesis about something they think customers want. They build a minimal version with the most critical functionalities and push it to production. They then examine the feedback of customers, improve the feature accordingly, and reiterate. These short feedback cycles usually take six weeks.

One can wonder if security measures are part of that absolute minimum version shipped to customers. It would be too rude to blatantly ask that now. We'll circle back to it later, for sure.

---

[11] The Lean Startup is a book by Eric Ries that summarizes these principles.

While these onboarding sessions were going on, our inbox has been continuously flooded by invitations to open accounts on the dozens of tools used by the company. One email from the infrastructure team naturally catches our attention. It contains plaintext credentials to AWS and GitLab, the code management application. Are these people for real?

We hurry to the AWS console sign-in page to input the password, and thankfully we are invited to choose a new one right after logging in. A second authentication factor is not required to browse the infrastructure, but given what we have seen so far, it's hardly surprising.

We refrain from exploring AWS services and permissions. There will come a time for that. For now, we patiently wait for the rest of the presentations to finish so we can calmly process the thinly covered security holes.

The next day, we head to the development onboarding session, where we are greeted by Tony, the backend developer who interviewed us a month ago. He starts his session with a rather impressive figure of 50 small circles with complex interconnections:

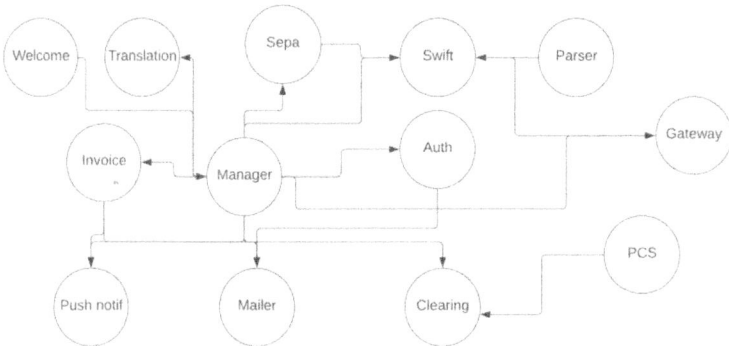

Figure 4-1: Partial view of the inter-connected apps at Mirage

"This is our application architecture. Each circle is a microservice, an independent app, with its own code repository and deployment lifecycle, that performs a specific business need. We have a microservice for authenticating customers, another for handling payouts, and so on. These microservices all run within containers on our Kubernetes[12] cluster."

He lingers on a few services that fulfill core values for customers, presents some banking jargon like reconciliation and settlement, then ends the presentation with a Q&A session. There are only tech people at this session, so I guess it's okay to shoot an honest and naïve question:

"Tony, just so I understand, this Kubernetes cluster is running on AWS and all these microservices are hosted on the same cluster, correct? Is there any isolation between them? How do we separate the most critical microservices from the unimportant ones?"

Tony pauses a few seconds then answers: "Interesting question. Yes, these apps are running on Kubernetes, which is itself running on AWS machines in the eu-west-1 region in Ireland. We decided to group all microservices into a single cluster to ease deployments. You'll have to talk to the infrastructure team to get more details about that. Right now, indeed, any application can talk to any other application in the cluster. We don't have a system of authentication and authorization to handle inter-app communication."

We respond back, "So, wait, you're saying that if I get into one of these minor apps, such as the one doing translations, I can contact another more critical app, say, the one performing wire transfers, send it an HTTP request, and bam, I have two million dollars in my bank account?"

"Well, you'd need to guess the right JSON payload and the proper HTTP endpoint. It requires non-trivial business logic also to set the values correctly!" says Tony in a highly skeptical tone.

---

[12] Kubernetes is a complex set of software components that schedule and run containers on a farm of machines. Think of each container as a single archive containing the files necessary to run a certain app. Kubernetes then takes this container, runs it in a redundant way across multiple machines, allows it to easily to communicate with other apps within the cluster and so on. A practical introduction to Kubernetes on freeCodeCamp http://bit.ly/3T9lmLu. In my book *How to hack Like a Ghost*, we deep-dive into hacking Kubernetes, http://bit.ly/3TP8vwU.

There is no point in continuing the debate during an introduction session in front of eight other new developers. We likely won't change this entire application architecture right here. It is, however, telling when a company's developers are tricked into modelling a weak attacker that cannot even figure out a simple JSON payload. People always go to the extremes. Either they argue for the mindless hacker who is too dumb to understand a HTTP payload, or they flip the narrative around and declare hopelessness against the FSB and the NSA. Meanwhile, hackers in the real world are thriving inside that artificial and invisible chiasm woefully ignored by most companies.

Reflecting on what we uncovered in these two days, from the lack of basic workstation security to deep architectural flaws, it's delusional to think that we will single-handedly solve these issues. These are symptoms of a more fundamental problem: erroneous threat modelling. The people thinking and developing these systems do not have an accurate picture of real-life attacks. Maybe some have none. They forget to design their systems for the adversarial reality it will live in. That's how we end up with four-character passwords, a free-for-all production environment and a team focused on trivial CSRF vulnerabilities.

We have an hour before meeting with Nina, the VP of engineering who has been handling security operations on the side for the past few months. We start pondering over the flaws we've discovered so far:

```
Workstations with feeble overall configuration
Clear-text passwords sent through email
No authentication between microservices
No multifactor authentication on tools
Broken password policies
Broken threat model
```

We can clearly see a primary theme emerge around authentication. This company is one password leak away from being hacked. Maybe it already has been.

Addressing this threat can roughly go one of two ways. Diving into each tool and configuring a robust password policy coupled with a second authentication factor or, opting for a single login solution that centralizes that configuration and instructing every application to trust this central entity when it forwards the identity of an employee.

This latter setup is commonly referred to as single sign-on (SSO). Now, we can argue that in making a tool or provider the central authority, we also promote it to be the single point of failure for our security. That's very much on point. But the reality is that not every application supports a malleable and robust password policy. Most SaaS products won't let you tweak the password's minimal length or forbid dictionary words. And even fewer will support multifactor authentication. However, many of them do support delegating authentication to a specialized third party, i.e., an SSO solution.

Furthermore, the SSO mitigates the much bigger threat of employee and contractor churn. We cannot go around each app curating the list of accounts, deleting old employees, adding new ones, sending passwords through emails and instant messages... All that goes away, or is in large part automated through an SSO. In exchange, sure, we accept a new kind of risk related to centralization of access. If someone tampers with this centralized platform, they gain tremendous access to the company's resources. We'll need to mitigate that through robust configuration and detection measures.

Skeletons in the closet

While we're scheming over the broad authentication issue, a person collapses on the adjacent seat and engages us in a happy tone: "Hey, I'm Nina. Nice to meet you! I can't tell you how excited I am to finally have a security expert amongst us."

"Thank you! Pleasure to be part of the team!" we smile back

"I hope the onboarding session was not too tough. What do you think of our app—did you manage to hack it yet?" asks Nina in a provocative tone.

We admit that we did not even ask for permission to connect to the app yet. It's a payment platform, after all. Isn't it subject to strict regulation?

"Well…" responds Nina, "we have a dummy account on the production platform, but I guess it's more appropriate to just set up a new test environment dedicated to your security tests. Here, let's do it now. Go to the Jenkins service at *https://jenkins.mirage.co* and run the job called `Create-staging`. It will deploy a version of the current app in our Kubernetes staging cluster. Pretty neat, right?"

That is indeed very cool. We search our flooded inbox for Jenkins credentials but cannot find any.

While Nina is busy searching for ways to grant us access, we absent-mindedly type the URL for Jenkins into the computer to prepare the sign-in page, but something weird happens.

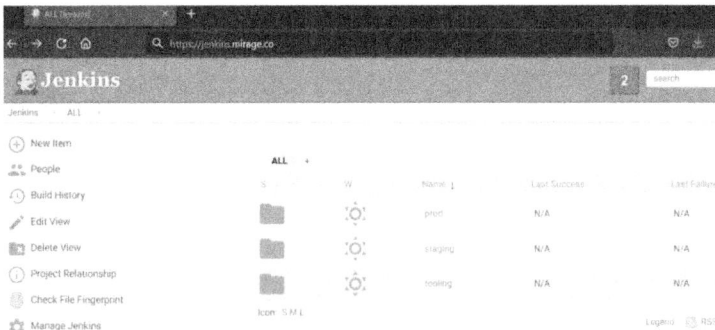

Figure 5-1: Welcome page for Jenkins at Mirage

We are greeted with the Jenkins homepage listing all of the jobs that can be executed. Nina looks over and points out:

"Oh yeah! I completely forgot that we don't need authentication on Jenkins. You just need to be in the office or have the VPN up and running," she explains in a light tone.

Huh!?

"That's big, Nina. We only have a single AWS account that hosts all our servers. Jenkins must then be running on this same account, I presume. So right now, I can execute any command on a server located inside the AWS production account, right?"

"Well, hold on… how would you execute any…?"

Before she even finishes her sentence, we're already going to the classic */script* page that allows admins to execute groovy scripts on Jenkins and enter a harmless proof of concept in the input text area to run the whoami command on the server:

```
println "whoami".execute().text
jenkins
```

Nina gulps her words. "…oh, I see. But. I mean, it's just one single server that is not supposed to run any critical…" she starts uttering defensively.

We swiftly return to the script console of the Jenkins server to execute one single additional command. There is no need to argue with words what can be easily proven with data. We know that Jenkins is typically used in companies for scheduling scripts and commands. The names of the jobs under the prod folder on this instance confirm it: Create-DB-Snapshot, Deploy-application, … These scripts most likely would have to interact with production resources: databases, servers, Kubernetes clusters and so on. That means that nested somewhere on this server are credentials to perform these jobs. Probably highly privileged credentials. We go after an easy win by displaying the current environment variables:

```
println "env".execute().text

JAVA_HOME=/opt/java
GOPATH=/opt/go
PYENV_SHELL=bash
AWS_ACCESS_KEY_ID= AKIAIOSFODNN7EXAMPLE
AWS_SECRET_ACCESS_KEY= wJalrXUtnFEMI/K7MDENG/bPxRfiCYEXAMPLEKEY
JWT_TOKEN=eyJhbGciOiJIUzI1NiIsInR5cCI6IkpXV…
…
```

"…workloads. Oh my god—wait! How did you get these AWS access keys?" exclaims Nina.

We load them to a terminal session on our computer and retrieve their associated user to confirm that they are indeed valid:

```
$ export AWS_ACCESS_KEY_ID= AKIAIOSFODNN7EXAMPLE
$ export AWS_SECRET_ACCESS_KEY= wJalrXUtnFEMI/K7MDENG/bPxRfiCY…
$ aws sts get-caller-identity
{
    "UserId": "AIDASAMPLEUSERID",
    "Account": "123456789012",
    "Arn": "arn:aws:iam::123456789012:user/jenkins"
}
```

We push the button even further, much to the dismay of Nina, by listing the permissions associated with this account through a call to the AWS API list-attached-user-policies API call:

```
aws iam list-attached-user-policies \
--user-name=jenkins \

"PolicyArn": "arn:aws:iam::123456789012:policy/Administrator",
"PolicyArn": "arn:aws:iam::123456789012:policy/iam-admin",
"PolicyArn": "arn:aws:iam::123456789012:policy/jenkins-ci-write",
```

"We've just gained admin access to Mirage's production environment," we respond, proudly pointing to the Administrator policy attached to this user. "So, to answer your earlier question: yes, we just hacked Mirage."

We watch the blood drain from her face as she stares intensely at the screen to replay the chain of events and make sense of this madness. Finally, she accepts the reality of the outcome and sighs.

"I mean, yes, you're right. We really need to fix this, but if someone has the skills to pull this off, then they can do whatever they want inside the network. We cannot possibly defend against a hacker with such skills. The defenders are always disadvantaged and doomed to lose."

Here we go again. Either the attacker is some doodling baby or an NSA wizard able to whisper any computer into obedience. If we can find and exploit a hole in five minutes, then surely there are other people who can do it in one or two minutes. Jenkins is such a classic in the pentesting world, there is really no excuse for this type of vulnerability.

"Well, at least we put it behind a VPN, right?" says Nina in a self-reassuring way.

A part of us wants to scream a screeching "Of course it's not enough! We're talking about tangible customer money here!", but our second day on the job is hardly the time to enter into a confrontational argument with the VP of engineering. Clearly our visions on security are not aligned. We must correct that first before arguing over sensible security measures. We let it slide for now. Since she has been overseeing security for the last few months, we will need her full cooperation during the handover phase.

We change topics and ask her about any security issues or projects she was currently working on.

"I got roped into security at Mirage because of the increasing customer reports of account take over. These nasty hackers... They brute force passwords until they find the correct credentials of customers. They log in and transfer the money to another account. Customers even told us about phishing websites that look exactly like our payment applications. You know how gullible people are. It's really our weakness. We are powerless."

Ah, the old user-blaming fallacy that plagues the tech world. There are many tangents we can follow here, but it's so alarming that we cannot help but stay laser focused on the brute force issue. Mirage is a payment institution after all, aren't there any regulations or standards that require multi-factor authentication before authorizing payments?

"We do send a unique code by SMS before validating a transfer, for instance, but these clever hackers, once inside the account, call the customer, and armed with every transaction detail, they easily impersonate Mirage support, then trick our customers into communicating the secret validation code. We track the brute force attempts in a Slack channel. Let me show you," Nina says as she pulls up a Slack channel flooded with bot messages that all share the same format:

```
IP 34.1.3.31 successful authentication on account ID fcd900fe-
d3bf-4a1b-84ae-75f3ba68a1e8 after 5 failures
```

Most of the messages seem to spark long-threaded conversations between roughly the same three people who follow up on the alerts, sometimes directly blocking the account, other times contacting the customer for feedback and so on. We ask about the accuracy of the alert and get a resounding:

"Oh no, these are almost all compromised accounts. The alert is quite straightforward. If an IP address fails multiple times on many accounts yet succeeds on another, we raise an alert."

"Wait, what?! But there are...a dozen a day! How long has this been going on?"

Nina explains that they have been targeted by a constant brute force campaign coming from different IP addresses. It has been targeting many accounts for about four months. Attackers always stay under the lock-out threshold for each account. Each day, 12 customers get hacked—that's roughly 360 a month or more than 4300 a year. It's ridiculous that any company would put up with this sort of charade. It is doubtful that any regulator would look too kindly on this. It's pure and simple negligence.

"Oh, let's not get too dramatic. We're on top of these alerts," Nina argues back. "We have three people dedicated to securing accounts as soon as an alert pops up on the *#alert-bruteforce* Slack channel!"

"Yes, but Nina, this is not a video game app. Can you imagine if your bank was continuously breached...every single day? Would you trust them with your money?"

"Well, when you put it that way... I guess we've been in this situation so long that we've become desensitized to the gravity of it all."

Nina then proceeds to explain how her team set up an ELK stack that parses customer authentication logs. ELK stands for Elasticsearch, Logstash and Kibana, three common tools used to collect logs, store them and allow easy visualization and parsing of data. They wrote a rather intuitive rule: for each IP address that has at least five authentication failures followed by a successful one, an alert is raised on the Slack channel. An operations person would then suspend the account and call the clients to help them change the password. Sometimes the operator comes too late to the party or forgets to suspend the account, which results in losses.

The technical setup that Nina described is great. It's the premise of a security information and event management (SIEM) tool, a platform that collects logs from various sources looking for configured malicious patterns. However, a defense approach that mainly relies on detection as its primary gate is fundamentally flawed and limited. The fact that it monopolizes three people full time is the best evidence of that. Three people who could otherwise be adding value to some critical production cycle to achieve business growth.

Brute-forcing robot scanners are the most basic threat level with which any company with an Internet-facing login form must deal. If a payment institution is vulnerable to brute forcing, the app's security is broken. There is no sugarcoating it. Salvation, in this case, lies, first and foremost, in protection measures to neutralize 99% of brute-forcing attacks. Then we complement the risk coverage of that residual 1% with detection measures. Otherwise, we will never escape the rat race of scaling. Nate's presentation said that the customer base grows by 10% every month. That means, statistically, one additional alert per month. We will double the cases in a year's time, and with it the number of human operators who perform the menial grunt work of remediation. Detection by itself is simply not scalable. We need to fix the root cause, and it's probably located somewhere in the application.

We ask Nina to invite us to the *#alert-bruteforce* channel and give us admin access to the nascent SIEM her team set up.

"All our slack channels are public so you can just join it freely," she replies. "I will also ask Marc from the infrastructure team to give you admin access to the security ELK stack."

We diligently join the channel and marvel at the number of customers whose accounts have been breached. This is frightening. As we scroll up the channel, each day numbers at least 10 to 15 breached accounts. We speak with some of the operators on the channel to better understand the whole process. They grant us access to a Google spreadsheet describing every case of customer account takeover. There are 620 cases and counting. Total losses: $350,000... so far.

While the infrastructure team is preparing the credentials to the ELK stack, we do what we do best. A quick audit of the authentication phase of the app to search for the root cause of these constant bruteforce attacks. How bad can it really be?

We download Burp *(https://portswigger.net/burp)*, our faithful web proxy to intercept all HTTP requests made by the browser. That way, we can tweak parameters before they reach the server and test the app's response to some edge cases. We head over to Jenkins to stage a new test environment. Just as Nina promised, 10 minutes later, we have our own staging environment running inside the production AWS account. Simply saying it out loud sends chills down our spine.

We follow the job's instruction and go to our dedicated environment *https://audit-test.staging.mirage.co* where we get to enjoy an exact replica of the Mirage app. The minimalist layout with hues of azure and blue does have a charming and inviting appeal. We have to give it to them for making a beautiful app. A broken app, but a beautiful one nonetheless.

We want to understand why so many of our customers get pwned. Do we have a fundamental flaw in the application that makes these bruteforce attacks so effective, or did the attackers get a lucky wordlist from a neighbor company?

We follow the registration flow to create our first user account on our custom staging version. We are invited to choose an email and a password. We input a random combination, hit enter and intercept the HTTP request with Burp so we can replay it with different values.

Figure 5-2: HTTP request to create an account intercepted by Burp

We try a trivial "test" password, but receive the following error on Burp's right-side panel:

```
HTTP/1.1 422 Unprocessable Entity
Server: server
Content-Type: application/json; charset=utf-8
Content-Length: 166
Connection: close
```

Alright. The backend server rejects the request, as it should. Let's add a single character to the password:

 # Request
```
POST /api/users/signup HTTP/1.1
Host: auth-audit-test.staging.mirage.co
User-Agent: Mozilla/5.0 (Windows NT 9.0; Win64; x64; rv:97.0)
Gecko/20100113 Firefox/136.71

{
    "email": "test-audit@gmail.com",
    "password": "test1",
    "first_name": "test",
    "last_name": "test",
    "world": "onboarding",
    "language": "en"
}
```

 # Response:
```
HTTP/1.1 200 OK
Server: server
...snip...
```

Huh...was that a "200 OK". Did the backend app just accept a five-character password?

This surely must be a bug. We go back to the browser window and stare blankly at the password instructions: it clearly states that a password should have at least eight characters. We slowly start typing a password in the input form and, lo and behold, at the fifth character, the "Next" button beams up, indicating we can move on to the next page... Mirage is basically encouraging users to be content with a five-character password. Isn't that a hoot!

We finish the registration process, ignoring the 50 or so additional requests made to the backend. There will be time later to look for injection-type vulnerabilities in these queries. For now, we're focusing on the authentication phase. Once the account is all set, we head to the login page, input the email with the fabulous five-character password and are greeted with a beautiful animation leading to our payment homepage.

We inspect Burp's HTTP history and confirm that authentication is just a matter of sending a single HTTP request with the right username and password to the endpoint */api/users/signin*. No captcha involved, no JavaScript challenge to confirm the browser's identity, no second authentication—nothing. It is so easy to automate this single request and flood the server with thousands of authentication attempts.

We change the password and start bombarding the endpoint in an attempt to simulate a classic bruteforce attack. It's only after 10 attempts that the error message changes to "account locked".

We register five new accounts and alternate authentication requests on each account with fake passwords. So long as we stay under the 10-attempt limit for each account during a 30-minute period, we don't get blocked.

To recap, we have an app that invites users to choose poor passwords, does not care for multifactor authentication and does not counter any automated behavior to replay authentication requests. The only protection it has is an old-fashioned account lockout, which is useful against vertical bruteforce attacks (one username, many password candidates) but is hopeless against horizontal password attacks (one password, multiple usernames) and credential stuffing (username/passwords gathered from leaks retried on other websites).

In the midst of our tests, we get interrupted by a slack notification from Tom, an infrastructure engineer who hands us a private pastebin link to access the ELK stack acting as a SIEM.

"We don't have a password manager at Mirage," he says, "so I set up this open-source local privatebin *(http://bit.ly/3Vhucar)* on a server and use it to securely send passwords to people."

Bless you, Tom!

We connect to the Kibana interface of the SIEM and load the authentication logs of every user on the app. Given our previous tinkering with Burp, we know that authentication requests are materialized by HTTP POST queries to the URL */api/users/signin*. We filter on these parameters in Kibana, then aggregate by status over time:

```
status_code:(200 or 401) and path:"/api/users/signin"
aggregate by @timestamp, interval:1 day
```

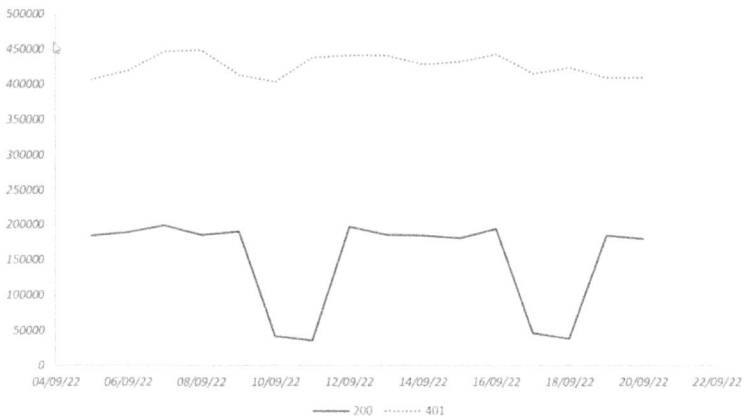

Figure 5-3: Graph showing successful vs failed authentication requests

There are two times more authentication failures than successful logins. In terms of numbers alone, this app's most dominant visitors are attackers, not customers! What an irony that all the infrastructure scaling one expects of Kubernetes and AWS has been to serve the attacker's needs. We filter these requests, receiving 401 responses and aggregate by IP address:

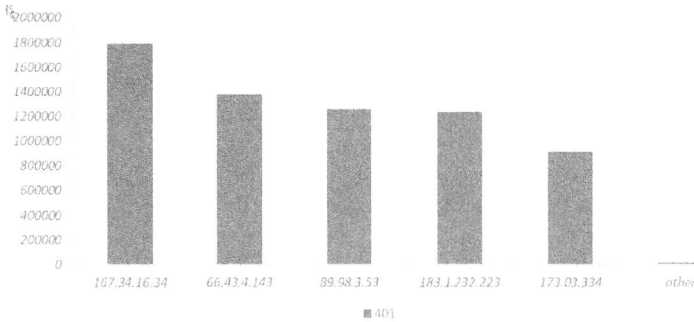

Figure 5-4: Distribution of IP addresses with the most failed authentication requests

Five IP addresses are causing 99% of this mess. Attackers did not even bother hiding behind proxy servers. The bar is very low indeed. We could ban these IP addresses, but they would just get new ones in a matter of hours. We need a more subtle trait to ban or rate limit these requests.

We start grouping these requests by different HTTP headers to find such a trait.

The user agent, that characteristic string that identifies browsers, is a good candidate, but it would surely block legitimate users as well. Many people do share similar browser versions. We notice a custom HTTP header sent by the Mirage app called Lead-User-ID. All the offending requests bear this same ID no matter the IP address.

We quickly drop a slack message to Nina asking about this Lead-User-ID header:

"Oh, I think it's a cookie we stick to a user the first time we see them. We don't exploit it much once the user has finished registration, but it keeps being appended to all requests, I guess. The backend code is defined here in the `tracking.rb` file inside our repo *https://gitlab.mirage.co/backend/register-service*."

We clone the repo to our machine to easily navigate files using our local editor…

```
git clone git@gitlab.mirage.co:backend/register-service.git
Cloning into 'register-service'
```

…then open the `tracking.rb` file and find the custom method generating these Lead-User IDs and sending them back as cookies to the browser:

```
def lead id
  SecureRandom.uuid
end
```

The front-end app must somehow grab this cookie and insert it as a separate header for all subsequent requests. It is very plausible that these brute-forcing maniacs just copy-pasted a full HTTP request and started bombarding our app without really understanding the meaning of the headers they were replaying. Naturally, then, all their authentication requests for different users are sharing the same Lead-User-ID, which is almost impossible under normal conditions given that it's a randomly generated UUID through the `SecureRandom.uuid` method. Maybe we can leverage this attribute to block or rate limit them.

Placing a hard limit of 30 authentication errors per IP or Lead-User-ID would significantly thwart the current attack. It could even buy us enough time to rework the authentication flow and permanently fix the issue with multifactor authentication and a more robust password policy. In fact, we could even argue that we don't need to fully solve the issue. We just need to make it more expensive to attack Mirage than the next startup on the list.

As we continue gathering metrics about the current bruteforce attack, we get a delightful notification from Google calendar: "*Compliance meeting in five minutes*"... Damn, we were making such good progress!

Tetris game

We climb the stairs to the third floor where the head of compliance is waiting for us in a small meeting room delightfully named "Excellence". The allegory fails to capture the imagination given what we have witnessed so far.

"Hello, I am Robert, in charge of compliance at Mirage. Welcome to the team! I hope your onboarding experience was pleasant so far?" he asks with a gentle smile.

"Pretty intense, truth be told. There is a lot of work to be done."

"Yes, I understand. It was time we hired a security expert to help scale safely and protect this company. Let me tell you a bit about my background. I joined Mirage seven months ago after spending a decade working for various bank regulatory bodies within the government. My expertise lies in the financial risks, but as you know, banks are increasingly exposed to cybersecurity risks. I want to make sure that our company is covered against such hazards. Can you tell me more about you and which framework and controls you intend to follow to reduce the cyber risk at Mirage?"

We recount our adventures as pentesters for financial institutions. The sweet and shortened version of interview questions we have so dearly memorized by now.

"I am not sure that I see any immediate value in any of the most popular frameworks," we respond back in a calm tone. "ISO 27001 is, to put it mildly, an outdated list of constraints used by auditing companies to charge massive fees. PCI DSS, pushed by the cartel of Visa and Mastercard *(http://bit.ly/3VccGmK)*, involves more auditing shenanigans and wordplay than actual security. CIS controls *(http://bit.ly/3URpjEN)*, another framework for managing security, tries to adopt a more pragmatic approach, but it fails like all other frameworks in the most critical aspect of cybersecurity: it scarcely offers any advice about prioritization. All of these frameworks can give us good ideas about security measures to implement, but I will not tie us to any one of them in particular. Personally, I feel like the five macro steps of the NIST framework fairly summarize how a company should approach cybersecurity and fits the model of breaches as we see them in the wild."

He is taken aback with the bluntness of the response—we're not exactly punching with gloves, but it's hardly an original opinion. CIS cannot be clearer in its official guide: *"You can get a credible list of security recommendations from many sources—it is best to think of the list as a starting point"*. Big corporations rushing to print a list of controls and sending it to all their branches with a memo requiring full compliance with each control point is pure madness.

Robert clears his throat and responds: "I am not familiar with NIST, but if you feel like it's the best one to follow, alright. As a banking institution operating in a few countries, we have to abide by many legal requirements. Some of them directly apply to cybersecurity, of course. I did a self-assessment a few months ago using a combination of Sarbanes-Oxley Act of 2002 (SOX) cybersecurity controls and European Banking Authority (EBA) guidelines, where I focused on the 10 most important shortcomings. Let's review them together quickly to decide of an action plan, alright?"

Oh, boy! This will be fun. He slides over his computer to show us a full Excel page with a list of controls, all marked with big cap red letters reading "NOT COMPLIANT."

Robert goes on: "So, the first thing that shocked me when I joined Mirage was…"

We hold our breath. The "test" password? Lack of authentication pretty much everywhere? Dozens of customers hacked every day?

"…the absence of any sort of security awareness training. This is mandatory in many financial institutions. We need to train users and customers to identify phishing, adopt the right reflexes and protect themselves. Otherwise, one wrong email and we'll be toast! I mean, you probably know this better than I."

Flabbergasting. This company really is the gift that keeps on giving. We stay politely silent and fixate on the screen, indicating we should move on to the next point. Robert takes the hint and goes through his spreadsheet one line after the other: lack of accreditation framework to assign privileges and roles, no risk and threat matrix, absence of logging and traceability, data tampering, and so on. He finishes his Christmas shopping list, turns toward us and bluntly says:

"OK. What estimated deadline should we put for closing these recommendations? Let's start with a quick one: the awareness training. If you start working on it now, we should have a draft early next week—what do you think?'

"Sorry, come again?" *That was some fast dribbling.*

"Yes, the goal is to have these tasks done by the end of the quarter to meet our regulatory obligations. We're a private company for now, but if we want to move forward and go public, we must be compliant with SOX requirements. In Europe, our branch is receiving even more scrutiny. The European Banking Authority (EBA) guidelines already apply to us right now, and as you can see, we're currently breaching many of them. These are mandatory actions, so we have no choice." says Robert in defense.

"I understand that, and I agree with a lot of the actions you mentioned. The accreditation framework, for instance, is vital, and I came to the same conclusion. In technical terms, it would probably come down to having a single sign-on solution to centralize authentication, role assignment, onboarding and offboarding. But this is, at best, a five-month project, not a one-week task. Some companies are still swimming in the middle of it after two years of hardship," we reply almost impatiently.

Robert looks at us dubiously. We shatter his composure with the next statement:

"…and I could make that argument for almost every other control you listed."

"You cannot possibly mean that," he defiantly retorts back. "We need this right now. If—or rather when—we'll be audited by a regulatory body, which will happen this year or next, we must prove that we have all these items in place. Every financial institution follows these same guidelines. What do you need to make it work by the end of the quarter? We can hire the best consultants if you need help."

He won't budge. He must think this is a negotiation tactic to scrub more resources or lower expectations.

"I understand, Robert. I have audited a number of banks during my career that all pretend to tick off these boxes. We still broke them in three hours. I am not exaggerating. Ask any security auditor worth their salt," we respond sternly.

The abstraction level of these common security framework is staggeringly deceptive to the untrained eye. Data integrity is, of course, paramount. No one could argue against that, but one cannot take it as a project and slap a deadline on it. It's impractical. Let's explore what this specific control entails in a Mirage, for instance: First, we need to enumerate all storage environments, from Postgres databases to messaging queues like Kafka or RabbitMQ to memory databases such as Redis and so on. There can easily be a dozen types of databases with different versions. Then, we need to identify every app, user and job that communicates with them and find out the least they need in permissions.

One way to ensure a certain level of integrity is by implementing authentication and rigorous authorization over an encrypted channel, such as TLS. That entails creating dedicated service accounts and roles with minimum permissions for each application. This is usually a given for Postgres databases, but other storage mediums, such as Redis, are not so security-oriented.

Some database clients won't support authentication, so we need to upgrade libraries. Quite a dangerous operation, for every upgrade entails the risk of a deprecated API or method that can blow up the application. Libraries that cannot be upgraded for whatever reason need to be locally patched to support authentication—again not an easy task given the vast array of libraries and the low-level code that must be changed.

Even if we clear all these obstacles, we still have to switch all Mirage's app configurations to use the new authentication scheme when connecting to databases. Mirage has close to 50 apps, so that's 50 upgrades times the number of database types. These are complex migrations that could each easily bring down the entire production environment several times over if we miss a single permission.

Sometimes authentication can be activated in place on the existing database cluster, while other times, authentication can only be enabled at creation time. So, one might need to create a new database cluster, migrate data to a new cluster with minimal downtime, handle concurrent access and duplication of data, update applications and so on.

Of course, this scenario supposes that we have a full working business knowledge of almost every app at Mirage, and that we can carry out these sorts of migrations, handle their side effects, perform quality assurance tests on every business edge case and so on.

That's one super-project that gives us some kind of assurance related to data integrity. One out of many. Need I go on?

This long monologue is not an excuse to wave a white flag when it comes to data integrity. It's simply a hard reality check that unpacks that deceptively brief little line present in almost every security framework.

Reasoning through such generic abstractions will not yield pragmatic security improvements in the field. We need a better mental model for defining, implementing and tracking projects. We try to explain that to Robert.

"If you want to check boxes in a compliance sheet that does not map to anything tangible, then you don't need my help. I am here to tell you that, when done properly, every one of these requirements is a stream of never-ending projects, some of which cannot be started without deep structural changes to the way Mirage works. That does not happen in a month. I am committed to working on it, of course. That's why one of my first assignments will be to design a roadmap for this quarter that should help make great strides in the most pressing requirements listed here. How does that sound?" we respond back.

Robert considers us for a few brief seconds and then reluctantly agrees. He knows we're just buying time with our roadmap rebuttal, but it's the best we can provide him for now. We have more pressing issues to focus on.

We rush out of the conference room for our next appointment. While swiftly running up the stairs, we cannot help but marvel at the chiasm between the people running compliance and those in the engineering department. Robert has no idea what "assuring data integrity" actually implies in terms of authentication, authorization, deployment strategy, backups and so on. It is very difficult for anyone doing real engineering work to take these controls and requirements seriously when they are being thrown around by a compliance officer who cannot not measure the weight of their words.

Security frameworks are another good idea turned into a catastrophic disaster. Some fare better than others, but they all fall prey to the same issue: the absence of any prioritization. A corporate executive in their ivory tower decides that the ISO 27001 is the way to go. They descend tablets of hundreds of control points upon its security officers in different branches to apply them all!

Oh, how easy it is to blindly start with the easiest or most familiar countermeasures and leave behind the most relevant control points. That's how we end up in a discussion about user awareness when the banking app resembles the most perforated Swiss cheese.

As previously stated, one could even argue that these cybersecurity frameworks only serve the agenda of the many consulting firms that feed off the complexity and pointlessness of the controls required. The majority of security audits performed by the big accounting firms consist of futile interviews with managers, policy and documentation reviews, and occasionally, a meager audit on a sample of machines. One would score a higher note on these audits if they had a patching process rather than actual up-to-date machines. These frameworks have bred a new industry of policy-writing junkies who scribble down unrealistic security measures and never bother to actually implement them or indeed check their effectiveness. So, as long as one has an access-right policy, a procedure to describe how permissions are assigned and a process to review that policy every quarter with some KPIs, they are golden. They can float in a policy bubble for all of their existence, blissfully ignorant of the public databases exposing all their customer data to the Internet…until an attacker pokes a hole in that fantasy world, causing it to crumble like a house of cards.

We jump over the last set of stairs and rush into the small meeting room where Henry is furiously typing on his computer. He looks up with a smirk and asks: "So, how is your onboarding going so far?"

"A lot more turbulent than expected, that's for sure!" We wonder for a split second if he is somehow aware of Mirage's issues. We were barely looking for them, yet we uncovered enough to occupy a small team for a year or two.

"Great. Things are moving like crazy around here, so that's precisely the spirit. We are always trying to push the envelope. If we deliver a feature in three weeks, next time, we want to do it in two weeks. Same quality, but better lead time. Next time around, we would push for one week and so on," he gleefully responds back. "Look, I know this is only your first week so you don't quite have the full picture of the company and product, but here is what I am expecting of you in the coming weeks: I would like you to design the future of security at Mirage. What do we need to achieve that vision? What's the acceptable trade-off to user experience? And how can we get there in the shortest timeframe possible."

"Hmmm…so a roadmap?" we ask.

"Not quite. A roadmap is usually a projection of multiple tasks on the axis of time to reach a certain goal. It's a tool, but not the goal itself. I want you to first work on the goal, the mission, the model. What does security look like at Mirage if you had to explain it to someone in three sentences? What are the founding principles that guide our decision-making when it comes to security? How do we handle user friction caused by security measures?"

This is quite an ambitious and exciting task that requires a good helicopter view of Mirage, and more broadly, the security universe. But at the same time, to form a coherent mental model, we must immerse ourselves in Mirage's culture, its application and infrastructure.

Henry asks if we uncovered any hidden gems, almost in a matter-of-fact tone. We do not want to sound too alarmist in our first meeting, but there is no way of putting it nicely, so here goes:

"To be honest, it has been one stroke after the other. From laptops secured with "test" passwords to unprotected Jenkins servers. Any employee can be admin over the whole infrastructure in five minutes, and when they work out the database structure, wire millions of dollars to their account without leaving much of a trail. I was not even looking for these vulnerabilities; they just keep popping up. I still need to perform a full audit to account for everything, look for quick fixes, prioritize actions and so on."

Henry, in a feat of perfect synchronization, managed to both drop down his jaw and close the lid of his computer.

"Really? This is some serious shit. Can you show me?"

We proceed to replay the series of commands we performed in front of Nina on the Jenkins server: dumping environment variables that contain AWS access keys, listing the policies associated with Jenkins and showing that we indeed had an admin account on the infrastructure. Henry's eyes were beaming through the whole process.

"That's mind-blowing… how did you find this so quickly?"

"This is a text-book vulnerability. Jenkins is probably one of the favorite targets of pentesters. It's always 'in-decommissioning' or 'soon to be replaced' so nobody takes the time to really secure it. Yet most Jenkins servers are used to schedule production jobs, database workloads and other important tasks. These tasks often require credentials to various critical resources…that's how we end up with admin access keys on a poorly protected server. The sad thing is that people think this is some advanced attack. It's not, and that's one of the main perceptions we need to shift around here."

Henry is fascinated, and we can sense it in his excited tone. He asks about the immediate action plan to resolve the issue, which is understandable, but the truth is that there may be 20 other Jenkins-like apps out there. And whatever we may think about the VPN's shortcomings, at least it reduces the attack surface of this particular flaw. Other exploits don't have that luxury:

"Well, Jenkins is a problem, but it's not *the* problem right now. I learned today that a dozen customers have been hacked on a daily manner for a few of months now. As in, the attacker found their password, logged into the account and sometimes took money out. Our sole current countermeasure is a bunch of alerts that trigger a manual response from our back-office operators. We cannot continue like this. We're under attack from a poorly sophisticated attacker that is slowly bleeding us dry. We need to stop it right now."

"What's the total loss so far?" asks Henry, very poised.

We show him the excel sheet of 620 clients and the $300k lost in transaction reimbursements.

"I was aware that we started having bruteforce attacks, but had no idea it escalated so quickly to these numbers. What do you need to remediate this?"

We tentatively reply: "I have some ideas to stop the bleeding, but I am still unfamiliar with the code base and the platform. Ideally, we need someone from backend and the infrastructure team to help us, do you…"

"Hold that thought," he interrupts.

Henry furiously types on his computer. Thirty seconds later, Tony and Marc's faces magically appear on the screen as he positions the laptop in the middle of the table.

"Thanks for being available, folks. We have a situation that requires our immediate attention. You can take it from here," says Henry as he turns to us.

We briefly explain the ongoing bruteforce attack, the losses the company has absorbed so far and the many weaknesses of the app that made it possible: a non-existent password policy, the absence of two-factor authentication on login, no rate limiting and so on. Tony interjects, almost on the defensive:

"But we were in such a hurry when we developed that authentication component a few years back. Plus, we had intense pressure from the product to manage the user experience. These are important issues, but we cannot fix them overnight, our roadmap is full for at least six months…"

That's a classic rebuttal that one will often hear in any company. A security officer points to an urgent vulnerability only to have the holy roadmap with its unyielding timeline thrown at them. The discussion suddenly shifts into a Tetris-like game where people around the table fit together imaginary and approximative deadlines. We lose our power frame and get sucked into the project management frame controlled by people who quickly oppose security in order to protect business growth. It's a twisted, modern-day Sophie's choice.

Fortunately, we heavily investigated the brute force's behavior, so we hurry to stop Tony in his apologetic and generic monologue and force him to step into the real world:

"We are not looking to fix all the root causes. We can do that in a later phase. Let's stop the bleeding first. Over 90% of all authentication failures are caused by four IP addresses. No regular customer does more than 30 failed authentications in an hour. We clearly see it in the logs. Can we quickly set up a rate limit of some sort, maybe based on the IP address in our infrastructure or directly in the code? If an IP address fails authentication more than 30 times in an hour, we reply with an error message regardless of the password."

Tony looks horrified. Marc, more stoic, responds back that Mirage does not have any security component that can perform this kind of countermeasure. He mentions that they can simply block the IPs using an access list at the network level (NACL) but it's limited to a handful of IP addresses. He suggests looking into the AWS Web Application Firewall (WAF) given that the infrastructure is tightly integrated with AWS services.

We quickly look up the WAF service on AWS. It does offer a rate limiter, but it only takes into account the IP address, not a custom header such as the Lead ID that we wanted to leverage to steel man our first patch. Also, and this is crucial, WAF rules apply the rate limit to the IP address irrespective of the server's response, i.e., we can limit an IP address to 100 requests in five minutes, but that would apply to all customers, not only those who fail authentication. The impact on user experience is not negligible and will require a profound study over many days to even find an approximate threshold.

Leveraging the strength of a more prominent commercial WAF is most probably the best solution going forward, but we cannot afford the luxury of time. There is no choice; we have to commit to a solution:

"I know you don't like it, Tony, but I don't see any other choice than to do it at the code level. Do you have any idea how we can proceed?" we ask.

Tony does not take too kindly to this attempt to drag his team into a hot mess at the last minute, especially for what he perceives as infrastructure limitations. After all, why should his team stay late at night to fix other people's incompetence?

He replies rather coldly:

"I suppose, yes, in theory, but this would require extensive testing and quality assurance. I know you're new Alex, but at Mirage, changes like these must go through a product manager who writes a product specification document that describes the user experience and the final value to the customer. Engineers then write a technical document and submit it for review to other developers. Only then do we dive into the code. We cannot just hijack the entire development process, compromise our quality commitments and delay the roadmap."

Tony is playing his trump card, the ultimate excuse to block any audacious initiative from moving forward: due process. Of course we want to ship quality code to our customers, who could argue with that? But due process is a means to consistently ship value to customers, not the end goal itself. Processes should be flexible, bendable and adaptable to new circumstances, not wielded as inflexible tools to deny progress. So, again, tirelessly, we drag him down to the field. We share our screen our pull up the repository of the application:

"I looked briefly at the code this afternoon. It seems we use Redis to cache some objects. I bet we can easily repurpose it to code a simple rate limiter. We store an IP address as a counter with an expiration date of an hour. At each failed authentication, we increment this counter. If the count surpasses 30, we know that it hit the limit during that one-hour window. Redis is a cache in memory, so the fetch time is fast and constant. This is a textbook use case of Redis. They even have the code on their blog… I am sure we have decent engineers who can assemble this in a class in two hours and call it in the authentication controller. We can write a short technical document together and test it on the staging platform. I am more than happy to take the bulk of the development process. I just need some brief assistance and review to deploy the changes as it's really my first time at Mirage."

As previously stated, the one who controls the frame controls the narrative. Tony is focused on identifying roadblocks to justify inaction. We, on the other hand, are looking for solutions to the problem. If we give in and start arguing about due process and roadmaps, we're done. We will be constantly trapped in this problem-finding cycle, whereas the path to salvation lies in the opposite direction. We need solutions, ideas to reach the goal faster, innovative insight that solves the issue without delaying business goals. To bring Tony onboard, we borrow pieces of his frame and inject them into our own narrative. We still focus on a quick fix and pragmatic solution, but also address the quality and test issues. We steer the wheel a bit to give him enough reasons to jump aboard our own narrative.

Bringing up deadlines and prioritization before converging on a solution is futile at best. Harmful in most cases. People engaging in such discussions are not looking to solve or help you solve the problem. They're justifying inaction. Learn to recognize this pattern and disrupt it. One potential way of doing it is leveraging technical skills. In this particular case, being a tad familiar with the code base and having a solid understanding of the components involved gives us a tremendous advantage to do just that.

In a scale-up, almost everyone is busy working on what they conceive to be the most important feature of the moment. One cannot win these roadmap arguments, as I call them, with a simple display of authority. Yes, the first time a head of security might escalate to the CTO or CEO to report a blocking issue. But how many times can one really play that card before conveying a severe lack of leadership and competence? That's why I adamantly and wholeheartedly believe that a head of security or CISO in a scale-up of under 500 people must have technical skills or a team of technically competent people who are capable of rebutting bullshit deadline arguments that make it look like writing an "if" statement is a two-week job.

Tony could show a little more team spirit, but his spontaneous reaction to defend the sacred availability of his team is a classic management reflex to which many revert. It is so easy to adopt that "us" versus "them" attitude, even when everyone is playing on the same damn team. The infrastructure team, "them", cannot even put together a decent WAF. The security guy, "them", wants us to spend the night working on his feature. We, "us", are the poor victims who have to make it up for everyone's incompetence.

However, by showing that we took the time to dive into the code and come up with a reasonable solution, we move the discussion toward the engineering realm, away from all the blaming and finger pointing. Furthermore, we actively propose our help to implement it, thus shattering that invisible reactionary glass wall. We are in this together.

Tony considers his options and looking at the code replies: "Well, now that I think of it, we do use Redis for rate limiting the SMS one-time password, so I guess we can repurpose it to rate limit the IP as well."

How strange that this little factoid did not come up at the beginning of the conversation. Again, Tony is not really to blame. He instinctively shifted into "protection" mode and started conflating the problem instead of actually solving it. Had he adopted the latter position from the beginning, of course, he would have cracked the case in 30 seconds.

We latch onto this moment of openness and continue the discussion about the SMS rate limiter and how we can use it to block not only the IP address but also the Lead-ID header to effectively counter bruteforce attacks. We decide to reconvene in 15 minutes to look more in depth at the code. Henry steps in before the meeting ends to help us find a product manager familiar with the authentication flow. They will help us test the code and confirm that the proposed blocking thresholds won't affect users.

The following day, the anti-bruteforce code is almost ready to go to production. The fix was relatively simple. Together with Tony and another developer, we instantiated a new instance of the already-present SMS rate limiter class and used the IP address as the key for the counter:

```
def login_rate_limiter
  @sms_rate_limiter ||= begin
    options = {
      lock_period: 3600.seconds,
      max_attempts: 30,
      renew_lock: true
    }
    RequestsLimit.new("auth:failed_login", request.ip, options)
  end
end
```

We then added a couple of checks in the authentication method to increment this rate limiter and deny access if the counter exceeds the limit.

```
def authenticate_user
  ## Horizontal bruteforce
  render_429 if login_rate_limiter.exceeded?

  current_user = sign_in(param[:email], params[:password])
  ## Password and email not correct
  if not current_user
    login_rate_limiter.increment
    render_401(reason: "Failed auth") unless current_user
  end
  login_rate_limiter.reset
  ...snip...
end

def render_429
  render(json: {errors: "Too Many Requests"}, status: 429)
end
```

We implement the same logic for the Lead-ID header.

The product manager reviewing the changes in the pre-production environment is not that thrilled about the user experience. "We just send back an error if a customer performs too many failed attempts? Don't we risk blocking legitimate users?" he complains. We present him the figure of user authentication errors showing that regular IP addresses manage less than 10 authentications an hour on the worst days, far below the proposed threshold.

"Oh, I see, we are really only annoying bad actors. Not regular customers. I love it," he proclaims before giving his approval.

The code goes into production in the afternoon while we dutifully follow the distribution of authentication status codes. We immediately see a major drop in the number of failed authentications (401 error codes):

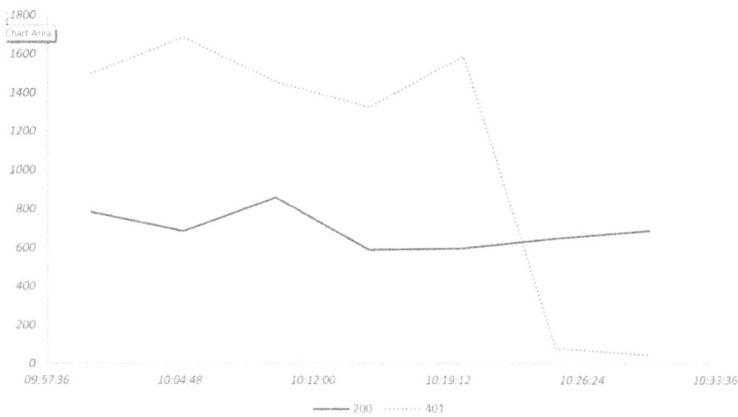

Figure 6-1: Authentication dashboard showing a sharp decrease in the number of authentication failures

Beautiful!

It's always rather stressful to ship such radical changes to production. One small bug and thousands of users could be blocked from accessing the app, causing an uproar on social media. Even after extensive tests in staging, we nervously ask a nearby developer to test the login feature in production. They confirm it's working.

"You don't have access to the test account on production?" they ask. "Wait, let me invite you. You're the new head of security, right? I'll put you as admin then."

We put the authentication dashboard on the second monitor to keep an eye on it and carry on with our new priorities.

Now that the crisis is averted, time to prepare for the medium-term solutions. As soon as the attackers figure out the limitations placed on the IP and the Lead-ID header, they'll heavily invest in giant pools of IP addresses to perform their attacks. It can take them days, maybe weeks, but they will surely be back. We need to be ready.

We ping Melissa, the head of product, to talk about passwords. Luckily, she is immediately available for a quick chat. We grab a coffee together in the atrium and explain the situation with the daily hack of accounts. She calmly listens to the story and nods her head along the way.

"There are two important measures we absolutely need to put in place: a stronger password policy and multi-factor authentication. We fall prey to the most basic attack types. I am sure we can do better," we argue.

Melissa does not seem convinced. "I understand, but adding more constraints to the user journey is against our core value and the product's vision. Our customers choose to stay with us because they don't have to jump through the meaningless hurdles of compliance and bureaucracy found in incumbent companies," she responds almost in a scripted way.

She is absolutely right. There is always a trade-off between security and user experience. The most innovative companies place the cursor at just the right level and infuse security into their user experience to make it a seamless experience. How many times has any of us screamed at their computer for being disconnected after five minutes of inactivity on an app? And just who is that monster who forbids pasting passwords on login forms?

"Of course, Melissa. We want 90% of our customers to have the most straightforward flow possible. No security prompts, no hassle. But those 10% who present odd characteristics or security risks, those are the ones we want to challenge. For instance, we could store the IP and user agent of a customer. Whenever they log in from a new location or a new browser, we ask them for an SMS. People don't change computers every day. We'd be protected against the majority of account takeover schemes while still providing the best user experience."

Melissa thinks about the proposal for a minute and nods in approval.

"That would be nice, yes. I still need to see some concrete data to support this before we go forward but it seems like an interesting take."

She sighs and continues: "But anyway, no matter what we do, we all know that the human factor is always the weakest link."

How strange it is that product and compliance, who rarely see eye to eye on things, seem to mutually agree on the same fallacious argument that *customers, being human, are the weakest security link, so they need continuous awareness and training.* Never mind that the app and platform spectacularly fail across all the authentication flow: suggesting and accepting weak passwords, no rate limiting, no second authentication factor, weak detection measures and so on. It's the user's fault that their account gets hacked. What a lazy way to deflect responsibility.

"I have to disagree, Melissa. It is our duty to build the most secure product for our customers. We cannot invite them to enter a five-character password, then blame them for getting hacked because of that same password. We must create an environment where they have no choice but to be secure. To borrow a design metaphor, it would be like presenting them a dialog box with the word "Cancel" in flashy green, and then blaming users for clicking on the wrong button. This one is on us."

Melissa nods in agreement. We seem to win her over with our argument for a fluid and seamless user experience. We continue discussing the possible mitigations and finally settle on a couple of actions to pursue. First, we should increase the minimal character length of accepted passwords. Rather easy to agree on this one, you might think, but our instinct, shaped by years of hard-core security recommendations, was pushing to fix the password check in the backend part of the code. Meanwhile, Melissa was adamantly against this move since it breaks compatibility with previous versions of the app.

Any security professional knows this mantra by heart: "*we put checks in the backend because it's so easy to bypass JavaScript and HTML verifications.*" That's completely true when fixing code injection vulnerabilities, but Melissa is suggesting something more subtle. We want to nudge users to choose the right password. Almost all customers will just keep typing characters of their passwords until the "Next" button lights up on the app. Therefore, a simple change to the front end (web and mobile apps) would yield much more secure passwords in general.

Why not do it both in the front end and backend? Melissa sums it up in one word: *mobile.* We cannot introduce such a breaking change in the backend without forcing all mobile users to upgrade their Mirage application. Some customers use old versions of the application. A forced upgrade could mean a total loss of service for hundreds of customers until they replace their phones. The product team is therefore very careful with these breaking changes and limit them to once a year.

"The next breaking change on mobile is scheduled in six months," she informs us. "That will be our window to ship the password upgrade in the backend as well. We want to reshape our registration form anyway, so we'll just bundle it with that. By the way, Maria will come back to you about these future changes. Is that okay with you?"

We move on to the next mitigation item: Second-factor authentication on the login form. "I will wait to see your data, but please keep in mind that SMS authentication is a pain for most customers," she insists, "They already don't like it when requesting a payout."

We are not going to win her over with hunches and guesses. We need to know exactly how many people would be bothered with a two-factor authentication on login and prove that it's a viable strategy against the type of account takeover we are facing. We need data before engaging in a meaningful conversation. We thank Melissa and wave goodbye as we ponder these questions.

Many hard-core security professionals would not at all approve of the direction this is taking. Playing footsie with the front-end to fix backend problems, and now going around chasing SMS as a form of double authentication. They have every reason to be upset. Their technical analysis is sound. SMS is a lousy double authentication factor. Attackers regularly trick operators into giving them already assigned phone numbers (SIM swap). The SS7[13] protocol used to deliver SMS is completely based on trust between nodes and is therefore as resilient as a wooden house in a firestorm. Most importantly, SMS, and any other time-based or hash-based OTPs, do not solve phishing. Tools like Evilnginx *(https://github.com/kgretzky/evilginx2)* are notorious for proxying requests between the phishing site and the legitimate web app in real time. Both passwords and regular OTPs fall prey to this attack scenario.

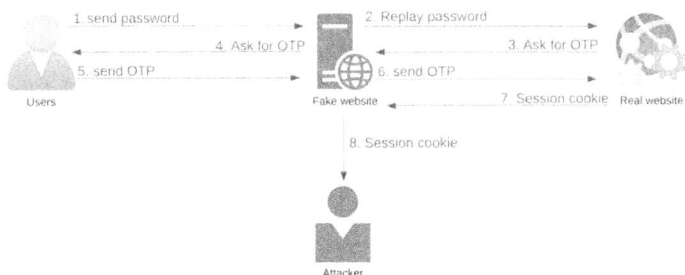

Figure 6-2: Illustration of how an attacker can replay the OTP

---

[13] DEF CON talk about SS7 issues by Sergey Puzankov : *https://bit.ly/3FGUaNQ.*

Note: HMAC-based OTP (HOTP) is a standard algorithm to generate unique tokens based on a shared secret. Using this common secret both the client and the server generate the same six- or eight-digit code by calculating the hash of the secret along with an ever-increasing counter. Time-based OTP (TOTP) is a special case of HTOP where the counter is the number of intervals (e.g., 30 seconds) elapsed since a defined timestamp.

Then why are we after this broken second-authentication factor? Like I said, it's a lousy technical solution, but it's the best decision product-wise. It will completely shut off bruteforce attempts and we can deploy it on all our current user base with a couple days of effort. Literally every customer has a cellphone. It will take one week to develop, tops, since it's being used for other features of the product. All the bricks are already there.

So, what if some attackers can bypass it using carefully built phishing platforms? If we can destroy brute force, credential stuffing, and significantly reduce phishing while we work on a more sustainable 2FA solution…fantastic! Better to deliver some value in one week and then improve step by step than stay naked for six months while we work on the next best feature that should supposedly solve all our issues.

Are there forms of authentications that resist phishing? Yes. WebAuthn[14], the protocol developed by the FIDO2 alliance *(https://fidoalliance.org/fido2),* relies on a private/public key pair specific to each user. Authentication involves signing a challenge sent by the server, which includes the URL of the website. So, the attacker cannot simply forward that response to the original website as part of a man-in-the-middle attack. That signed URL will contain their fake website, thereby invalidating most forms of credential grabbing phishing attacks.

The attacker can bypass this check by hijacking a legitimate subdomain, compromising the browser, pushing users into installing a browser extension or a malware on their computers, or finding a flaw in the protocol itself. These types of threat are real, but they could be addressed through additional security measures.

The cold, hard truth, however, is that WebAuthn is not that easy to implement at scale. Many not-so-old browsers and operating systems currently used by a significant portion of the population do not support WebAuthn. And if they do, they don't support software authenticators, such as MacOS Keychain and computer TPMs[15], which protect the public/secret key through the computer's password, Touch ID and Windows Hello.

---

[14] A good summary of WebAuthn by Tweag: *https://bit.ly/3YnXOF4.*

[15] Trusted Platform Module is a secure computer chip within computers to store secrets and perform cryptographic operations *https://bit.ly/3hhN2PU.*

The only reliable alternative is Physical FIDO2-compatible USB keys (e.g., YubiKeys), but they can be quite expensive and pose other types of challenges, such as distribution, renewal and maintenance of the inventory.

Only very recently, in 2022, did iOS and Android start rolling Passkey in their latest operating systems, a WebAuthn-based protocol that leverages Bluetooth to remotely sign the browser's challenge. This will probably help adoption, but not today and certainly not in the next couple of years.

It would make total sense for a company to impose such a stringent authentication form on its own employees. The company controls their browsers, computers and can easily distribute $50 FIDO2 keys. But a business trying these novel protocols on its customer base? That's rough. You cannot reasonably force a customer to either upgrade their browser, buy a new phone or change laptops before accessing their finances. Distributing $50 keys to hundreds of thousands of customers creates a lot of friction and directly impacts the business' fundamental economics—how much does a customer bring in and how much does it cost?—and therefore its viability. Does the risk of hindered growth and customer adoption really trump the losses induced by the punctual inefficiencies of regular OTP forms? No matter how you slice it in the real world, and unless there is a technological revolution in the user-experience flow, the answer tends to be no.

These are just a subset of the hard product considerations we will have to solve before rolling out a something like WebAuthn-compatible features in a mandatory fashion to customers. These will take more than a week to solve. We should solve them. But after we stop the bleeding with good ol' fashioned SMS authentication.

We turn our attention to fixing the password length. We know it's a front-end issue. Somewhere in the JavaScript code, there must be a line that says that five-character passwords are acceptable. We ask the person sitting next to us to send us the link to the GitLab repository of the front app. We clone the repo and start warming up the keyboard. JavaScript was never our specialty. This app relies on the ReactJS framework[16], which further complicates matters for us. But we don't want to develop a new feature; we just want to hack an existing check. Surely, we can do that.

We grep for every occurrence of the term "password" and "length" in the code base:

```
$ grep -ERi "password|length|pass"
```

---

[16] https://reactjs.org/

Among the many leads that pop up, we notice `HookValidators.js`. The name sounds like a promising lead! We open the file and find a beautiful constant named: `minLengthRegExp`:

```
...snip...
if(passwordInputFieldName==='password'){
 const uppercaseRegExp = /(?=.*?[A-Z])/;
 const lowercaseRegExp = /(?=.*?[a-z])/;
 const digitsRegExp = /(?=.*?[0-9])/;
 const specialCharRegExp = /(?=.*?[#?!@$%^&*-])/;
 const minLengthRegExp = /.{5,}/;
 ...snip...
 const minLengthPassword =
minLengthRegExp.test(passwordInputValue);
...snip...
```

Hurray! We change this from five to eight, register a new branch, then commit and open a merge request on GitLab to apply the change. Before we hit enter, a small doubt creeps in… Is it okay to touch other people's code in this uninvited way? It seems kind of rude, no?

We search for the manager of the web app team in the internal organizational chart and send them an instant message. We tell them about the brute force, the number of clients that were breached and our plan to submit a simple fix on the web app to prevent that from happening in the future.

Seconds later, we receive a reply back: "Sure, go ahead. Thank you so much for taking care of this. I agree. The fix should be simple. Send us your code update proposal on the channel #web-review, and we'll have a look at it."

Great! We proceed as he suggested, test the flow in the staging environment, and patiently wait for feedback.

We push the keyboard away and relax on the chair for the first time since the morning…

We assuredly have many flaws to fix, many broken thought patterns to recalibrate, but as long as we keep scoring these small wins, we will succeed in the long run. Slowly but surely, as they say. It's only the beginning.

Trial by fire

"If liberty means anything at all, it means the right to tell people what they do not want to hear."

George Orwell

Web of attacks

We can finally press the pause button after these eventful days. We stopped the hemorrhage of hacked accounts that was gushing for the past five months. The number of failed authentications on the app is at a healthy 20 occurrences per hour. Down from 20,000 per hour in the previous days. Our nasty and hasty patch seems to have impeded the attackers, and we don't see any attempt to bypass these protections for now. The fix of the password length check on the web app was dutifully deployed by the Web team. We missed a unit test in the code, but the team was kind enough to quickly help us fix it.

We drop a brief message to Henry to let him know that the incident is over.

We can finally stop improvising and devise a coherent strategy that takes Mirage's security to the next level. We stare at our agenda for the day... No meetings in sight. Where do we begin?

We cannot indiscriminately, one by one, tackle every vulnerability that plagues Mirage as they rear their ugly face. We have limited resources and energy, and regardless of what political correctness may dictate, vulnerabilities are not all equal. We need a prioritization framework to identify and classify vulnerabilities to help us focus our energy on the most pressing ones. We cannot go chasing generic accounts, no matter how dangerous they are, when a single unpatched vulnerability on the web app can bring the company down to its knees. Our immediate task, therefore, is to figure out key projects worth focusing on in the coming weeks. Put differently, what small fires can we suffer to ignore for now while we tame firestorms?

To figure out how to prioritize vulnerabilities, we have to step back to the most fundamental questions in security: who are we fighting against and what are we protecting? These questions literally define our field and therefore should govern our decision making. We model them as the two extremities of a graph, as shown in this rudimentary figure:

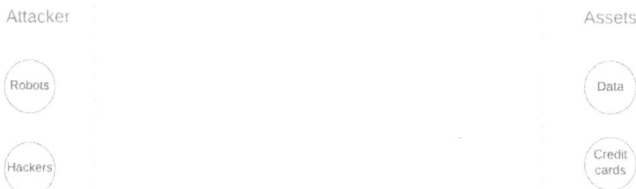

Figure 7-1: Draft of an attack graph

On the left, we have different types of attackers, each with their own properties: robots that routinely scan the Internet, script kiddies, stubborn hackers and so on. On the right, we find assets that make up the value of Mirage: customer data, databases, transaction systems, etc.

The vast in-between is an unstable vacuum ripe with potential attack patterns that can materialize at any moment. For instance, a script kiddie may find an SQL injection on a web app, retrieve clear-text passwords, connect to the public admin interface, plant a webshell on the server, and then pivot to other critical assets by replaying passwords until they dump all of Mirage's data. That's an attack pattern chaining half a dozen vulnerabilities to reach assets at the right edge of the graph.

Some attack patterns are more probable than others due to the tech complexity, surface exposition, opportunity, and so on. It is these properties that will govern our decision-making when choosing which attack paths to focus on. Our first projects must deter and neutralize the most likely attack patterns to emerge on that graph.

Notice that our drill-down from first principles is forcing us to consider and reason about attack patterns as the primary unit of our decision framework. Each attack pattern may be composed of one or many vulnerabilities, such as SQL injection, password reuse, public admin interface, but we're not prioritizing vulnerabilities, nor are we prioritizing security solutions for that matter. We're focusing on the full thread of the attack pattern.

Often times, security teams take the opposite road. They start debating solutions: *Should we install an antivirus or an email sandbox?* That's a misleading argument. They are comparing apples to oranges. Worse yet, they are already deciding on the solution to their underlying threat scenarios without taking the time to fully state the attack pattern. That's a flawed decision-making process. Maybe we don't need an antivirus to address that malware threat scenario. Perhaps there is a different project with a lower cost and quicker deployment timeline that neuters the attack pattern. We won't know for sure until we explicitly graph out the threat scenario from the source to the destination and explore the hypothesis and flaws that make this scenario possible and damaging. Only then can we evaluate the full the scale of the issue, its impact, probability and therefore the necessary energy and resources that we choose to effectively spend to resolve the problem.

Beware of these substitution arguments, where one gets caught debating solutions as proxies to the problem they are addressing. Always go back to the underlying threat scenarios, starting from the attacker and ending at the target assets. Evaluate the probability and impact of each one, all the conditions that make such a path possible, and then come to a meaningful conclusion.

Let's get cracking on Mirage's threat graph!

Mirage is a classic up-and-coming scale-up. It manages a few hundred million dollars for its clients. Right off the bat, we can broadly model four types of attackers. First, we have the regular robot scanner coming from the Internet with neigh any resources. It's mostly looking for low-hanging fruit, such as easy public exploits, bruteforce simple passwords and so on.

The second type of attackers would be the single hacker with a few hundred dollars and a rudimentary knowledge of security. They jump from site to site looking for easy and already published exploits. They reuse existing off-the-shelf tools with only a superficial knowledge of their inner workings. They might even go after customers directly using prepared phishing kits.

The third type of attacker is much more experienced. Once they set their eyes on a target, they're ready to deploy the necessary skill and patience to find a crack in their defense. They are capable of crafting stealthy exploits that land them directly on the internal network. It is best to assume that these folks always have access to a corporate computer or network because that's what usually ends up happening.

The fourth type of attacker is what we commonly refer to as organized crime. They have access to many third-type attackers and can invest significantly in exploits and toolkits to break into a company. They are looking for big payouts. Their attacks range from spending $150k on the latest Exchange exploit to acquiring old corporate computers looking for residual data.

Let's put these four types of attackers on the left edge of our graph.

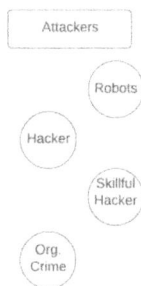

Figure 7-2: Types of attackers

We can be more granular, but that's a first macro approach that will yield plenty of interesting scenarios. We'll drill down on each one of them in a moment.

Notice how we did not consider nation state attackers. How do we protect against the NSA and Beijing's ever watchful eyes?

We—and I cannot stress this enough—don't.

A small fintech serving regular businesses with a few tens of thousands of clients should not worry about nation state attackers. Period. We may revisit this statement if and when we climb to a few billion dollars in revenue and start contracting government agencies, but for now, taking into account this type of threat when building our security is a dangerous distraction that could expose us to other types of attackers. It's not the NSA's secret iPhone exploits that cost Mirage $300k. How can we justify spending time NSA-proofing the executives' laptops and phones while silly bots are poking holes in the platform with simple bruteforce attacks?

Now that we can clearly picture who is attacking us, let's move on to the second question. What are we trying to protect? Mirage is a payment institution, so naturally our customers' financial data are the crown jewels of this company. Customer personal data is another obvious war chest. We also have employee data, strategic corporate information and so on.

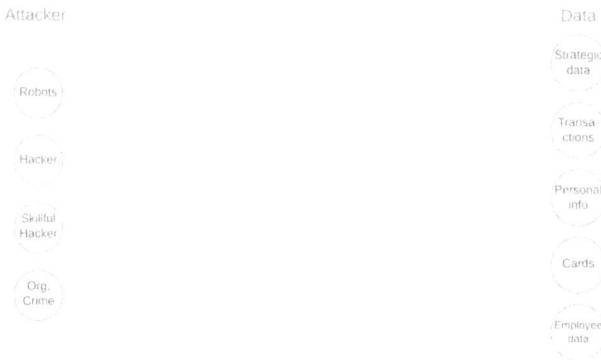

Figure 7-3: Types of attackers and assets

We don't currently have a full picture of where this data is, but the purpose of this exercise is to highlight this missing knowledge so we can remediate it. We will schedule 20-minute one-on-one sessions with managers from the various teams at Mirage: tech, acquisition, sales, etc. Aside from getting answers related to customer data storage, we'll also use these precious minutes to bond with them and build the trust necessary to pierce through the classic corporate bullshit when we face the next security crisis.

Alright. Now the million-dollar question… How do we get from the left part of the graph to the right one? What are the obvious paths? How likely is an attacker to prioritize one path over the other? Do we have adequate protection and detection covering each critical path?

Since it's our first time approaching this in the context of Mirage, we don't care about pure exhaustivity. That triple-hop leveraging spear phishing, CORS and CSRF can wait. We want to find the big whales, ideally one-hop vulnerabilities that get us straight to the right part of the graph in one hefty stride.

Let's revisit those cringeworthy vulnerabilities we picked up during the first few days and transpose them over this graph. The first one is rather obvious, we barely contained it a few hours ago: the weak authentication system on the Mirage app. Any attacker with a large enough pool of IP addresses can try millions of passwords unhampered until they land on a valid customer. Our dim protections would fall under the weight of a big enough IP address pool.

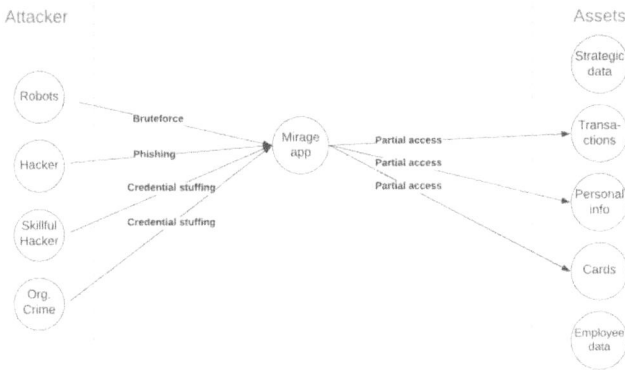

Figure 7-4: Authentication vulnerabilities on the Mirage app

Attackers can follow different paths: phishing, vertical bruteforce, horizontal bruteforce (one password for many accounts), credential stuffing (replay of leaked credentials), but their reach is limited to the data of one customer at a time, hence the "partial access" above. The impact, on the other hand, can dramatically extend to hundreds of victims over time.

While this scenario may seem like it's limited to the Mirage app, it's actually far more pernicious. This exact scenario can play out on any of the dozens or hundreds of SaaS tools used by the company. Every onboarding email sharing a simple password is a symptom of this problem. From Salesforce to the HR tool.

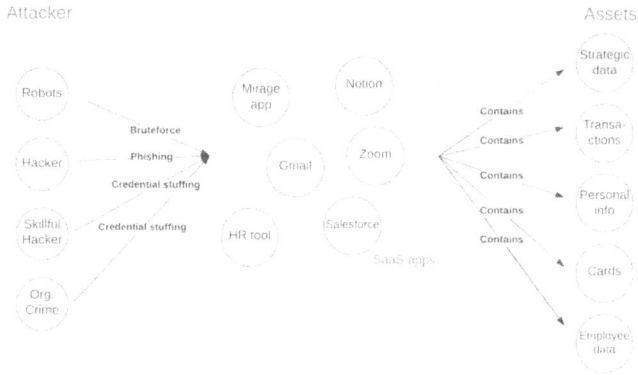

Figure 7-5: SaaS threat graph

We only displayed six apps, but this attack pattern extends to all SaaS products holding any of these aforementioned critical data. Representing the actual attack pattern through a graph really highlights its potency.

Phishing, brute-forcing, credential stuffing, and similar attacks have a very low entry ticket. Anybody can download a phishing toolkit and spam Mirage's employees to collect credentials that may just give them access to the critical data we're trying so hard to protect. It is downright crazy to have such a simple attack impacting almost every facet of Mirage's business. That's the sort of whale we are looking for.

All these types of password-based attacks have similar cures, and it's not user awareness. I don't know who insists on propagating this fallacious take, but user training and awareness barely count as security measures. Certainly, not effective ones, yet it's probably one of the first countermeasures many security experts hurry to implement. In a speech addressing the French security ecosystem, the director of the national French cybersecurity entity (ANSSI) said, and I quote, "*my dream is to have five minutes of the people's attention to talk to them about cybersecurity.*" Really? That's the dream? Five minutes to tell them not to click on links and check for syntax errors? How about asking for the attention of vendor executives that ship insecure software to begin with? And since we're dreaming, why not make it a good one? Let's patch all vulnerabilities on the face of the planet or create the perfect computing platform that is immune to exploitation. Those dreams would at least solve actual hard problems in cybersecurity and would definitely neutralize attacks. Waving a finger at people praying they will catch attacks made possible by a sloppy tech environment is wishful thinking.

People open emails and click on links all day long. That's how the Internet works. Hoping that a training delivered once a year to check grammatical errors in the message's content will magically immunize them from phishing is foolish. People are not the problem. The issue is the tech environment that allowed that email through. The computer configuration that did not stop that malware from executing is faulty. The vendor that hurriedly shipped an insecure tool to cash in profits is accountable. The platform that allows users to choose a weak and broken authentication method is responsible. The lack of network segmentation and isolation is to blame.

Every single attack scenario involves countless deficiencies in software design, system architecture, network policies, financial delegation schemes, and many other technical and procedural aspects, yet everyone is keen on blaming the accountant who opened that bad email that one time. One bad email out of 2500 good ones a month. Where is the logic in that?

Any of these deficiencies, if fixed, could 100% impede the attacker's kill chain, yet everyone seems to be actively working on user awareness and phishing simulations, even though they keep yielding the same results: 10 to 25% of people open attachments or give away their passwords, irrespective of what training they had. What a surprise... We seem to forget that analyzing emails and attachments requires hard technical skills. It's actually a job. It's called being a digital forensics investigator, and the people who do that are paid well, quite rightfully so. These folks did not simply sit through a two-hour session to master this skill. Any hour security teams spend on this kind of nonsense is an hour wasted neutralizing attacks using other measures that yield provable results.

If we force WebAuthn on apps accessed by employees (either through embedded authenticators such as Touch ID and Windows Hello or through YubiKeys), we can almost entirely eliminate the risk of credential grabbing through phishing. Let me repeat that sentence once again. *We can almost entirely eliminate the risk of credential grabbing through phishing with a robust protocol such as WebAuthn.* Good luck with your user awareness slides[17].

That was a long digression, but I feel it was worth it as I witness the Twitter world going crazy after yet another QR code advertisement on national US television because it supposedly teaches people to click on untrusted links, whatever that means.

---

[17] A refreshing article by NCSC about the inefficiencies of user awareness to combat phishing http://bit.ly/3En4Lh1

So, to recap, we identified a series of threats targeting many apps, including Mirage's product, that all seem to exploit weak authentication schemes. We don't have the full list of apps yet, but it's imperative to build it. We'll leverage our upcoming one-on-one session with the different departments to build this inventory.

We continue exploring other vulnerabilities that activate dangerous threat scenarios.

Of course, poorly protected workstations! We check a couple of machines of colleagues sitting nearby to confirm that they all share the same settings: disabled Firewall and hard-drive encryption. Some colleagues did not even bother changing the default "test" passwords. Others replaced it with "mirage". Hardly an improvement...

An attacker need only gain physical access to one of the machines to dump the data locally saved by the employee. If they target the right people, they might even recover saved passwords to SaaS tools and perhaps access to the production environment:

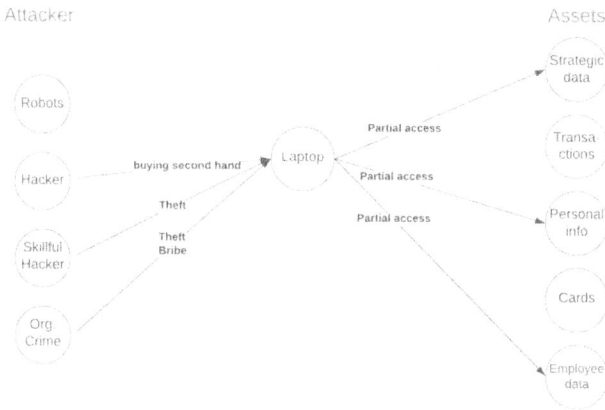

Figure 7-6: Laptop threat graph

This risk will continue to increase in severity as the company keeps on recruiting and scaling. While we're lightly probing the workstations settings to better qualify the threat level, we notice that shared IT account installed on all computers. We send a brief message to John to confirm whether the password is indeed similar to all computers. Twenty seconds later, we receive written confirmation. Of course, it is...

"But we don't use it except as a last resort, when the user is locked out of their computer," he argues, ""and we store the password in a vault, so it's only accessed by IT."

It turns out that the IT department subscribed to a password manager solution, which is refreshing news amidst this influx of disconcerting observations. At least that password is not scribbled on an Excel spreadsheet in a shared network drive. It does not negate, however, the devastating effect should that password somehow leak. Fortunately, macOS has the SSH service disabled by default, which severely limits lateral propagation between computers using this or similar means.

To recap, then, we have a couple of threat scenarios that require physical access. This access can bear great damage if it targets the dozen people with admin privileges, but otherwise, the impact is mostly contained to that single computer and any SaaS tools available to its user. These are important issues that we need to address for sure, but given the current security landscape, we will probably seek a subpar quick win while we focus on more urgent matters:

"John, can we schedule a quick 10-minute meeting to go over some macOS settings and upgrade the process please?" we ask.

We won't close the loopholes through good will and a manual process, but perhaps we can score a quick fix that will dramatically lower the risk of such attacks. In any other context, these workstation flaws may be top priority, but the absence of lateral propagation between workstations is heaven-sent. It's the single setting that allows us to deprioritize this issue, and buy us time while we work on more pressing problems, such as that Jenkins with zero authentication.

Speaking of the devil, how does this particular annoyance fit in our threat graph?

From an impact perspective, this is clearly one of the biggest threats out there. Complete dominion over the infrastructure just because we are on a particular network shared by all employees is as reckless as it gets. This vector can be exploited by disgruntled employees. For example, malicious applications can be run by employees on their laptops while connected to the VPN, thus compromising the Mirage application. And there are many other avenues that we have yet to discover.

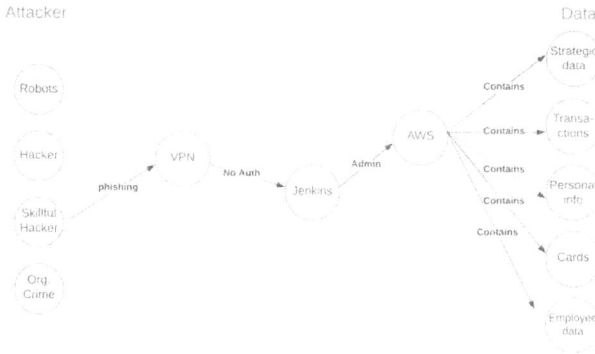

Figure 7-7: Jenkins threat graph

This graph may illustrate what it looks like to gain multi-hop access to the data, but the attacker only faces one real hurdle: the initial entry point to the network (phishing in this case). Following that, they just cruise peacefully to the data, bouncing from one component to the other.

We can narrow down the entry points of this threat scenario by slapping authentication on Jenkins, maybe tie the whole thing to our authentication efforts, but the potential impact on production following the compromise of this service will remain the same.

The original sin of this design, the root of all evil if you will, is breaking the sacrosanct least privilege principle. Ninety-nine percent of developers probably simply run predefined jobs on Jenkins. They don't need access to job settings, much less admin consoles. Similarly, the Jenkins user on AWS probably does not need admin permissions on all the one hundred AWS services. It performs pre-defined commands on a fixed set of maybe three to four services. Its permissions should not grant it more wiggle room than that.

Fixing the Jenkins flaw will likely be relatively easy. We'll activate authentication, limit admin rights to the infrastructure team and reduce the scope of Jenkins' AWS user to the strict permissions it needs. It could take a couple of days to coordinate the whole endeavor, but it seems fairly straightforward. The more interesting question is, how many other Jenkins-like apps do we have out there? Was this misconfiguration an honest mistake, or is it symptomatic of a more systemic issue, such as bad threat modelling that led to a plethora of apps without authentication? The exchange with Nina leans toward the latter. And if that is indeed the case, just how many other internal apps have suffered the same fate?

Our next big action to take is clear: we need to identify all internal apps and assess their level of interaction with the production environment. We do not yet have the resources to control how apps are deployed on the network and what their configuration should be like, but we can make sure that even if they are compromised, they would not bring down the whole production environment.

We take note of discovering all internal apps to assess their security level in the coming days. For now, we plot them as a single node in our threat graph until we shed light on the issue:

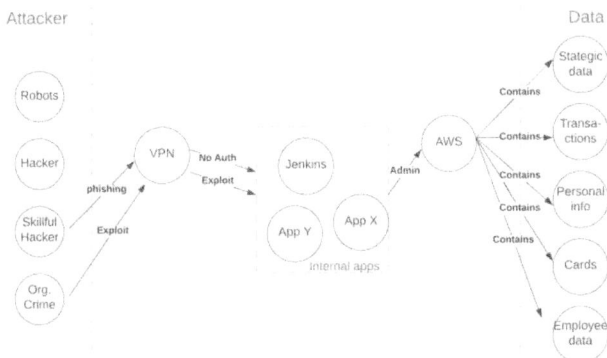

Figure 7-8: Internal apps threat graph

We step back and look at our graph to appreciate all the possible one-hop scenarios we've covered so far: phishing, bruteforce, insecure admin apps... Any one of them leads the attacker directly to some or all of Mirage's treasure trove.

There are additional pathways that we did yet not consider—for instance, a vulnerability in an Internet-facing application. We don't even have a clue of all the public domains owned by Mirage, and we have a feeling that no one else does either. We quickly message Nina only to have her confirm our suspicion. We recall the onboarding slides presented by Tony where he showed that all applications developed by Mirage were running on the same Kubernetes cluster, within the same AWS account.

One critical vulnerability on any of these apps means game over for the entire cluster. Once an attacker is in the context of a trusted app, they will quickly find a way to contact other apps, fetch data from databases and sneak into the most valuable assets. Mirage may be hiring the best developers in the market, but we still need to hedge against classic mistakes that lead to dreadful SQL injections.

We add this type of web app exploit as a viable threat scenario.

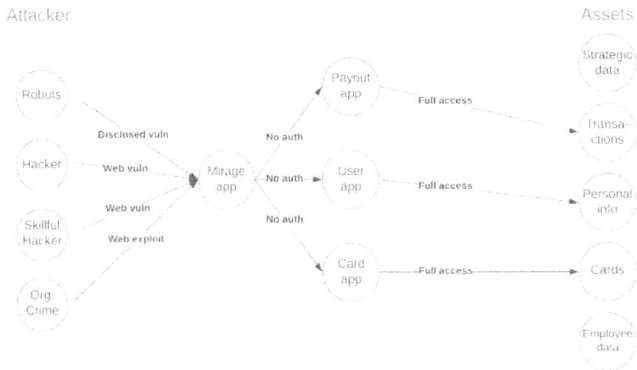

Figure 7-9: Web vulnerability threat graph

We continue this exercise of building threat scenarios out of the vulnerabilities and misconfigurations we've observed. We draw additional attacks, such as the delivery of a malware through phishing or the backdooring of our app through a compromised third-party package. These are all valid scenarios, but ultimately, their probability and impact will fall below our current line of urgency.

We cannot be exhaustive in this first iteration because we lack the mastery of the environment, but it will come bit by bit. We will refine this graph every day, every week, as it will be the foundational piece of our prioritization and decision-making.

We step back to admire the threat landscape, artfully laid out. We can clearly see our top priorities for the moment. These initiatives will most surely heavily impact the product and the infrastructure and will require all the buy-in we can get.

We send a message to Henry: "Have you got 10 minutes for a chat? Let's talk about that roadmap."

Baby steps

Henry carefully listens to our argument. We present the threat graph and diligently go through the most important threats currently looming over Mirage's business:

- An attacker abusing the weak authentication scheme, thus affecting the product and every SaaS and internal tool used by the team

- An attacker exploiting a vulnerability on any of the apps exposed by Mirage
- An attacker abusing the wide permissions attributed to apps over the production environment.

We illustrate each scenario, their underlying vulnerabilities and naturally conclude: "We need to dig into each scenario to confirm our hypothesis, but at this point, given all the data we have, it seems reasonable to believe that these are our top priorities."

"I see," he responds, "your prioritization model to determine your area of focus is interesting. In product design, we usually start from the customer and work back our way to the features we think they want. You've followed a similar approach, but took the attacker as a starting point. The parallel is striking. Yet I would still like to keep the customer in the discussion. I don't want you to get lost in implementing security measures without thinking how it will impact the customer."

Henry makes a crucial point. We are not solving authentication just for the heck of it. We're solving authentication for the sake of protecting Mirage's customers and business. Entirely ignoring the customer may bias our judgement toward technically sound security measures that may be detrimental to the growth of the company and its user experience.

Oh, how easy it is to vainly assume that every security vulnerability is an existential threat to the business and milk that argument over and over to justify the most ridiculous restrictions that make customers want to rip their computer to pieces. The reality is that many companies not only survive but thrive after even the most decimating hacks: CapitalOne, Maersk, and so many others. Yes, it is a dicey outcome and the pain is acute for a couple of months, but one may argue that the odds are fair to gamble on. A security breach that costs a dozen million dollars pales before the prospect of exponential growth that could yield a $10-billion-dollar valuation. One could almost be forgiven for taking such a risk.

I am not advocating for throwing caution out of the door and surfing naked on the wave of growth. I am simply reframing the context of our work in a much broader perspective where we can see and appreciate the trajectory of the company. That's basically Henry's point. Security is not an isolated artifact in this company that we should optimize no matter what. It's a cog in a bigger machine that should work toward advancing the global mission. This dilemma of local vs global optimization transcends security.

The classic example being a sales department that promises ghost features just to close a sale and reach their numbers, even though it will lead to unsatisfied customers, high churn and loss of trust, all of which impairs the business down the road. Or a product manager whose only concern is to ship the feature on time to collect their bonus, no matter the poor quality or the broken technical architecture that cannot withstand the expected load and ultimately hurts the company. Examples abound of such locally optimized decisions that hurt the overall system, and it is acutely relevant in our case because many potential measures could easily hinder the company's performance despite having stellar security properties.

The minute one starts to argue security measures for the sake of security, they will inevitably lose the support of every company executive. Rightfully so, as they are no longer pursuing the same goal, which is achieving the company's mission[18].

So, to circle back to Henry's point. Where does the customer fit in our decision framework?

"You're right, we currently model each threat path by taking the attacker's perspective. When designing and arbitraging solutions to neuter these attacks, we'll adopt a more product-based approach. We'll consider the customer user experience and target the best trade-off that keeps the same user experience while severely reducing the threat landscape. Take the authentication scheme, for example. One robust solution is to slap a 2FA on the login form of the Mirage app. But we don't want to annoy 100% of customers, 100% of the time, just to stop an attacker who may or may not target one account out of 20,000. We will probably devise a way to remember the browser and only ask for 2FA when the customer signs in from a new IP and browser. We have not worked out the details yet, of course, but that's the approach we'll take for all the security measures we'll devise."

This answer, while resting on many hypotheses, is no improvisation feat. It faithfully derives from our commitment to a pragmatic security that accelerates the business while protecting its interest and growth. A vision that we stated well before joining Mirage and that crystallizes through these decisions and projects that we lead, thereby answering one of Henry's main questions about the type of security we want to pursue at Mirage.

Henry seems reassured and quickly shifts gears to talk about project management and how to properly follow the value we bring to customers.

---

[18] An inspirational lecture by Fred Kofman on this specific issue of goal alignment: https://bit.ly/3Yc8uGF.

"We need a set of measurable goals to track the success of the projects. Let's take that bruteforce problem. It shows up clearly in your graph and cost us $300k in the past few months. One goal, for example, would be to keep these losses under $5000. What's the earliest we can achieve this goal? And what projects should we work on to achieve this as fast as possible?'

The discussion veers off the rail of security and enters the realm of lean project management. The build-measure-learn cycle, where we postulate a statement, build a quick proof of concept that can help us validate or invalidate that statement before scaling the effort to implement the real deal. We think that a WAF can help us block vulnerabilities and protect against bot attacks. How can we quickly test this hypothesis before contracting a $50,000 tool? We think that managing identity requires a single sign-on solution, but how many apps really support this integration? And does it really solve the issues we're experiencing? We need to quickly test this hypothesis before initiating a three-month project to integrate the solution.

"Alright," concludes Henry, "How can I help you deliver your first project in the shortest timeframe possible?" he asks.

We cannot sustain our current exposure to the outside world. Our main app is laid bare in a predatory environment. Yes, there are some quick fixes that we started doing on our authentication app, a sort of band-aid to buy us time, but it won't resist much longer to increased scrutiny. We need a proper web application firewall (WAF) acting as a first layer that can set up flexible rules on the fly to ban malicious and bot-like traffic. Not only will it heavily slow down novel types of bruteforce attacks, but it will also raise the bar against exploit-type attacks such as potential SQL injections and so on. That's one of our most pressing attack scenarios. It's a big-ticket item with proper payout. The sooner we put it in place, the longer we'll be able to breathe and carry out other projects. We can work in parallel with the product team on improving the authentication scheme of the Mirage app, probably through some sort of 2FA protection. We'll figure out the details soon enough.

"We need the infrastructure team's support to implement a WAF. They can show us around the current setup, how it works and how we can plug this additional component. Marc already expressed eagerness to work on the WAF project. We just need to snatch the first availability of one of his engineers," we respond.

"A WAF can cost as much as $4000 a month so..." we start laying the groundwork, but then Henry cuts us short:

"If you deem it necessary for the company, and from what you're saying it clearly is, then we'll happily pay for it. I see security as one of those life-threatening risks for a young company. We're not in the business of saving thousands of dollars on an issue that can cost us the entire enterprise," he responds.

A web application firewall (WAF) may seem like an expensive joke to many experienced hackers—hell, even I may have written some words to that effect—but in the context of a company exposed to attackers with a variety of skills and resources, a WAF, a good WAF, can buy us critical time to patch systems when there is a serious vulnerability spreading like wildfire on the Internet. It can help us diffuse a dangerous situation, like that bruteforce scenario, in a matter of seconds, while we work on a permanent fix. More importantly, it adds another hop to any Internet-based threat scenario on our graph.

A bruteforce needs to first bypass the WAF before crashing on 2FA and password complexity. An attacker wishing to find or exploit that SQL injection vulnerability will first need to bypass the WAF. Which can be done, but not without leaking some weak signals that can help us detect a potential attempted breach early on.

"One other thing. I asked the recruiting team to find us some security engineers to help you carry out your tasks. They won't be hunting full time as we have many important positions to fill first, but who knows who might show up. Try to find five minutes to send them a brief description of the job."

"Oh," he adds, "I am glad to see how hands-on you were during these last few days. We need that around here."

Great news!

We head back to our desk and prepare our email for the compliance team to inform them of our top priorities for the foreseeable future. As a precaution, we export the graph in a nice Excel file that auditors love so much. We chuckle at the idea of Robert trying to map these concrete topics to his list of absurdly generic controls.

The next day, we schedule a call with Marc from the infrastructure team to bootstrap the WAF project. He quickly jumps onboard. "I always told Henry that we were in dire need of a WAF, but I guess we needed to suffer an attack for him to realize that. I can ask Steve on my team to look into the AWS WAF. It integrates very well with our ecosystem. He'll be available next week to look into it."

Hum…

"Marc," we say rather carefully, "I am not entirely sure that the AWS WAF is the best option. It may very well be, but I would be more comfortable testing it alongside other products to confirm it covers all our use cases."

"Yes, of course. I understand. It's just that we try to keep a homogenous infrastructure as much as possible, and if an AWS service meets 80% of our needs, we should go with that, in my opinion. In any case, whatever solution you recommend will have to go through our tech approval process. Are you familiar with that?"

Henry did mention something to that effect during the interview process, but it's just a foggy memory by now. Marc explains that every new feature or project at Mirage requires writing a technical document detailing the problem to be solved, the chosen solution, its implementation steps, test phase, and finally, its rollout plan. This document aligns tech stakeholders around the key deliverables and their quality.

Fair enough.

We message Steve to grab a quick coffee and bond before working on the WAF together. He quickly responds back with what we can only guess is a smirk:

"So, how fucked up is the security of this place?"

"Well, it is challenging to pick up pieces after the fact, but we have got to start somewhere, I guess," we respond.

"You have not seen the half of it yet. It blows my mind that half the developers have access to production servers and databases. It just takes one bad SQL statement and the whole banking app is down. What are we going to do against that?" he questions expectantly.

This is a classic conversation with an engineer who had the privilege of witnessing one too many shortcuts. They have been in the company long enough to know where all the bodies are buried: the hard-coded credentials, the generic admin accounts... All of it! We want, nay, we need the feedback of such people to help us accelerate the discovery process. Give them a thoughtful ear, and they will throw critical vulnerabilities your way that would otherwise take deep digging or sometimes chance to uncover.

It's easy to be dismissive of the avalanche of vulnerabilities that Steve and his peers will throw at us. Some security teams might feel overwhelmed by the sheer number of flaws that need fixing. Others, especially those who have been there for a while, can have their ego bruised, as if the mere existence of such vulnerabilities stains their hard work. It is precisely for these reasons that we spent time building our prioritization framework. We have clear rules around what we should focus on and what we should let burn for the moment.

The most important thing is to submit each new flaw or vulnerability to the same analysis we performed earlier. Steve is talking about developers having write access to production servers. We can almost visualize our threat graph. First, we need to get a valid VPN connection, either through phishing or other means, and then we must steal those database credentials. That's a two-hop compromise scenario that only works on a handful of developers. It's severe. The potential impact is huge, but not as serious as our current three priorities. We explain our reasoning to Steve:

"I understand your concern; it's very valid. From a security perspective, though, I am currently addressing the much more pressing web vulnerabilities on public apps that can be exploited by anyone. I'll add the scenario to my threat graph and probably look into production access in the coming months, once we successfully reduce Mirage's public exposition and threat levels. That being said, maybe we can easily address availability and integrity risks by enabling database backups every hour or every day, for instance. I did not take the time yet to inspect our databases, but if we rely on AWS's service, they should propose snapshots and backups that can be configured easily, right? That's a quick win that would ease recovery and buy us time while we address other urgent security matters. What do you think?"

Steve seems satisfied with the answer. We listened to his concern, qualified the menace and agreed on a course of action.

We continue chatting about the next big architecture moves planned in the infrastructure team. At some point, he sneaks rather snarly: "You should have seen the outrage of the executive team when I forced that 2FA on the VPN. They went mad!"

Oh...so it was Steve in the end!

We continue bonding over war stories of crazy security measures and pentesting escapades. We even lean toward the same two WAF solutions that we both came across independently a few years back. We quickly discuss the pros and cons of each, and decide to meet again in one week's time to start working on the WAF.

Marc will be disappointed about not getting his AWS WAF, but working with Steve will be fun!

We take a look at our calendar and it's almost time to meet John to go through the configuration of workstations. Securing workstations against physical loss and malware propagation usually requires enforcing security settings through some sort of device management solution. It's the only way to guarantee safety with a certain level of confidence. However, we have more urgent vulnerabilities to remediate. The apps are naked on the Internet with a broken authentication scheme, so, if we can find some quick hacks to mitigate 80% of the workstation issues with a couple of tweaks, then all the better. That would greatly reduce the surface attack and give us leeway until our prioritization framework clearly indicates that workstations are the next major threat.

We head over to the dedicated IT desks and are surprised to find John in front of 10 new computers, jumping from one to the next to configure their settings. The man does not stop!

We hesitantly engage him for fear of disrupting his ritual and take it as an opportunity to ask about their laptop preparation process:

"I noticed some crucial security settings that were missing, and I wonder how we can easily incorporate them without adding constraints to your process," we tentatively ask.

Judging by the 10 laptops spanning three desks, it's very clear that the IT team is having a hard time scaling the onboarding process. We can't just show up with absurd recommendations that would triple their already long touch time. They will never go along with it. Call it emotional intelligence, empathy or simple observation, but this is the tactical advantage of having a security team that can immerse itself in the day-to-day lives of the teams it's assisting.

"We receive computers and equipment from the local Apple store every week, and as you can see, we line them up and manually configure them. We install the VPN, Slack and other tools. We create local accounts for newcomers, then register the computer-user association in our Excel file, so we can keep track of who owns what. It's a very laborious process," complains John in an almost desperate voice. "Every week, we onboard 10 to 15 people. Easily about a day's work just preparing computers."

"Did you ask for a device management solution? I bet that would help automate much of this setup, no?" we ask.

"Yeah, but Rachel, the CFO, thinks the cost is prohibitive. She is not really into this IT stuff, so she cannot quite understand how life-changing this solution could be for us," he retorts back.

We nod in agreement. Sadly, that's a common trap that plagues many companies. They're too small to hire a dedicated IT director or CIO, and the CTO, who is responsible for the product platform, does not want to deal with printer and workstation issues. The IT department ends up affiliated with the CFO or HR director or in another transversal direction. Of course, these executives don't understand squat about computer technologies, so the conditions and processes of the team heavily degrade, leading to shortcuts, such as putting "test" as a password for everyone. As is often the case, bad security practices are symptoms of much bigger structural issues. Curing the symptoms may be the short-sighted solution to tick a checkbox, but the underlying issues are bound to spew new symptoms, new security flaws.

"I think I might be able to help here, John," we say with a bright smile. "Do you have a device management solution in mind? Does your team have experience managing one?"

"Yes, I installed a device management solution from scratch in my previous job and was operating it for a couple of years. I know exactly what to do. We just need the budget," he responds back.

"Alright, I'll write an email to Rachel saying that the current state of affairs is absolutely untenable and that we need device management to square things off. You can start pushing on your end as well. What does it cost, really? $65 per computer? What would the damage be if someone's computer got stolen with a plaintext hard drive containing all our business data on it? I know for a fact that it's more than $65…"

John interrupts us: "Actually, at least one laptop gets stolen about every month. People go to a nearby pub to have a couple of pints, and before you know it, we receive an email asking for a replacement."

That same computer with "test" as a password and no encryption? There goes our hypothesis about physical access being rare…

"Damn… do we disable their access at least?" we desperately ask.

"Yes, we notify the infrastructure team so they can reset their VPN profile. We also disable their access on various tools, but I am sure there are SaaS tools that we don't have access to…it's a bit complicated and it takes time to reach out to all teams," responds John.

We reassure him that this process will get much easier once we solve the authentication issue across all SaaS tools. In the meantime, we ask him to be included in the loop of these alerts. We'll take a look how efficient the offboarding process is.

"I will send an email to Rachel right away. This thing is a no-brainer. It will probably save your teams days of work, provide a better experience for new joiners, and it is much more secure. Furthermore, I heard that we're planning to recruit 20 to 30 people a week. How are you going to handle that without some form of automation?"

"Exactly! Thank you very much! I owe you one…"

"No worries, in the meantime, however, please, can we make two small adjustments to the onboarding process? Can you enable File vault systematically when setting up computers? We need, at the very least, to encrypt laptops before handing them over employees."

"Yeah, sure. Let me add it to the setup procedure. Consider it done, starting with these ten computers," he promises.

"Great. Also, can we choose a better password than 'test'? I believe there is no way to force people to change passwords on first login on MacOS, so we have no choice but to set up a more complex password right from the start."

Johns looks hesitant. "I understand, but we configure these accounts manually, so it's really cumbersome to choose a unique password for each user and type complex characters. The keyboard layout may differ from computer to computer so special characters and numbers are hard to get right. How would we even give that password to the user? Should we send it to their personal email?"

"How about automatically generating passwords for users and printing each username/password on a single sheet of paper that you give with each laptop. It does not have to be a complex password with weird characters. A two-word password separated by an underscore would work just fine. In the onboarding session, we ask everyone to update their passwords. Again, this is all just temporary until we get that green light on the device management solution."

"That…could work. But we don't have a way to generate such passwords. Is there a tool that we can use?" responds John

"I will take care of it. I'll send you an AppleScript by email that you can add to the Finder app. Prepare a list of usernames in a text file, one name per line, double click on the script and it will generate as many PDFs as there are usernames. You can then print them and slip each one in the computer accordingly. What do you say?"

John could not be happier that we took his concerns to heart. Sure, we may have added a couple of steps to his regular procedure but we will fight to help him secure the budget for that device management.

"One last thing, John. Could you please automatically install that password manager that you guys use for everyone in the company. You can even instruct people in the onboarding session to store the VPN pin code in the password manager. If someone complains about the costs, say it's a security requirement and send them my way."

"You got it!"

We return to our desk and work on that quick AppleScript to generate long passwords for new joiners. We'll keep it nice and simple. There's no need for weird special characters, length is the only criteria that matters. If this simple hack helps us avoid the "test" password, then it's already a big win.

We also drop a brief message on a couple of company channels to ask everybody to encrypt their laptops using File Vault or an equivalent solution if they use Linux. We keep it short and sweet, with a quick video on how to do it on MacOS. Again, it's a band-aid at best. Only 20% of the people reading that message will likely take the time to do it, but it only takes 30 seconds to post, so why not?

The infrastructure and IT teams holding the most privileges on the platform are the ones most at risk. We individually message them to confirm that their settings are configured properly.

Finally, as we promised John, we send a quick email to Rachel with Henry in copy to talk about the need for a device management tool highlighting the cost-to-benefit ratio. A payment institution that loses its data because of a single stolen computer... Can it get more absurd than that?

Poking around

The next day, we crack our fingers and flex our muscles. Now that we've taken care of the workstation threat as best as we can, it's about time we truly pentested this bank!

Out of all the things that we could be doing, from preparing the 2FA implementation on the app to comparing WAF products, why in hell are we taking a few days to pentest this app?

Steve's warning about developers accessing production is symptomatic of much a deeper problem in our beautiful threat analysis. We only dealt with the known knowns—that is, we only considered the flaws we were lucky enough to witness while haphazardly interacting with the company during the onboarding process. These first flaws were the essential first pawns that allowed us to bootstrap our prioritization framework, but the tech environment at Mirage is large and there may be other one-hop vulnerabilities lurking out there. We were cautious enough to take a high-level approach to account for this bias: we extrapolated specific flaws (Jenkins remote code exec) into classes of vulnerabilities (authentication and extensive permissions) to factor in potential blind spots. Still, we need to look under the hood and make sure we did not miss any crucial pieces of the puzzle.

In an ideal setting, flaws and cracks in the system should never be news to a decent security team. Just like an efficient market, everything should be priced in. This or that vulnerability is only present because it was deemed less critical than that other vulnerabilities that the team chose to prioritize.

This little pentest adventure will surely occupy us part-time for the following couple of days. Furthermore, it may be the only time where we will lack any bias regarding the app and can therefore earnestly explore every request and parameter without any preconceived notion of expected behavior. We have the skills to do it, so let's take advantage of that. Many security teams would simply delegate this exercise to an auditing firm that would review the app, the infrastructure and everything in between. This decision depends on the technical abilities and inclinations of the team in question, but I would argue that this first pentest is about more than just the vulnerabilities. Yes, finding remote code execution is important. But equally important is the intimate knowledge of the product and its underlying tech.

A hacker friend of mine was adamant in believing that pentesters ended up knowing the app better than its developers. While it can be perceived as a bold statement, it echoes a parcel of truth familiar to many pentesters.

A developer will test the expected behavior of their code: *does the code correctly perform function X that was drafted in the specification document?* A pentester, on the other hand, will try to find a way to make that piece of code perform functions Y and Z instead, to which developers usually respond: "*Oh, I did not know it could do that...*"

We need such a comprehensive understanding of Mirage's platform as we have impactful additions on the horizon, such as adding 2FA to the login page and putting a WAF in place to cite only a couple. We must present a convincing and thorough case for these changes: how will they impact the end user? How do they fit in the current tech environment? Which code to add and where? We cannot outsource this analysis to other teams and be content to follow their progress every couple of weeks. The more autonomous we are, the faster we will deliver our projects. This intimate, first-hand knowledge of the app and its infrastructure will free us from the shackles of people's roadmaps and absurd justifications. It will give us powerful leverage when negotiating solutions. We'll be able to call on everyone's bullshit when they dismissively raise imaginary problems in an attempt to impede the work that needs to be done. We will be actors of our own will rather than simple beggars of time and means.

You either make propositions or you take them. You either make things happen or you wait for them to spontaneously appear. The former stance confers more power and is likelier to yield actual results.

Let's get to it, shall we?

The first step of any hacking job is, of course, reconnaissance. We must weed out all of Mirage's assets exposed on the Internet, from websites to databases and other esoteric servers. The classic way to do so in your typical hacking guide is to bruteforce DNS domains using tools, such as DNSRecon *(https://github.com/darkoperator/dnsrecon)*, leverage specialized search engines from *https://crt.sh* to *https://censys.io* and scan the full network for viable hosts using a broad Masscan *(https://github.com/robertdavidgraham/masscan)*. We could do that for old time's sake, but today, we have a distinctive advantage. We are already on the inside. Why bother with DNS brute-forcing when we could just dig our way through AWS to identify all registered domain names? It's much faster and more accurate, and we know the right people to help us. We send a quick note to Steve:

"Hey, Steve. I would like to start poking around our current apps exposed on the Internet. Do you happen to have a list of all public domains in Mirage? It will also help us for the WAF project."

Steve kindly takes 10 minutes to explain how they set up domain name resolution using Route53, an AWS service to handle domain resolution.

Each DNS record, such as *app.mirage.com,* is declared on Route53 within a hosted zone, a high-level domain container of sorts. In this example, the hosted zone would be *mirage.com.* Hosted zones marked as private can only be resolved from within specific networks, such as the employee's VPN and production networks. Those that are declared public can be resolved from the Internet.

"So, we can query the Route53 service to list all domains and therefore all applications, correct?" we ask.

"Well, it depends. Public applications, yes. Internal applications, however, are set up a tad differently here. They can also be reached through our internal HTTP routing engine without a corresponding hostname on Route53. We can dive into it if you want, but for your immediate purposes, just focus on the public domains within Route53," responds Steve.

We take a few minutes to go through the Route53 documentation[19] and its API reference. We start hacking together a Python script that will call these APIs, go through each hosted zone and query its declared DNS records.

We first initialize a connector to the Route53 service using the Python boto3 library, then call the `list_hosted_zones` method to list all hosted zones:

```
import boto3

client = boto3.client("route53")
response = client.list_hosted_zones()
```

For each hosted zone in the response, we call the Route53 API method `list_resource_record_sets` to fetch its DNS records:

```
for zone in response["HostedZones"]:
   zone_id = zone["Id"]
   response = client.list_resource_record_sets(
                    HostedZoneId=zone_id,
                    MaxItems="300")
```

We then filter the output to only keep A records (DNS names pointing to IP addresses) and CNAME records (DNS names pointing to other DNS names). The full script can be found on the book's GitHub repository[20]. It's a little bit more organized than the crude examples above, but its core functionality remains the same. We obtain the following output when executing the script:

```
alex@computer:~/ python list_domains.py
```

---

[19] *https://docs.aws.amazon.com/Route53/latest/DeveloperGuide/Welcome.html.*

[20] *https://github.com/sparcflow/Blitzscaling*

```
renewal.mirage.com.
entry-1790935582.eu-west-1.elb.amazonaws.com
public
--
dashboard.mirage.com.
entry-1790935582.elb.eu-west-1.amazonaws.com
public
--
auth.mirage.com.
entry-1790935582.elb.eu-west-1.amazonaws.com
public
--
jenkins.mirage.co.
10.2.2.12
private
--
*.production.mirage.co.
tooling-1201436684.elb.eu-west-1.amazonaws.com
private
…snip…
```

We get close to 30 public DNS records, some private, others public. All the publicly facing domains, such as *dashboard.mirage.com*, point to an AWS load balancer, as is evident by the "elb.eu-west-1.amazonaws.com" suffix. These machines must, in turn, forward traffic to the servers hosting the apps within the Kubernetes cluster. We confirm these hypotheses by clicking our way through the AWS Cloud console.

Now that we've compiled this list of targets, we can explore each one of the public endpoints looking for the most blatant vulnerabilities. Forget about XSS and CSRF, we only want to unearth the most critical vulnerabilities that directly lead to the compromise of the app and therefore access to customer data. We're looking for SQL injections, remote code execution, path traversal, server-side request forgery and so on.

We jump from one website to another, clicking on every parameter, visiting every page we can find. Our instincts are on fire; this has been our job for a few years now, so it all flows almost naturally. Burp proxy is running on the background intercepting every HTTP request. We tweak the parameters of the most interesting queries, sometimes injecting special characters such as " ' ` ( ) ; | &ddddd in the hope of triggering an error, other times changing object identifiers to test for user segregation[21].

---

[21] My first book *How to Hack Like a Pornstar*
https://www.amazon.com/dp/B01MTDLGQQ walks the reader through techniques for finding and exploiting vulnerabilities.

As we wade through the many pages of the Mirage app, we stumble upon a form uploader that expects PDF invoices. In trying to understand its nominal behavior, we upload a regular document and observe what happens. The app responds by displaying a beautiful thumbnail animation of what seems to be the first page of our PDF document.

Great user experience, for sure, but as that delightful animation is dancing around, a spark of opportunity kindles in our eyes. This app is parsing user-provided PDFs! PDF parsers are notorious for harboring glaring vulnerabilities. Maybe we can do something with that...

We isolate the HTTP endpoint on Burp that is responsible for this conversion.

Figure 9-1: PDF upload request in Burp

We can see that the host is set to "convert.mirage.com". A quick search on the company's GitLab server reveals code repository behind this endpoint. We clone the codebase and open it in Visual Studio Code *(https://code.visualstudio.com/)*. We abuse some of VSCode's plugins to jump from one class definition to another, foraging our way through the deeply nested code of Rails[22] controllers and services until we land on the little piece of code that parses the PDF file:

```
def build_converter(src_path, dest_path)
    converter = MiniMagick::Tool::Convert.new
    CONVERT_OPTIONS.each { |_, v| converter.merge!(v) }
    converter << src_path
    converter << dest_path
```

---

[22] Ruby on Rails is a web-application framework that makes it easy to spring a new app from scratch: *https://rubyonrails.org/*

Mirage is using MiniMagick to convert a PDF to a PNG file, which then ends up as the thumbnail we saw earlier. MiniMagick is a popular Ruby package or gem to convert files between different formats: PNG to JPG, PDF to JPG and so on. It's a wrapper around the executable ImageMagick *(https://imagemagick.org)*, which itself relies on yet another tool called GhostScript *(https://www.ghostscript.com)* for certain formats.

But how does the app determine which file type it's actually receiving? Can it guarantee it's a PDF file?

We scroll back to the calling class and find that this type of check is delegated to yet another third-party package, the CarrierWave gem *(https://github.com/carrierwaveuploader/carrierwave),* which expects a method called `content_type_whitelist` to define which types to allow through.

```ruby
class ApplicationUploader < CarrierWave::Uploader::Base
  include CarrierWave::MiniMagick
  include ApplicationHelper

  def content_type_whitelist
    %w[
      application/pdf
      image/png
      image/jpeg
    ]
  end

  process convert: "png"
  ...snip...

end
```

Mirage developers seem to leverage this method to enforce strict acceptance of PDF, PNG and JPG files. However, the Rails framework operates a lot of magic behind the scenes. We cannot reliably infer whether the content type is blindly accepted as is from the request headers or if it's derived from the file by inspecting its content (a more robust check).

Luckily for us, it's fairly simple to check this hypothesis. We send an XML file with an altered content-type header set to `application/pdf`.

```
POST /apis/v3/documents HTTP/1.1
Host: convert.mirage.com
Content-Disposition: form-data; name="Content-Type"
application/pdf
Content-Type: application/pdf

<?xml version="1.0" standalone="no"?> <xml>test</xml>
```

In theory, this request should fail, because XML is not an accepted type, yet...

```
HTTP/1.1 200 OK
Server: server
...snip...
```

```
{"file":{"id": "98a78e-e8e7err...","thumbnail":
""https://files.mirage.co/..."}}
```

Lo and behold, the app returns a 200 OK. We can download our uploaded file and confirm that the XML file was indeed converted to a blank PNG image. We have just found a faulty file type check that allows us to pass any file to the ImageMagick class. Maybe we can send a dynamic format that embeds executable code? We search the Internet for known payloads to abuse this type of behavior and find a rich list of scripts and blog posts about leveraging PostScripts and SVG file formats to execute code through ImageMagick[23]. We download a template of such a payload.

Below is an SVG file that embeds an image based on the content of the /etc/passwd.

```
<?xml version="1.0" standalone="no"?>
<!DOCTYPE svg PUBLIC "-//W3C//DTD SVG 1.1//EN"
"http://www.w3.org/Graphics/SVG/1.1/DTD/svg11.dtd">
<svg width="720px" height="1080px" viewBox="0 0 720 1080"
version="1.1" baseProfile="full"
xmlns="http://www.w3.org/2000/svg">
<image xlink:href="text:/etc/passwd" x="0" y="0" width="100%"
height="100%"
transform="scale(0.5, 0.5)" />
</svg>
```

We submit the file falsely labelled as PDF and collect back the processed image with a full copy of /etc/passwd:

```
root:x:0:0:root:/root:/bin/bash
daemon:x:1:1:daemon:/usr/sbin:/usr/sbin/nologin
bin:x:2:2:bin:/bin:/usr/sbin/nologin
sys:x:3:3:sys:/dev:/usr/sbin/nologin
sync:x:4:65534:sync:/bin:/bin/sync
```

A nasty command local file inclusion, just like we like them. We can effectively read files on the Convert Mirage app. We are officially in!

---

[23] https://bit.ly/3WVhKgN, https://bit.ly/3WRSs3e, https://bit.ly/3vrT9EI.

We dump environment variables located in `/proc/self/environ` and with them the database credentials, AWS API keys and other useful passwords. If we tweak our payload slightly or use another format, like PostScript, we can even achieve persistent code execution. We are in a flat architecture, so we can call the private HTTP endpoints of other services to move money, create users and so on. None of these endpoints are protected with authentication as Tony confirmed in our first few days. This is effectively game over for Mirage.

The perfect illustration of one-hop vulnerabilities that validates our WAF project, as any decent WAF would have rejected that obvious payload. It also gives us the proper leverage to stack deeper levels of security, such as container hardening, intrusion detection at the system level, service authentication, network segregation and other fun future projects.

We continue roaming around the apps and find other instances of the same ImageMagick vulnerability. We stumble upon some XSS here and there, even an XML injection issue, but thankfully, it requires compromising a partner to inject that malicious payload. A possibility for sure, but less urgent than straight up remote code execution available to all.

The fact that this vulnerability is present on every endpoint accepting files is telling. This is a systemic issue. A false assumption or lack of knowledge by Mirage developers that warrants a written standard to align everyone on secure file uploads.

The timing could not be more adequate since we are meeting Charles, a backend tech lead, in a few minutes to discuss data storage and the location of critical customer information.

Charles has been with Mirage for over two years and is one of the most senior tech leads in the company. One can almost always find him commenting on technical documents and merge requests or debating hot technical topics on Slack.

"I heard about your work with Tony on the bruteforce issue!" he says. "Thanks for helping us take care of that. I really wish we could extract all of that rate limiting logic from the authentication app and delegate it to a different service specialized in that."

"Yes, it was really just a band-aid to stop the bleeding," we reply. "Next week, we will start working on a web application firewall with the infrastructure team. It will inherit much of the logic of the rate limiting and anti-bruteforce we implemented. Expect an MR to remove that code in the coming weeks!"

"Oh my! I love MRs that chop off lines from the code base," he joyfully says.

We trampoline from the WAF to threat modelling and the prioritization framework we have created and explain how he can help us fill in the gaps about data storage facilities.

"I can guess that our most critical data is stored on different AWS services," we start, "but it's still fuzzy a little bit. Could you please shed some light on that? Where is our most critical data located? It seems like a simple question but I have trouble getting a straight answer when I asked around informally."

"Alright. The first thing you need to understand is that our team, the backend team, is fractioned in two. Following Conway's law[24], our code base is similarly composed of two main galaxies of services. The first group of services, all written in Ruby, is centered around a monolith called "manager", the first Mirage application. It provides most of what the customers see on their dashboards once they log in. We're trying to dismantle this gigantic app into several micro services to ease maintenance. We extracted authentication last year into its own service, for instance. That's where you did your anti-bruteforce changes. We still have a long way to go, though.

The second galaxy of services revolve around the low-level payment services (PS). These services, written in Golang, handle the actual communication with the financial ecosystem. They handle XML payment files, receive notifications from other banks and so on. Each business domain is isolated in its own micro service that does one thing—and one thing *only*. You'll find a service for initiating SEPA transfers, another for parsing SWIFT messages and so forth.

Now, to answer your question, every piece of critical data handled by the manager app is stored in a single S3 bucket called `mirage-manager-data`. There, you'll find several folders containing customer's proof of identity, receipts, and invoices. On the payment services (PS) side, each service has its own S3 bucket, often starting with the prefix "mirage-banking-". These bucket names are often defined as environment variables in the config file `prod.yaml` in each code repository."

Charles proceeds to open the SWIFT service on GitLab and navigates to the prod.yaml file that contains, among other parameters, the list of environment variables loaded at run time in the application:

```
...snip...
env:
  S3_BUCKET_NAME: mirage-swift-prod
  PASSWORD_KEY: AQICAHqzseCql3AxM7bJv37...
  API_DOMAIN: mirage.co
```

---

[24] Conway's Law states that organizations who design systems are constrained to produce designs that are copies of the communication structures of these organizations.

```
API_KEY: b70901b545e8ffb3ec186bb62de00bb76744012c
AWS_ACCESS_KEY_ID: AKIA44ZRK9DQ4D7XCL8Q
AWS_SECRET_ACCESS_KEY: AQICAHjzgvEvyCMkG5cJd66ydBGfBOcUKZ...
...snip...
```

We can spot the S3 bucket name used by this app. More interestingly, we notice that a few variables contain some ominous words, such as "secret" or "password". We hesitantly blurt out: "Uhh... Charles. Do you see these AWS secret keys as well or am I already going senile?"

He nervously laughs. "Haha, yeah, about that...We never really settled on how we should handle secrets at Mirage. But I believe someone developed a routine to store encrypted passwords in the code and decrypt them when the code is deployed. I don't know the exact workings of it all. You'll have to check with the infrastructure team."

We take note of this suspicious encryption scheme employed by Mirage apps. Storing encrypted secrets in the code is better than having plain old passwords, for sure, but if the key is easily retrievable by any developer, then that defeats the whole purpose. In our minds, almost immediately, an exploit line is being drawn on the threat graph, going from attackers with access to the VPN, then breaking the encryption scheme on GitLab, then achieving full access to business and customer data on AWS. A deadly two-hop threat scenario. This is a huge problem and a big challenge to tackle. Changing how passwords are stored and deployed within apps can blow up the whole deployment process and cause customer friction and waste. This will be an exciting project when we're done dealing with one-hop scenarios.

Ideally, developers should not be bothered to know production secrets. A secret should be referenced through a public identifier that can be shared and written to the configuration. However, the app and the app alone should be capable of fetching the secret tied to that identifier, loading it and then using the secret to access the target resource. This is the basic premise of secret management solutions, such as AWS SecretsManager, Google SecretsManager and HashiCorp's Vault. It's too early to start such a complex project, but it will definitely pop up on our radar very soon.

Charles continues describing the different storage mediums leveraged at Mirage: Redis clusters for caching and scheduling jobs, Elasticsearch for some aggregated data related to customer behavior, Postgres databases as the main storage engine on AWS RDS and a nascent attempt to use Kafka as a message queue to transmit information between micro services.

"Right now, much of our inter-service communication relies on synchronous HTTP messages, where the client expects the counterparty to be healthy for the message to get through. If the communication fails for any reason, then the payload is simply lost, unless we have built-in retries, but even that has its limits. We want to break this tense communication circuit by introducing a component in the middle, an event streaming platform, such as Kafka, that can collect messages from one service and make it available to any service that wishes to use that data. Services producing messages can "fire and forget" events, knowing that it will be stored in Kafka and delivered when the other services are able to consume them. Kafka libraries have, of course, embedded retries, tracking of the last message read and so on. We can scale message distribution using partitioning and have better fault tolerance," explains Charles.

We soak up as much information as we can about distributed computing[25] and make a mental note to deep dive on event streaming whenever we get the chance. If it's the future of the tech landscape at Mirage, then we better level up on it to make meaningful contributions when the time is right.

After a couple of minutes discussing inter-service communication, we transition almost anecdotally to our latest findings: "I was doing some pentesting work earlier today to get familiar with the app and I found some interesting vulnerabilities if you want to take a look."

Charles went from a state of mild intrigue to wild disbelief as we demonstrated a remote code execution on the app. He quickly dove into the code and came to the same conclusion we did: the ImageMagick class had no business interacting with system components and the CarrierWave gem did not properly validate the file's type.

"Would you care to present this at the next tech weekly meeting? I think this will highly interest other backend developers. I suppose you'll want to fix this as soon as possible, but if you could record the attack and show it to everyone, it would help illustrate real security issues. I'd also recommend you write a quick doc that explains what went wrong and how to fix it. I think everyone, myself included, have gotten so used to seeing security issues mishandled. Almost neglected. After a while, people just stop caring about them since no one has the right expertise to really help and guide us. If you demonstrate that you have a say in the matter and are here to help, I think it will encourage people to care more about the quality of the code they produce and probably reach out to you when they have questions."

---

[25] Designing Data-Intensive Applications by Martin Kleppmann is a must-read if you wish to know more about distributed databases

"Thank you, Charles! I will do that! Yes, I would like to fix this vulnerability right now, if possible. According to the documentation, tweaking the ImageMagick policy to only allow a subset of file types would help neutralize the exploit. I will prepare a fix in an upcoming merge request. It should closely resemble the following changes on the policy.xml file:

```
<policy domain="module" rights="none" pattern="*" />
<policy domain="module" rights="read | write"
pattern="{GIF,JPEG,PNG,WEBP,PDF}" />
```

"Awesome. Post it on the Slack channel *#backend-mrs*. It should be reviewed rather quickly. You can do quality checks on the staging environment; I believe you already know that. A simple upload of a PDF and JPG document should do it. You can also follow errors on the Kibana and Sentry dashboards[26]—that's where we output our exception stack traces," Charles advises.

We spend the rest of the day playing with different implementations of the fix to the upload form. Neutralizing ImageMagick was easy. A configuration tweak in the policy.xml file did the trick. Restricting uploaded files to a few type files, however, proved a bit more challenging. The Rails framework is full of conventions and obscure methods that just seem to be automatically defined and called out of nowhere. A fellow backend developer was kind enough to give us a quick hand and, finally, three hours later, we had a full fix that we validated in the staging environment.

We send the request for changes on the #backend-mrs channel, ping Charles' team, and 30 minutes later, the new code was on its way to production.

We cannot help but marvel at the speed of releasing new code at Mirage. Releases are not planned annually or even quarterly. There is no strategic committee that follows a scheduled roadmap defined nine months ago. Releases happen continuously, all day long, on any one of the 50 micro services that compose the app. This setup is more and more common in tech companies following the principles of lean manufacturing that encourage small batches and short feedback loops to quickly refute or confirm a hypothesis about a feature's success.

---

[26] *https://sentry.io*

The byproduct of this continuous release cycle is that vulnerabilities can be fixed almost instantly, so long as we confirm the validity of the fix and handle its potential edge cases. Which brings me to my second point: it's much easier to change an app that has decent unit tests, a quality assurance plan and can be deployed and reverted easily. All of these elements give us the necessary confidence to try things, push new code and alter existing methods, knowing very well that there are many safety nets that we can rely on to catch any misguided errors. Of course, no test is perfect and no QA plan accounts for all edge cases, but it's sufficient to empower not only the security team but any tech team to make the necessary changes to move the company forward. A code that everyone is afraid to touch is an obsolete code that endangers the company, no matter how modern its technical stack is.

Once the changes are live, we hurry to the production environment and test the upload feature once more. Deploying new code is still a nervous step for us.

Everything is working right. Sentry reported no errors following the deployment. We let out a big sigh of relief and send a message to the tech team about the quick change…some day, we will bring production down with a hasty change…but today is not that day!

We follow Charles' advice and write a one-page document explaining the vulnerability, the fix and send a message to Henry to book a slot at the next tech meeting to present the issue.

Following our conversation with Charles, we update our threat graph to reflect the new storage databases.

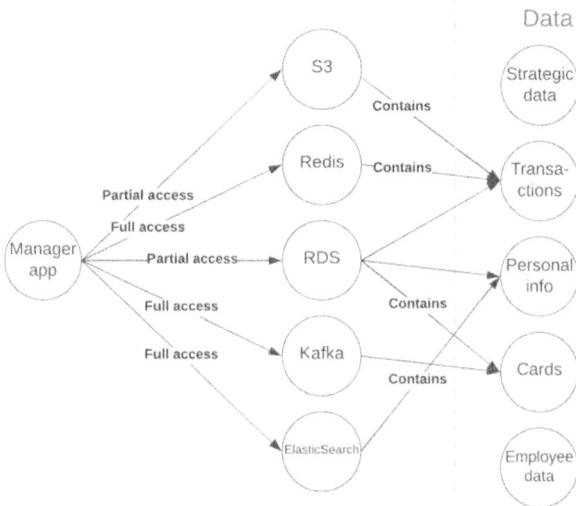

Figure 9-2: Threat graph

This graph tells only a partial story. We implicitly assume that access to S3 and other datastores can only be performed through the Manager app, but that may not be entirely true. S3 buckets can be exposed on the Internet, just like any other resource: virtual machine in the AWS EC2 service, RDS databases, Redis cluster, etc. They can be secured by limiting various entry points, but that takes a robust configuration. So maybe, just maybe, we have a direct line between attackers and our storage spaces that we may not be aware of.

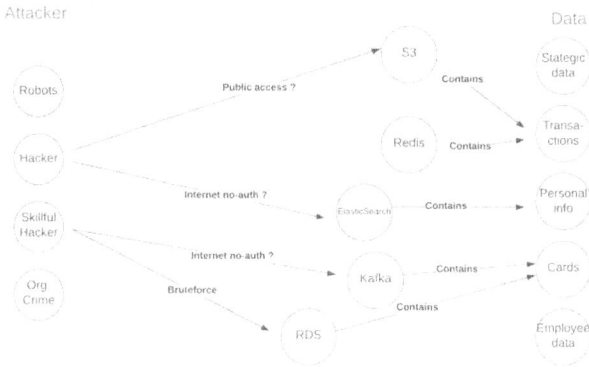

Figure 9-3: Public access to datastores?

This goes to show that our discovery using DNS enumeration on Route53 was very limited. It only gave us the custom apps developed by Mirage, not the cloud resources available on AWS. Asset discovery is the foundation upon which we build our security. We don't have to protect every asset, nor set up detection covering every scenario, but we do have to account for every asset, lest we get burned by an unauthenticated Elasticsearch on the Internet[27].

Armed with this new knowledge, and in continuation of our audit, we set out to list every AWS resource. The closest AWS API call to do that is resourcegroupstaggingapi. It is limited to resources that bear a tag or label, but Mirage has the good habit of adding default tags to all their resources so this API is a good first start. The code is rather simple as can be seen in this rough skeleton.

```
client = boto3.client("resourcegroupstaggingapi")
res = client.get_resources()
for r in res["ResourceTagMappingList"]:
    print(r["ResourceARN"])
```

---

[27] http://bit.ly/3lQl12O

You'll find the full version of this script in the book's GitHub repository[28]. It takes into account pagination of resources, extracts the service, region, account and presents it nicely in a CSV format that is readily exploitable.

We spend the next couple of hours reviewing all these resources, looking for easy one-hop vulnerabilities: public S3 buckets hosting customer data, firewall rules with 0.0.0.0/0 exposing unauthenticated databases on the Internet, and so forth. It's a first cursory check that will feed our threat graph and may challenge or shift our current priorities.

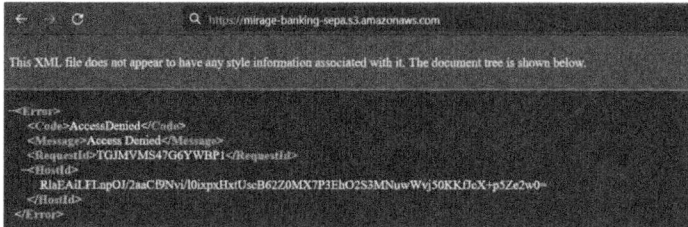

Figure 9-4: Access denied to an S3 bucket

I added a few scripts in the book's GitHub repository to find such quick wins, but so far, nothing critical stands out. Mirage built a strong network fortress around its cloud resources. Except for some public API endpoints, every resource is subject to tight network filtering that denies Internet access. Of course, once within the circles of the VPN and the production network, everything is allowed, sometimes without authentication but that's a different story. We'll pick it up in due time in the coming months.

Somewhere between the continuous audit of the Mirage app, cloud resources and the fixing of the ImageMagick vulnerabilities on the rest of the apps, John pops over to our desk and gleefully declares that they got approval for the device management project!

"Thank you very much for the help. That email exchange you had with Rachel really helped push things along! I will let you know how it goes and invite you to setup your security settings when we get it ready for rollout," says John.

There is nothing more rewarding than witnessing improvements in real time! Especially in areas that have been stuck for such a long time. Our small contribution will better the life of the whole IT team and solve troubling security flaws...That's a solid win!

---

[28] *https://github.com/sparcflow/Blitzscaling*

The Friday of that week, as we are busy digging into the code for the last XSS vulnerabilities, Robert from compliance, in a weird sort of cosmic coincidence, sends us a pentest report performed last year on the app.

Working in the industry for five years and not recognizing the pentesting company's name is never reassuring. In which obscure corner of the world did they find this company? We browse through the report and land on the first critical vulnerability: "No CSRF tokens on the Mirage web app." Oh, that's where Tony and Marc got their interview talking points! We continue reading the report, but every new finding feels like a pebble stuck in the throat. You know that a pentest report is a waste of disk space when TLS v1.1 is highlighted as a medium vulnerability.

In his email, Robert added a link to a Jira board listing all the findings of the report. Not surprisingly, all the issues are marked as "to be done" by the tech team. Not a single finding was addressed in almost a year.

Many security veterans reading this will have a sense of déjà vu. "*Of course, nobody gives a crap about security, least of all developers and IT administrators.*" None of the issues they raise get prioritized by the tech and product teams. To quote a fellow hacker, "*security is a failure.*"

Yet…we just fixed multiple vulnerabilities in a couple of days, thanks to the same tech team that one might chastise when reading compliance's Jira board. What gives?

Failure to address security issues is often symptomatic of a broken organization model and misaligned incentives. With the security field being heavily focused on the offense and the hacker mindset, companies often start by building an offense team. A group of people who perform pentests all day long, reversing binaries, doing phishing simulations, the whole nine yards.
They mistakenly believe that their goal is to find vulnerabilities and delegate the remediation process to other teams. At the end of each assignment, they send their 30 or so findings to developers and infrastructure admins, thinking they really contributed to the security of the platform, before wandering off to the next target.

Of course, none of these vulnerabilities get fixed. How dare this team of outsiders who understand nothing of the app's intricate features and the development lifecycle hijack everyone's priorities? Why should the product and tech team drop everything to work on these security issues? Their key performance metrics are about shipping features and fixing customer-facing bugs, not spending time fixing TLS vulnerabilities. … And who could blame them?

Unless a vulnerability directly damages user-experience or impacts a measurable business metric, it's very hard for product managers and tech leads to prioritize fixing them. They can always make the case that shipping a feature that boosts acquisition by 20% should be prioritized over a vulnerability that could one day far in the future cost $100K. That's not only the reality of many scale-ups that prioritize growth, but the case of almost every company.

Security teams end up chasing product managers and developers, arguing over roadmaps and deadlines, helplessly warning everyone about the boogeyman around the corner.

Even if some naïve and willing developer finally decides to step in and follow some of the recommendations, they have the beautiful surprise of discovering one-line unrealistic recommendations written hastily by a pentester who barely understands the business and the tech environment. They often don't account for half of the nominal customer business flows. Let alone edge cases. With no elaborate technical details, no test plan and no quality assurance scenarios, the team snoozes the recommendation and get back to working on features, vowing never to indulge the security team ever again.

Pentesters in the security team end up having fun for a year, get frustrated by the status quo around year two, and eventually churn while complaining about lack of meaning and impact. The company's security posture is as miserable as before and continues in a downward spiral until it's too late and too complex to reverse course, even with the best intentions.

A team that sits on the bench simply shouting instructions from the sideline will never make a dent. It's too easy to write a recommendation to "*bump the Redis Ruby package from 4.2.5 to 4.3*", completely oblivious to the breaking changes that such an update requires. Had the pentester tried to implement this change on any single app, they may have realized that some critical features of the product would stop working due to a change in the behavior of the `exists?` method in the Redis 4.3 package. In the context of Mirage, that would mean that rate limiting, caching objects and many other features would fail to behave as expected, causing a major degradation of service to the end customer.

Is upgrading that Redis package really worth the effort of updating the code base of the 15 apps using it, testing the dozen or so behaviors of each one in a dedicated staging environment, and deploying the change 15 times? Maybe these days of effort are better spent fixing a more important vulnerability. Maybe not, but the security engineer writing such a recommendation must fully appreciate the complexity and nuances of these laborious tasks before handing them over to the target team.

Once you hop on the reality train and start taking your own medicine, you realize how intricate and complex it is to perform so-called simple tasks, such as upgrading packages and systems, how any seemingly small change may break production. When you take ownership and responsibility of your recommendations, you naturally pay more attention to their impact and feasibility. Try implementing a mock-up of that recommendation in a production-like environment, perform a solid quality assurance (QA) of the technical and business cases, and then detail your recommendations in light of these learnings. Not only will they gain immense credibility and trust, but the developer reading such recommendations will feel more confident carrying out the change if most of the side effects have already been carefully modeled, tested and accounted for.

I will go as far as saying that a successful security team should actively participate in implementing the recommendations they're issuing. When you have skin in the game, I assure you that you will revisit the priority and severity of that CSRF. Most importantly, when you can actively help remediate flaws, you won't have to wait two months until the product manager prioritizes that string-encoding flaw.

Consider what happened in the last couple of days: we found vulnerabilities, followed standard coding practices adopted by the tech team to make contributions to their code base, fixed the vulnerabilities with a little help, tested and validated the change and deployed to production. Developers continued working on features that improve the business. We only solicited them for reviews and exchanging ideas, which promoted a strong teamwork spirit. We scored important credibility points that we can later rely on to perform more impactful changes. Critical vulnerabilities were dealt with in a couple of hours instead of years, and everyone is happy with the collaboration. We were no longer the outsiders, but active members of the tech team! That's a huge shift in perspective. How empowering and fulfilling is that?

The best part is yet to come. The knowledge we harnessed about the apps we fixed will help us be more independent the next time we suggest a change. A virtuous circle making us more and more autonomous and therefore faster in remediating vulnerabilities.

Contrast that with companies where security teams are prohibited from carrying out changes in the system and code. Companies where they're part of a global audit team that proudly shits on other teams instead of helping them, or in the case of Mirage not so long ago: where the compliance team orders an external pentest and dumps the issues on the lap of the tech team. How can anyone be surprised that vulnerabilities in these types of contexts continue to prosper? These companies must change their operating system and empower security teams to conduct the necessary changes to fix vulnerabilities and not succumb to territorial power plays.

This is where the support of an executive is key. It may not be immediately apparent, but Henry's support is paramount to our success in following this hands-on strategy. We have a mandate to go and fix stuff, be it at the infrastructure level, at the application level or at the product level. We seek approvals, communicate changes, compromise on solutions and take responsibility if we cause a degraded service when carrying a risky deployment. But that's okay because Henry expects us to get shit done instead of passively waiting for others to prioritize our work.

This model is not without challenges. It puts an incredible strain on the security team. This single team suddenly needs to develop capabilities in various languages matching those of almost every tech department, from Ruby in backend to React on web. From AWS in the infrastructure to business logic and quality assurance on each app. It makes for tough recruitments and a steep learning curve, but the upshot is well worth it, as we have just witnessed.

Another key success criterion of this model is to have a tech team that welcomes such contributions by other team members. Of course, one cannot commit junk code to any code base and expect it to be approved. Ideally, each team should have its standards, linter, and rules that allow anyone to safely contribute to the code base. Exactly like an open-source project would accept contributions from virtually anyone.

If these conditions are cleared, no security problem could stand in the way of a company, big or small.

Back to our infamous Jira full of vulnerabilities. We scroll down the list and cancel all the TLS findings with an adequate justification. Missing CORS headers and the absence of a CSRF token on non-critical actions are not worth our time right now so we just cancel them as well. We've already solved all the XSS found in the report and then some. We mark them as resolved. All in all, except for the multi-factor authentication we're pretty much done.

We email back the Jira board to the compliance team and highlight the vulnerabilities we additionally found and fixed.

We receive a single worded email from Robert:

"Thanks."

We cannot help but grin.

First layer

The last few days of penetration testing and code review gave us precious insight into the workings of the Mirage platform. We are more familiar with the infrastructure, the business side of the product, the frameworks used, the internal libraries and can even almost trace a transfer of money through the code from the customer to the clearing house. We will continue to hone this knowledge over the next couple of weeks, dedicating a couple of hours here and there to diving into the code of a new app to shine light on a new piece of the puzzle. The code is the ultimate truth when it comes to the app's behavior. If we master it, we will make pertinent suggestions and debunk false assumptions thrown around in tough discussions.

In the meantime, Steve is finally free to work on the WAF so we set up a call to draw the contours of the project, the goal, the success metrics and so on. We both already have in mind the two or three distinguished actors in the market, but it's always good to jot down ideas of what we really desire of this WAF.

As stated previously, it is very unusual for a hacker or anyone leaning toward offense to endorse any kind of WAF to begin with. The first thing that goes through their mind when they hear the word WAF is the myriad of encoding and character plays to bypass their regex rules. Such bypasses thrive in nature and are bound to happen, but that should not disqualify the product or its necessity, as is often wrongly implied by many security experts. This is a textbook case of wrong threat modelling! Let's pull up that threat graph once more:

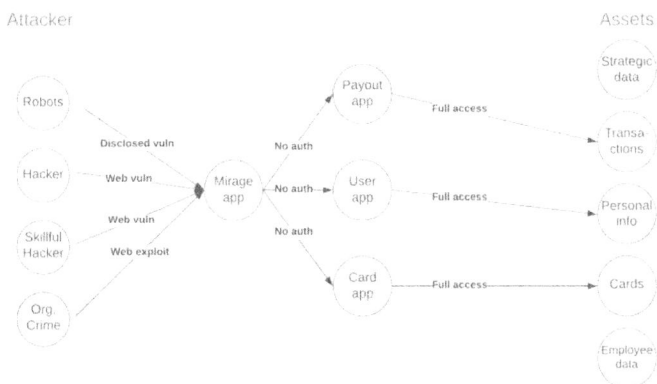

Figure 10-1: Threat graph of the web app

A WAF will get rid of bot scanners, those robots that automatically scan the whole Internet for any number of low-hanging fruit: new web exploits dropped on Twitter, unpatched CVEs, hidden admin panels, and so on. These attackers likely won't customize their payload to handle each and every WAF regex list. They're in it for the range not the depth. A couple of easy WAF rules will spare us 99.99% of the payloads in the critical hours following a vulnerability disclosure while we hastily patch our systems.

Not to mention that it will also protect against both vertical and horizontal bruteforce attempts, DDOS attacks and, if they're really good, credential stuffing by stopping bot-like behavior.

Now an attacker with enough resources will surely find a way to bypass that nasty SSRF rule and push your rate limiting to the edge of what's technically allowed. Maybe. But maybe they'll get bored of trying different payloads and fly off to an easier target. Maybe the next target on the list is 10 times easier and presents an equal payoff. Maybe their constant toying with the WAF will trigger enough alerts for us to take a more drastic approach than simply blocking a single request. This latter information is precious intelligence that we would not gather otherwise.

So, right there, the WAF helps us fully neutralize a sure threat (robot scanners) and greatly curtails a second one (hackers with moderate resources) and raise alerts on the third threat (hackers with advanced skills). That's a good enough bargain by any standard.

Together with Steve, we summarize these requirements in a technical paper and publish it to the rest of the tech team. It basically comes down to:
- Good protection against web-based attacks
- Rate limiting and various customizable firewall rules
- Event notification to detect bypass attempts
- API access to automate configuration and management

Steve sets up a dummy app on the staging Kubernetes cluster, then we reach out to the top contenders to schedule a quick proof of concept. We don't want to be stuck in commercial negotiations and partner selection based on an Excel sheet. We want to test these solutions in the field as soon as possible and roll out to production right after that. We set a goal to choose a vendor in two weeks and have the WAF up and running in front of the authentication service the week after that. Ambitious. Sure. But the return on investment quickly dwindles with each passing week. We can justify spending three weeks to set up a WAF and mitigate the aforementioned threats. Extend that period to six months, however, and suddenly the project's cost would outweigh its benefits, as we would be wasting too much time dealing with simple attacks. We'll be mindful of such tradeoffs on every project and constantly reevaluate the cost-benefit ratio.

While waiting for the vendors' response on this aggressive undertaking, we go through our ever-increasing backlog of emails.

_ "Hey, Alex, this is Serena from talent management. Henry told me you were looking to recruit security engineers. Can I pick your brain for 10 minutes about the ideal security engineer profile? Let me know if this slot works for you – Best, Serena."

We set up a call for the next morning.

After a short introduction where she highlights her experience as a recruiter of tech profiles, she asks us a seemingly simple yet heavy question: "so what is a good security engineer?"

Many tweetstorms and drama posts have torn through the industry, all attempting to answer this specific question. Is it technical prowess? An understanding of governance and compliance? Surely the ability to program must count? I have pondered over this question many a Sunday night, and every time I came close to a satisfying conviction, I found an abundance of counter examples that shattered it to pieces.

I think part of the difficulty is the diversity of the field, but also the fact that we are usually judging people by the final manifestation of a behavior, such as technical proficiency and communication skills. If we try to look beyond these obvious indicators, I think we'll more likely converge to two important and primary traits. These traits transcend information security. I refer to them as the hunger to learn and a bias toward action.

Looking for a security engineer? Hire someone who is hungry to learn and has the desire and ability to crack whatever needs cracking to get the job done. Is there a library written in Haskell that needs upgrading? This person will follow a tutorial on Haskell, find a way to upgrade dependencies, resolve conflicts, attempt an upgrade, test the changes and deploy them. Whether they know how to code is irrelevant. The real question is, are they willing to learn the skill required—coding in Haskell in this example—to solve the issue at hand?

Hire people who are eager to *do* stuff. There is nothing more counterproductive than someone who mistakes their job for strategic thinking and assigning tasks to other people. Get in the field, and help the team move the needle in the right direction. There is a time for strategic thinking, of course, but it must rely on fresh data from the operational ground. Otherwise, it's just masturbatory thinking. Hire someone who pounds on the keyboard to write a change management policy based on actual practices, rather than someone who creates a ticket for the compliance team to draft such a policy.

"Well, Serena, I am looking for people with potential. Hungry to learn. People who deliver tangible value. We need many different skills in this team, but I think it's easier to start with a security engineer who can easily slip into the head of an attacker. If I were to phrase my requirement in a single sentence it would be: *find me someone who is willing to learn, to act, and capable of thinking like an attacker*. Find me people like that, no matter their background, and we will work together to get them up to speed on everything else: AWS, Docker, Kubernetes, Golang, Python and whatever else is needed to get the job done."

We walk Serena through some of the tasks we had to perform to give her an idea of what a day in the life of a security engineer would be like. We also share a list of keywords that might help her find interesting resumes.

"Do you require any certification? University or engineering school?" she asks.

"Require is a strong word," we reply. "Not really. Like I said, anything on top is a bonus. A security diploma, PhD, certification, conference talks, open-source projects, etc. We'll probe for their relevance during the interview process. I am primarily looking for potential."

We write a short job ad together and center it around the hacker spirit and the hunger to dive into a cloud environment in order to build the security of a payment system. That ought to spike the interest of at least a few people.

We then move on to the infamous skill test. Serena presents a couple of examples used by other teams at Mirage: parsing XML, live streaming of data and other fancy exercises. All require coding an algorithm offline and dissecting it in a live session with the interviewer. These teams focus a lot on a few hard skills they deemed important. There is nothing wrong with that, but we'll do things differently. The skill test will be composed of two open questions:

- How would you hack Mirage? Describe a full scenario from recon to data exfiltration. Take any hypotheses regarding systems, processes and vulnerabilities.
- How would you defend against credential stuffing and password spraying where the attacker has access to unlimited pools of IP addresses?

These are factually problems we've had to deal with recently, so it will be interesting to discuss the trade-offs and implementation with candidates. Depending on their level of expertise, they may only provide a partial answer to these questions. That's fine. We'll go down the rabbit hole during the debrief session and evaluate how they approach a hard problem.

After the job ad is sent for HR validation, we join Steve in testing the PoC of one of the WAFs. He was dealing with some comments on the technical document, specifically from the mobile team. It turns out that Mirage's Android and iOS apps use certificate pinning: they hardcoded in their apps the public key of the TLS certificate served by all micro services behind the domain mirage.com. The WAF will necessarily act as the first SSL endpoint, decrypt all requests, analyze them, then forward them to the backend endpoints. It will therefore serve a new TLS certificate to mobile clients. This new TLS certificate will not match the hardcoded key in the mobile apps, leading to their pure cardiac arrest.

Seems important enough, indeed.

Before we jump into the discussion, we take a couple of minutes to dive into the code of the Android and iOS apps to better evaluate the situation. We need data if we are to find quick wins to unlock the situation.

We locate the certificate pinning routine through rough pattern searching of keywords such as "pin", "pinning" and "pinned":

```
val client = OkHttpClient()
    .newBuilder().certificatePinner(
    certificatePinner = CertificatePinner.Builder()

      // AWS ACM root certificate
      .add("mirage.com", "sha256/47DEQpj8…")

      // Pinned backup private key
      .add("mirage.com", "sha256/CAe6csQd…")
      .build()
    ).build()
```

When building its HTTP client, the Android app initializes a certificatePinner instance with two public key hashes. The first hash is associated with the current public certificate, as is demonstrated by this dirty script that calculates the hash of the public keys of a website:

```
# script display_pinning_hash.sh
host="mirage.com"
openssl s_client -servername $host -connect $host:443 2>&1 <
/dev/null |
openssl x509 -pubkey -noout |
openssl rsa -pubin -outform der 2>/dev/null |
openssl dgst -sha256 -binary | openssl enc -base64

# verification
alex@computer$ ./display_pinning_hash.sh
47DEQpj8HBSa+/TImW+5JCeuQeRkm5NMpJWZG3hSuFU=
```

There is little value in going over every command of the script, most of them are simply there to deal with OpenSSL's quirky formats: get the certificate, extract the public key, print it in der/pem format and calculate the hash[29].

More importantly though, notice that the second key in the previous code figure appears to be a sort of backup if we believe the comments. We perform a quick "git blame" to identify the author of this line of code:

```
$ git blame httpClient.tk -L 139
^05cd79f (nina 2018-07-06 21:20:27 18)
c1ad5b9c (nina 208-07-06 22:25:48 19) // Pinned backup…
```

Nina!

We find the same pattern on the iOS app so we send a quick message to Steve, Nina and Neil, the mobile tech lead who first identified the issue. We outline our findings and pray that Nina still has the private key that matches the hash we found in the code.

"I think I left it on a USB key somewhere at my place. I will bring it to the office tomorrow. I hope I did not lose it when moving last summer, though," she replies back.

"Awesome, thanks," we sigh in relief. "Steve, Neil, just so I fully understand, what would happen if we wanted to pin an entirely new public key? How long would that take?" we ask.

"We'd have to issue a new release of the app on both the Apple and Play stores. Usually, 80% of customers upgrade their apps in the following three weeks. After that, we'll have to sunset the previous versions since they won't be working following the deployment of the WAF. That will upset many users since we dropped support for old versions of iOS and Android a couple of months ago. We will force users to upgrade to a version that may not run on their phones. They will be effectively strong-armed into buying a newer phone to continue using Mirage. Needless to say, that will hurt our online reviews and user satisfaction scores," responds Neil.

We brainstorm ways to isolate traffic coming from the mobile app but since they point to the same backend endpoints consumed by the regular web app, there is no magical trick we can come up with. There is always the possibility to patch all web and mobile endpoints to use new WAF endpoints and spare old versions of the mobile app for now, but boy would that mess up the architecture, complicate debugging and make for a dangerous migration.

---

[29] The script is hosted on the book's GitHub page: *https://github.com/sparcflow/Blitzscaling*

"Well, Nina...We're counting on you!" we all say.

It is scenarios like these that keep me torn on the overall value of certificate pinning. It's not the simple cut-and-set tradeoff that many seem to believe. Come to think of it, why does everyone blindly agree that certificate pinning is an obvious good security practice? Let's explore this from first principles.

Certificate pinning allows the client to validate the certificate presented by the server. Its main purpose is, therefore, to fight against man-in-the-middle attacks, where someone with control over the network through a rogue Wi-Fi connection or some sort of packet subversion mechanism, manages to present valid certificates forging the name of mirage.com. They would then be in a position to collect and modify all the information sent by the user to the backend app: password, wire information and so on.

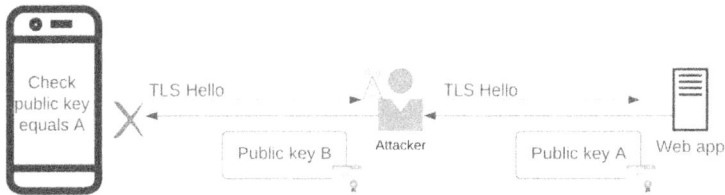

Figure 10-2: Interception of network traffic

Certificate pinning is a compelling countermeasure against this threat, often targeting mobile apps...But what makes mobile traffic so special? After all, we don't have certificate pinning on web applications, yet they often contact the same HTTP endpoints as the mobile apps.

One could argue that since mobile phones are always carried by people and connected to public and untrusted Wi-Fi hotspots, the probability of a malicious network device intercepting traffic is slightly higher than on a web browser in a laptop. This seems like a feeble argument at best, as is demonstrated by the staggering number of people working on laptops from cafés, airports, train stations and malls all around the world. Furthermore, the pinning protection on mobile does not extend to the WebView browser within the mobile app, which is often used to display HTML content not yet ported to the native app.

So, to sum it up, we have a slight increase of coverage against localized network attacks with rogue certificates, at the price of a huge burden in maintenance and change management on a critical piece of infrastructure, namely TLS certificates. If we need to change these certificates for whatever reason (compromised CA, leaked keys, putting a WAF in front, etc.), we have to deprecate apps used by dozens of thousands of customers…the security/business-cost tradeoff is not that evident.

In any case, it would be hard for Mirage to repudiate this architectural choice, so we will just have to live with it for now.

Speaking of the mobile platform, you'll notice that during our little tango dance with the app days ago, we only focused on the desktop version. We'll take a couple of hours when we can to look at the mobile app as well, even if only to validate the assertion that it indeed uses the same backend endpoints as the web app. A simple grep command should help us list all of the URLs, for instance:

```
grep -RE "https?://"
```

We compare the output of the command across different folders: mobile app, web app and confirm that they're indeed using the same endpoints. The web app even leverages more APIs than the mobile apps. We need to look at how the mobile app stores data locally, encrypts secrets and so on, but that can wait for a couple of weeks. The impact is localized to the device and would require a massive malware campaign that infects all customers for it to be of any significant damage to Mirage. The probability of such an event, while not zero, does put it behind more important tasks we still have to carry out. Still, we dutifully report this scenario in our threat graph to keep an eye on it.

Now that we have a potentially viable plan for the pinning issue, and following the vendors' response, together with Steve, we deploy the WAF products, test their settings, set up firewall rules, exclusions, rate limiting and other security features. We replay many web attacks on the dummy app to validate our assertions.

From a security perspective, we'll have four important settings to configure:
- Rate limiting to block IP addresses that perform more than, say, 30 failed authentication attempts in an hour. This is the exact rule currently living in the authentication service that we need to remove
- The same rate limiting rule on the Lead-ID HTTP header
- Activate the WAF to block SQL injections, remote code execution and other web-based attacks
- Block traffic from known bad IP address
- Configure alerts following a surge in blocked requests

One of the WAFs, ShieldSec, had an additional feature that prominently stands out: a bot protection that we can activate when the rate limiting is not enough. It blocks requests coming from automated tools, such as cURL and other known libraries. It's an interesting feature that leverages machine learning to recognize quirky attributes of such bot-like behavior and seems to work wonders against a lot of the automated tools. The rate of false positives is very low, but at the scale of tens of thousands of customers, we're bound to block a few legitimate requests. We'll probably end up selectively activating this rule when under highly resilient bruteforce. The product team will also love this feature as it replaces the traditional and annoying Captcha.

Can we bypass it with a custom, low-level HTTP library and a few additional tricks? Most probably. Should we disregard this feature because of that? Absolutely not. We are no longer in the confines of the threat we modelled for this project. We want to shut-down script kiddies and other low-level attackers using off-the-shelf tools. This feature is perfect for that. Whether an obstinate attacker can bypass it is irrelevant. That particular threat will have to be addressed differently.

We converge on ShieldSec and emit a recommendation in the technical paper. After a few negotiation rounds, we land on a $40k annual subscription. We synthesize all the arguments presented so far into a coherent list of bullet points to present to Henry in our next one-on-one meeting. Once the deal closes, we'll get unlimited access to the WAF console, deploy our security settings and work with Steve to update DNS records on Route53 to point to the WAF.

While we're waiting for these final approvals, we start thinking about identity management for clients and customers, our second highest threat scenario.

On the customer side, we have a weak authentication scheme where many customers are allowed to choose weak passwords with a weak second-factor authentication that does not extend to the login page. These two flaws make clients especially vulnerable to phishing, password guessing and social engineering.

In an ideal setup, customers should automatically be protected against the different manifestations of account takeover with a second-factor authentication. The large majority of account takeovers share the same tell-tale signs: the attacker connects from an environment different to that of the customer. They might use a Firefox browser when the customer is on Safari, or connect from a public hotspot using a different IP address than that of the customer. They can even come from different countries. As we pour over the data of recent account takeovers, we slowly gain increasing confidence that we could detect the majority of these attacks through simple discrepancy rules in these attributes. No need to build a machine learning algorithm or any fancy third-party tool to do that.

The Auth app stores every Lead-ID cookie and IP address used to access the Mirage app with a timestamp of first appearance. We can group the Lead-ID and IP addresses by date of creation to count how many users visit Mirage from a new IP address or with a new Lead-ID cookie and compare it to the total number of daily unique user connections.

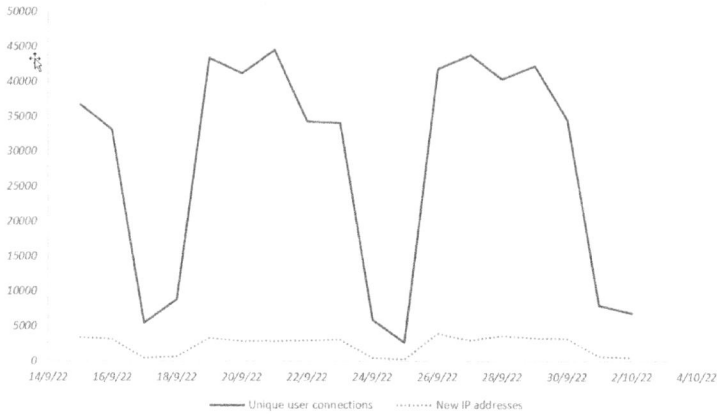

Figure 10-3: Count of unique user connections Vs user connections from new IP addresses and Lead-ID cookie

The dotted line represents customers connecting to the app from a new IP address and with a new Lead-ID cookie, while the continuous line tracks global connections. The ratio is 8%. That means 8% of customers connect to the app from a new browser and a new IP address that we've never seen before. We dive into these customers' behavior and notice that most of them got caught in the previous query because they just created their accounts that same day. We tweak the query to exclude them, which significantly reduces the population number to 3% of daily customers.

So, if a customer who created their account more than a week ago authenticates from a new IP address and a new Lead-ID cookie, we can consider it as suspicious behavior and automatically prompt them for SMS authentication. Otherwise, we just let them through unencumbered since we assume that only the legit user will reuse that same IP address and browser. We can tweak these trust criteria later on, but as a start, it seems like a good tradeoff between user experience and security.

As stated previously, we are limited to SMS 2FA, so it's still possible to trick the user into inserting that one-time code on a fake page. However, this introduces additional friction for targeted victims, which necessarily hurts the attacker's conversion rate and, more importantly, forces them to alter their phishing kits or purchase more expensive ones. A number of them might even go after easier prey with a better yield. Provided we can get this mitigation up and running with one week's worth of development, this would be a pretty good investment.

We share our numbers with the operations team to validate the results and apply this strategy on a few bruteforce and account takeover cases. Our intuition was right. The attacker would have been prompted for a second factor each and every time because they show up with a new IP and new cookie. We find a few odd ducks, of course (e.g., a wife stealing her husband's laptop to wire money) but they are marginal in the grand scheme of things.

We send a message to Maria, the product manager in charge of user acquisition, and set up a meeting to discuss the implementation of these ideas. In the meantime, we delve into the code to check how difficult the implementation would be. The rule seems like a combination of "if and else" statements, but some parameters are not readily available in that part of the code. We'll need to adjust some methods and classes to make it happen. Nothing too complicated but some rework will be necessary.

"Hey, Maria. How are you doing?" we ask.

"Fine, thank you/ I hope you're doing alright as well," she smiles back. "So, I gathered from your message that you want to talk about our new password policy, right? We are thinking of reworking the registration flow to simplify it as much as possible to boost conversion. Let me show you what we have got so far."

"Huh…yeah, why not, let's talk about that as well!" we blurt back.

She proceeds to display a succession of screens and layouts of the new registration app.

"We were thinking of removing the password confirmation field and, instead, giving users the possibility to display the password to check for typos. I know it's a big security risk but…"

"What do you mean big security risk?" we interrupt her. "As a user, I love it when I can check that my password is indeed correct instead of receiving an error at the end of a 22-field form page…The security risk is someone spying over your shoulder waiting for you to show the password. In that case, just don't show the password…It seems like an acceptable trade-off in my opinion. A lot of websites do this already, and if it can boost acquisition, then why not?"

There is no greater pleasure than knocking down inflated and exaggerated security risks. Banking apps are not getting pwned because they allow users to show their passwords in the registration form. They're not getting breached because they allow people to paste passwords. There are myriads of other vulnerabilities actually exploited by attackers to hack companies and customers, as demonstrated by our threat graph. It's our job to steer the focus of product managers and developers away from these non-scalable threats and help them work on the real-world issues.

On the same password page, we notice the six bullet points that summarize all the aching requirements that a password must satisfy.

"Oh, and those requirements that are supposed to be for the sake of 'security' can be greatly simplified," we say pointing to the current password rules. "They degrade user experience and push people to choose poor passwords. It's a lose-lose situation for everyone."

"I don't follow," replies Maria, perplexed. "You mean that we should not ask people to put in letters, special characters, avoid consecutive characters and so on? Every other fintech website is doing the same thing; are you really sure we can just remove them?"

"When we push users to respect convoluted password criteria, they will likely follow the laziest road to pass the test. That's just how our brains work. If asked to add a number, a person will probably add 1, 123 or 0 at the end. If asked to capitalize a letter, they will capitalize the first one. So, in effect, these rules reduce the entropy of passwords instead of increasing them. Look at the list of cracked and leaked passwords. Most of them follow these same patterns. You don't have to believe me, this was codified in appendix A of the NIST 800-63B standard for over a decade, yet everyone clings to outdated and intuitive gut feelings. Auditors, regulators and so-called experts are slow to catch up, but the verdict has been reached a long time ago."

"Oh, great!" responds Maria, positively impressed, "this will greatly simplify registration phase. Nate, our cofounder, initially wanted to only ask for a six-digit pin code on a virtual keyboard, you know, the ones they do at various other banks."

You give them a finger, they'll take the arm…

"Ha, yeah, let's not push it! We want to optimize for entropy, meaning randomness in characters. Six digits can be bruteforced in a million queries and guessed in even a fewer number. We really only need one rule: a long password that does not follow obvious patterns, such as dictionary word character, username, mirage keyword, etc. Let's ask for 10 characters, for instance."

"That's a lot of characters!" she pushes back. "Our acquisition numbers will be greatly hurt by this stringent requirement. People will drop at the password step. We need to keep the customer's journey in sight. Isn't eight characters enough?"

"I'd argue differently," we calmly reply. "People are trusting us with their money, so they expect a high level of security. Asking for 10 characters would send a strong signal that we take their security seriously. Every single character we add increases the cost of attack exponentially. If it takes one day to break an eight-character password, it will take around two months to break a nine-character password and so on. Given that we lost close to $300k to flaws related to authentication, I'd like us to close it with a strong measure."

"Can we measure the length of passwords currently defined by our users and then decide on a value close to the mean?" replies Maria. "Perhaps you are right and the majority of people actually choose long passwords instinctively given the sensitivity of the app, but I'd rather we draw this conclusion based on facts."

Love the spirit! Instead of bargaining between each other, Maria proposes to look at the data and draw a fact-based conclusion. We pause for a moment to think about it. The Auth app hashes passwords so we cannot count their length easily…but maybe there is a trick we can pull. When a user authenticates, the app pushes a corresponding log in the SIEM. We can add a field "password_length" to this log and calculate it on the fly. The password is already in memory so we don't add more risk exposure.

"Yes, give me a couple of days to draw statistics related to this, and I will come back to you with a proposition," we conclude.

Maria continues describing the slides until she arrives at a screen showing a Captcha before completing the registration.

"You know", we interject, "together with the infrastructure team, we are currently testing a solution that could be a substitute for that Captcha, if you ever want to reduce user friction during that last step."

"Really???" she says with glowing eyes. "Compliance is forcing us to put this Captcha in place to protect against fake user registration. Everyone is complaining about the heavy impact on user acquisition. Can we really get rid of it?"

"Yes, we just tested a new product with Steve. I believe we can achieve a similar protection without annoying customers with meaningless images that are getting so complex that only an AI can decipher. It analyzes the attributes of a request, and if it comes from a script, blocks it. It's not 100% effective, but close enough. We can selectively enable on certain pages it if registration metrics start to deviate from the normal expected rate, for instance. The goal is to have transparent security for the end user. As a customer, I don't want to be bothered with Captchas, security questions and other nonsense. I want the company to secure my account without wasting my time. I want my journey to be as smooth yet as secure as possible. That's the kind of security I want us to have at Mirage."

"That is so refreshing to hear," she says. "I'll tag you in the discussion with compliance to explain why we're dropping this."

"Awesome. If we're done with the registration phase, I have another point I wanted to discuss with you. I guess you're aware of the wave of phishing and bruteforce attacks that target our customers. Their accounts often get hacked as a result. One very effective protection is to automatically ask for an SMS code when the user connects from a suspicious place. I looked up the numbers and found a rule that only triggers for 3% of customers. What do you think?"

"Wait, walk me through it slowly," she says. "So, when I authenticate on the app…"

"If you come from a new IP and a new browser…" we slowly continue.

"I receive an SMS to validate the authentication? And if I use my regular browser from my regular WiFi…nothing?"

"Exactly," we say.

She thinks about it for a couple of seconds.

"Well, I don't find it shocking. Customers are used to SMS codes since we require it for money movement operations. That's 3% of how many customers?" she asks.

"We have 30k unique connections a day, so 900 customers will be prompted for an SMS every day upon authentication."

"That seems reasonable," she concludes. "Can you write the functional specification that details the user journey and the conditions to trigger the rule? We'll bring it to the tech leads to discuss engineering challenges. Do you have any idea how long it would take to pull it off?"

"Looking at the backend code, I'd say four days. I can pair with a programmer to move things faster. On the front-end side, we'll just have to reuse the popping modal, I guess, so a couple of days. Let me check with the web tech lead."

"What about mobile?" she asks.

Ah, those darn mobile apps...Every security fix on a mobile app will require at least a few weeks before full rollout, and will be trivially bypassed by using the previous app version, unless we deprecate all old versions, which puts ratings at risk.

"Ideally, we must include mobile now as well, but the realities of the field forces us to leave them out for now. First, we'll release the improvement on the web app, see how it fares against attackers, and then allow mobile to catch up a month or two later. By the time attackers figure out that we excluded mobile apps, we'll hopefully be ready to deprecate old mobile versions that lack this protection."

It's a strategic gamble that many might feel reluctant to make. But there are no perfect solutions in the real world. And we don't need one. We're fighting humans with their own trade-offs, limitations and biases. When the payoff of attacks dwindles due to the new stacked security layers, such as WAF, rate limiting and 2FA, a large fraction of attackers will more likely focus on less protected targets, giving us the needed respite to generalize the protection to all incoming requests.

As a rule of thumb, always strive to deliver maximum value as fast as possible. It's better to deliver 80% of the value now and incrementally rollout the remaining 20% in the coming weeks than to delay the whole endeavor until we can deliver 100% of the value all at once. Perfectionism is often cited as a cute make-believe flaw to the age-old question "*what are your weaknesses?*". In an environment of extreme uncertainty, such as the startup world or an adversarial setting, the risk of paralysis and delay induced by perfectionism can in fact turn out to be a deadly weakness.

We leave Maria with a last snark: "Oh, and please make the password field copy-pastable so people can use their password managers."

There is a special place in hell for people who forbid pasting passwords in forms...

The work on both the WAF and MFA on login keeps us pretty busy for the next couple of days. We closed the deal with ShieldSec. The security settings were fairly straightforward to setup given our extensive tests, but we tag along with Steve to help him plan the migration of all the HTTP endpoints, which gives us a unique insight into how DNS is configured at Mirage, how we can monitor incoming traffic for errors, and fully understand the life of a packet from the customer to the app.

Nina found her precious private key and we used it to generate a new wildcard TLS certificate on the WAF. The next day, we put the auth service behind the WAF by changing CNAME records on AWS Route53. Technically, it's a zero-downtime migration, yet we could not help but feel nervous at the idea of deploying such an impactful change to the whole customer base.

A soon as the change propagated, the first requests started to come in. We monitor the rate of connection, status code and type of browsers that went through. Everything looks OK, even mobile traffic. Perfect!

Our first app is live behind the WAF! Hurray!

To avoid wreaking havoc following this delicate migration, we put all security rules in audit mode: SQL injections rules, XSS, etc. We'll switch them over to blocking mode in a couple of days as we gather enough data to confidently verify that no customers will be wrongfully blocked.

This was only the start, of course. Following this successful first release, we migrate the rest of the exposed apps and write a quick how-to for developers and infrastructure admins to help them automatically put new Internet-facing apps behind ShieldSec. We also prepare a couple of runbooks in case we face an incident on the WAF: how to debug, how to view logs for errors and how to disable it through a break-glass mechanism.

As we finish these documents, we can't help but toy with the idea of automatically detecting future new public sub domains of mirage.com that are not behind the WAF. How great would that be?! We write down the idea in our backlog.

We set up email notifications on the WAF if the number of blocked requests goes over a hundred requests in a given hour. A very basic watchdog to spot nasty side effects until Steve connects ShieldSec to the classic monitoring infrastructure at Mirage.

In the midst of the WAF configuration, we come back to Maria with the statistics of user passwords following a quick patch we pushed on the authentication app to log password length in the SIEM. It turns out that more than 75% of customers who used the app in the last seven days chose at least a nine-character password. We happily settled with Maria on this lower limit for the registration revamp.

Ad astra

"It's hard to light a candle, easy to curse the dark instead."

Tuomas Holopainen

Spilled ink

The WAF ShieldSec has been operational for a few days now. We switch the firewall rules over to blocking mode after a small window of logging and adjustment. We also configure the infrastructure to only accept traffic coming from the WAF. Attackers will have no choice but to go through our first barrier to reach our applications.

All is working well, or so we thought...

"I think we have a small problem..." writes Charles in what, we assume, is a distressing voice. "We lost the IP address of customers in the logs. We only see the same couple of IP addresses everywhere. Do you think it's related to the new WAF?"

Yikes... Panic sets in!

We jump on the call with Charles and Tony and discover, to our horror, that indeed all IP addresses have been obfuscated by the WAF, which makes sense in hindsight. The WAF acts a web proxy after all, but we just assumed that the application would be smart enough to extract the real customers' IPs. Sadly, reality had its own plans.

Perusing the ShieldSec documentation, we discover that they send the customer's IP address in a custom HTTP header, so we quickly start patching applications to take this header into account when extracting the customer's IP address.

It's a small production incident that will prompt the most cautious customers to question the weird IP addresses and geolocation information visible on their Mirage history tab. An incident that could have been totally detected in our technical analysis and proof of concept, but we just assumed with Steve that the X-Forwarded-For header carrying all intermediate HTTP relays would be properly updated and parsed by the apps... So much for that. Once all applications were patched, deployed and tested, we close the incident and continue monitoring the situation the next few days.

No change is risk-free, but at least we demonstrated that we were willing to stand with the team, own our mistakes and actively work on a fix. Autonomy in conducting operational tasks is a double-edged sword that must be wielded responsibly.

"Oh, by the way," interjects Charles once the incident is cleared up, "Maria sent me your specification document regarding 2FA on the login page. I have an engineer who can probably start working on it in a few days. Can he reach out to you for clarifications, should he have any questions?"

"Of course," we respond, "I actually thought to pair with whoever works on the feature to get more familiar with the code base."

"Great. I'll let him know. Gary the lead web engineer should have someone on his team as well. He should swing by your desk today or tomorrow," he says before disconnecting.

Great day, if you don't count the incident, of course.

Melissa, head of product, was not excessively happy that we hijacked product priorities to push this feature, though. "If we have two engineers with a couple of days of spare time, then they should be working on important features, such as bulk payments!" she writes us in an angry message.

Her point is understandable, but we went through the proper channels. We wrote the specification with Maria from the product team, then presented the document to the lead techs, who decided to pull the feature and work on it as part of their improvement efforts. It's three to five days of effort to close a chasm in our app that costs us $300k. On the other hand, the bulk-payment feature she is referring to is a full-fledged six-month project involving a dozen engineers. The two tasks hardly compare. Any healthy tech must have the autonomy and latitude to prioritize such improvements, be it bug fixes, architecture revamps or security vulnerabilities. Some frame it as a maintenance cost or technical debt, but it's more profound than that.

A team that only delivers features will crumble under the load of the increasing complexity built along the way, which will ironically slow down feature development in the long run. Whether we file security vulnerabilities as bugs is a minor detail. The point is that every efficient tech team should have a proper mix of features and improvement projects. The role of the tech lead is to ensure that their team maintains this healthy mix and help the product team realize that feature quality and fast delivery go hand in hand with a good and reliable software platform.

We argue that much, but we know that we did not really win her to our side. Time will hopefully be on our side.

After three days working with the backend and web developers, we had a proper technical document and a working proof of concept. Funnily enough, writing meaningful unit tests took us more time than actually implementing the 2FA rules in the code. We had all the pieces scattered across the code: IP address, persistence cookie, user agent and web modal. We just needed to wrap them up together in the same class, define a new cookie dedicated to the 2FA setup, instead of relying on the old Lead-ID cookie, and create a few indices on the database to speed up the SQL query.

We wrote a QA plan, presented it to Melissa and Maria, and validated the launch the next couple of days… Just like that, we shattered account takeover attempts on the Mirage app.

Almost…

If you recall, we excluded mobile apps from this first release. The team will be able to pick up the improvement piece the following month.

We clean up the code and send a brief note to the customer support service to let them know of the upcoming change, should any customer complain. Then we crossed our fingers and hit the deploy button on the web application first. We then follow it up with the backend Auth service that will start requesting an SMS code when it does not recognize the browser or IP address.

We carefully monitor the release, pull up some dashboards on the SIEM and set up alerts if some key metrics go sideways: too many errors, too many SMS on login, etc. Basic watchdogs to make sure the feature is working as intended. One mistake in the code and we could be spamming every customer with SMS codes…

Again, the message to the teams is clear: we requested this feature, we helped develop it, we are here to own it and fix any unintended harm or strain it may cause. I cannot stress this enough: taking responsibility is a building block to establishing long-term trust and a key ingredient to helping prioritizing security topics within other teams.

One minute, five minutes, fifteen minutes…the first SMS requests started coming in. No spikes of errors…

We let out a sigh of relief.

The operations team celebrated this achievement that reduced their main source of toil. No more manual account suspension due to account takeover or brutcforce attacks, no more contacting clients asking for identity documents and video calls to verify their identities...and most importantly, no more losses!

Of course, the attacks will not completely disappear. They will lick their wounds only to retaliate with novel techniques in a few weeks or months, but these measures combined should drastically reduce the flood of attacks from dozens a week to maybe one or two a month…until the attackers get their hands on the latest phishing kit, start replaying SMS and other shenanigans… But, we'll be ready for them with new measures by then!

All of these actions slowly start brightening up our threat graph by adding new layers that the attacker should bypass before compromising the app:

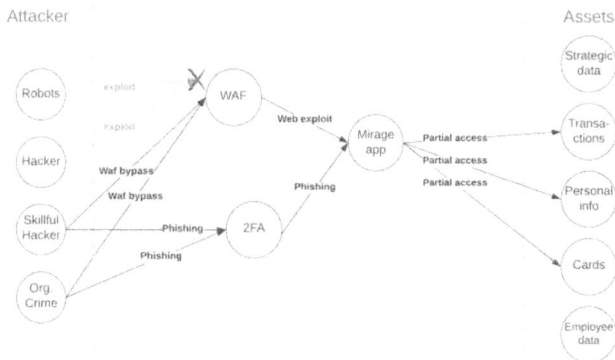

Figure 11-1: Web threat with new layers

Most importantly, though, our collaboration with the product and acquisition team on the registration revamp and the two-factor authentication echoed throughout the product and tech teams. Product managers, whose upmost priority is to maximize user experience, suddenly started to see us as valuable allies in their fight against senseless regulation and bureaucratic banking practices that watered down their bold features. Developers eager to ship new code and improve their technical stack happily shared their geeky insights about what they viewed as weaknesses in the system to help remediate them.

We were no longer seen as the gatekeepers of innovation and business, but rather the secret accelerators of the system. In the wake of this pressure, we felt compelled to create a chat channel "#security-requests" to centralize any question people throw at us in private messages. In this channel, one could often read:

"Hey, we're working on a feature that involves receiving webhooks from a partner. Is IP whitelisting enough to authenticate these webhooks?"

"We're introducing Apple Pay. How can we measure the trustworthiness of a device to avoid obvious fraud cases?"

"We want to convert HTML to PDF; can you please review this code?"

"Hey, we're working on an RFP for a new cash provider, do you have any security requirements?"

This sort of spontaneous interaction with various stakeholders is one of the clearest signs that we are moving in the right direction toward building a true teamwork environment based on trust and added value, rather than an autocracy with a Damocles sword hanging over the head of every employee ready to swiftly swing and chop off any daring idea. The latter setting is sadly very common in many companies where security teams feel left behind and excluded from key product and engineering discussions. It's easy to automatically shift blame onto others and loudly claim that *they don't care about security.* It's their fault, after all, if *they* don't know how to properly parse user input or anticipate how a behavior can be abused by an attacker. If, however, one manages to swallow their ego and reevaluate past interactions from the other party's point of view, they may unlock the real reason for such dissonance.

For instance, a security team perceived as nay-sayers, always exercising their veto to kill features, completely oblivious to the business, extending development time by 20 days just to cover seemingly silly and low-impact risks, will inevitably be left out of discussions. They may escalate that frustration all the way to the CEO and set up a complex validation process to review every change, but it won't matter. People will eventually find ways around processes that constrain them or get in the way of their incentives.

That's why a valuable skill of any security team is the ability to build things. Building things confers security teams almost unlimited power to assist others in finding creative solutions to difficult problems, including security issues. It's the special ingredient that helps security transition from a blocker to a differentiator and accelerator that helps deliver critical features with minimal risk, something competitors may struggle with in their old-fashioned setup.

If you cannot build tools, write specifications, technical documents, help draft legal terms, even deploy code in production, your response will axiomatically be severely constrained by the external help you may not get, or the availability of other teams over which you have no control or the limitations of your internal tooling, and so forth. A team that cannot build things will have no choice but to say "no" to the new ideas and twisted scenarios that are often required to ship great one-of-a-kind features to customers.

To come back to one request that was posted on the channel: *is it enough to whitelist IPs to authenticate webhooks?* Every rational person working in security would have to say "No". But, if that's the only type of hardening measure supported by both the partner and Mirage, you are effectively stuck. Whether you like it or not, you have two options:

- Bang your head against a white wall, aimlessly preaching about mutual TLS authentication. To hell with the technical limitations of both Mirage and the partner. It's their job to figure it out.
- Help them build an alternative to the damn thing!

Put yourself in their shoes. Who would you rather work with?

Speaking of mutual TLS authentication...Why is everyone such a fan of it anyway? It's horribly complex to configure and its protection only extends to the first TLS termination endpoint, often the very edge of the infrastructure. Past that point, there is no validation and an application that only relies on this protection finds itself exposing unauthenticated endpoints to the rest of the infrastructure (other apps, developers, corporate VPN, etc.). Anyone who spent any time debugging TLS errors would have to concede that there are solutions with a far better value/effort ratio.

In any case, my point is that a more pragmatic team would roll up their sleeves, dive into the specification, gather context, then reach out to the provider to negotiate and test potential solutions before settling on a compromise. And they can only do that because they have the power and mandate to change infrastructure components, deploy code, write tooling...in short, they can build things.

Case in point:

"On top of IP whitelisting'," we reply to the tech lead asking the question, "we can theoretically start with a simple token authentication. A sort of shared secret that the provider adds to every HTTP request. Put me in the loop with them and we'll write a quick product specification. It should not push development time by more than half a day, I believe. For IP whitelisting, we want to have it as close to the app as possible. Probably not within the code of the app itself. I'll check with the infrastructure team; maybe we can add a condition in our HTTP proxy to limit certain URLs and hostnames to a list of IP addresses. How does that sound?"

Not only do we help them implement proper IP whitelisting and token authentication, but we get to leverage this specific example to standardize the way we perform these checks by adding features in our infrastructure that can be reused later. This is the power of a team that can build things and ship improvements.

Every question or situation that arises on #security-requests is an opportunity to codify a set of standard security practices. We cannot expect every developer to keep up with the ever-evolving best practices: how to upload files securely, how to receive partner webhooks, how to put an app behind the WAF, and so on. Whenever we can, we steal a couple of hours here and there to write these documents and reference them in the channel *#security-requests* in a simple FAQ page.

We dive into the infrastructure components that currently allow external partners to communicate with our infrastructure. It's a classic setup found in many companies. A public load balancer sits at the edge of the infrastructure, filtering requests based on a fixed list of allowed IP addresses. All requests are then routed through Traefik*(https://traefik.io/)*, Mirage's HTTP router, to a single app called `external-callbacks`. This app processes requests before dispatching them to other microservices: *SEPA* for sending transfers, *Payout* for cash-outs and so on.

Figure 11-2: Partner access to Mirage

We stumble upon something quite odd in the load balancer's configuration. A rule that sends shivers down our neck:

```
Allow 0.0.0.0 any # debug rule
```

Oh boy... How did we miss this in our earlier audit of publicly exposed endpoints? This load balancer is not restricted to partners—it's open to the whole wide world!

We furiously type a message to Marc and the team to see if anyone has any context regarding this strange firewall rule. Meanwhile, we explore the code of the `External-Callbacks` service, only to be surprised by the variety of partners who rely on it. From Typeform to validate customer survey forms to IDFace to check customer identity cards, to Stripe for triggering payments. The risk profile is so heterogeneous that any potential vulnerability can wreak havoc. We immediately spot another problem: a lot of these routes do not implement authentication:

```
class PSController < ApplicationController
  # Disable signature following encoding issues when parsing data
```

```
# before_action :require_signature
def index
  PSCallbackJob.perform_later(webhook_params)

  render(json: {message: "success"}, status: 200)
end
```

You chain the two vulnerabilities together and suddenly Typeform, as well as the rest of the Internet, can not only register forms but issue payouts and make transfers by calling URLs in that microservice.

As is evident in the code above, someone did try to perform signature checks but just gave up because of the complexity of signing and verifying payloads produced by different libraries across different languages. They probably thought that IP whitelisting was indeed enough to cover the risk of unauthorized access. That is, until somebody accidentally allowed the whole Internet through the front door.

"I think I added that rule a couple of weeks back to debug the access of Typeform. Their IP address seems to change all the time," confesses Marc.

We hurriedly remove the faulty firewall rule and replace it with a more realistic list of Typeform IP addresses we found in the last three months' activity logs.

Yes, the 0.0.0.0/0 rule is bad. But are we really that much safer? In order to allow people to fill out a form, we exposed our banking endpoints to the entire Typeform company and, in turn, whoever they trust—and whoever those people trust down the road, ad nauseam. I'm certain that surveys are important, but not bet-the-company important.

IP whitelisting is not the issue per se, it's the fact that it's applied at such a low level of the stack (network level) completely decorrelated from its business purpose. Either a partner is allowed through the load balancer and can target any URL they want, or they are completely shut off. There is no granularity or IP/URL coupling. Partners with different business goals and security requirements are grouped together under the same risk profile, which needlessly over inflates the slightest problems. An issue with Typeform, which is solely in charge of survey forms, suddenly spills over the banking platform and could cost millions of dollars.

The second mistake of this setup is the infringement of another fundamental concept in security called defense in depth: we need to stack up security layers in order to block, detect or otherwise limit the impact of an attack that pierces through previous layers. Renouncing on signature verification and authentication because that request was subject to IP whitelisting by the previous component is a dangerous assumption that can quickly be dismantled with a single action, as we just witnessed.

Luckily, we already have a rough idea of what partner-mirage connections should look like, so we take a couple of days to rework this current setup to match this new standard. It scores high enough in our threat graph, given its Internet exposure, and Marc is eager to help fix his blunder.

First, we start by hiding this load balancer behind the WAF, just like we did for other load balancers that receive human traffic. We missed this entry point when doing the inventory with Steve, because we only considered customer-facing endpoints. It's time to rectify our mistake:

Figure 11-3: New partner access to Mirage

Next, we must move IP whitelisting closer to the app and tie it to the HTTP routing logic. Traefik should only deliver a request to an endpoint if it matches the list of IP addresses defined for that URL. This will prevent Typeform, for instance, from lying about its hostname to target URLs used by other partners.

Traefik offers a way of defining such controls in what they refer to as middlewares[30]. Marc helps us write the code required to take advantage of this feature[31]:

---

[30] A Traefik middleware is a component that processes the request before forwarding it to its destination. It can be used for IP whitelisting, authentication and so on https://bit.ly/3CvVeDs

[31] While we can achieve the same URL-dependent IP whitelisting on the WAF or at the app level, we chose to do it on Traefik because it's much easier for teams to maintain their own lists (contrary to tweaking the WAF configuration), and we're guaranteed a uniform behavior (contrary to app-level implementation).

```
apiVersion: traefik.containo.us/v1alpha1
kind: Middleware
metadata:
  name: ipwhitelist-typeform
spec:
  ipWhiteList:
    sourceRange:
      - 63.5.78.3/32
      - 45.57.6.78
    ipStrategy:
      depth: 2
```

We attach this middleware to the routing configuration of the service
External-Callbacks. Every request to the path /hooks/typeform
must go through the new IP whitelisting middleware and therefore be part of the
declared IP addresses.

```
---
apiVersion: traefik.containo.us/v1alpha1
kind: IngressRoute
metadata:
  name: ingressroute
  annotations:
    traefik.ingress.kubernetes.io.router.middlewares: ip-
whitelist-typeform

spec:
...snip...
  rules:
    - host: hooks.mirage.co
      http:
        paths:
          - path: /hooks/typeform
```

We will create as many middleware as there are different entry points to the
External-Callbacks service, and repeat this process for each of them,
thereby constraining each partner to its set of URLs. Only Typeform can call the
HTTP endpoint to register forms, only Stripe can call the /hooks/payout
URL and so on.

That's our second layer of protection and isolation.

Now to the third one. Typeform provides a way to sign payloads using a
shared secret, so we submit a merge request to the backend team to add this
payload validation. Their template code makes this a simple copy-paste job.

That concludes our three-layer protection of our partner access.

To recap, then, an attacker first has to land an IP address allowed by one of our IP whitelisting middleware to call our webhook APIs. Maybe they compromise a partner's app or coerce an employee. Even if they manage to do that, they still need to get that secret token used to sign or authenticate requests. Let's say they find it in an Excel spreadsheet or in a configuration file somewhere. Their impact would still be limited to the functionality exposed to the partner and have no side effects on other parts of Mirage's business. If they try to inject some shenanigans in the payload in an attempt to break this isolation, the WAF would block them and alert us to potential abuse of the endpoint.... Now that's defense in depth, not stacking up different firewall versions.

This little tangent around partner connection shed light on a whole new subgraph in our threat diagram: partner access!

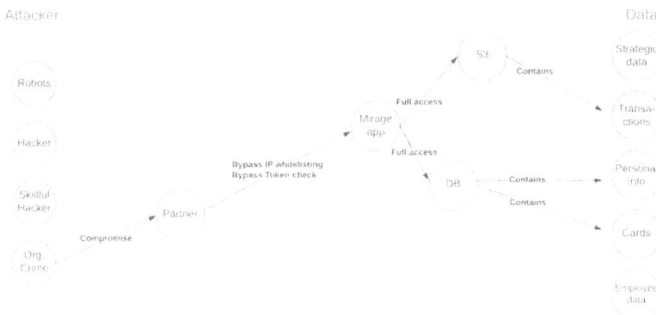

Figure 11-4: New partner access to Mirage

We mitigated the current issue for the External-callbacks app, thereby standardizing a new way of connecting to our infrastructure. We will do a quick session with the infrastructure and backend team to propagate this new design and incorporate into any new partner connection.

As we get out to grab a quick bite after the latest release of the callback service, we meet Robert, which, unfortunately for our lunch plans, starts an impromptu meeting. His team has been positively impressed with our closing of all vulnerabilities reported in the previous pentest. Something they struggled with for over a year. We talk in detail about the security roadmap, the rationale behind it, the threat modelling and so on.

"You're doing a great job with the tech team," he starts off.

Oh, a heartfelt compliment! We'll take it!

"...but you need to codify what you're doing in processes and procedures understandable for non-tech people. I have been in the auditing business for a long time; if we do not have a set of documents that explain how we protect our data, all your successful projects won't matter, we will be toast. Financial auditors will have trouble approving our books and the regulator will issue public recommendations, even sanctions."

Robert has a fair point. Cybersecurity has increasingly become the focus of regulatory controls from Singapore to the US. Even financial auditors ask for basic security requirements before certifying data extracted from accounting systems. These people rarely perform code reviews, penetration tests or other types of technical assessments. They swear by one thing and one thing only: documentation!

If you have a document explicitly stating that networks should be segregated and every packet be subject to firewall rules, then you get a green checkmark. They might ask for a sample or a screenshot, but even if you fail to provide one, you'll get a minor tap on the back of the hand. Almost no one will actually forage through arcane configurations to dig out that 0.0.0.0/0 rule that grants wide access to all partners. As long as we have tidy documents that faithfully rehash the accepted best practices, we're good. On the other hand, a company that fails to provide a document mandating network segregation will get a red warning, even though they meticulously filter every packet in the infrastructure. Showing them firewall rules won't help. I've tried...

This dark corner of the security industry where policies and procedures are conceived, where the legal jargon is the *lingua franca* and where ISO standards and PCI DSS are royalty, is abhorred by many engineers with a solid understanding of attackers. It is therefore populated by incompetent wannabe experts completely disconnected from the real world. They're responsible for writing policies with antedated requirements that are enforced across all Fortune 500 companies, or worse, enshrined in the law. Take the Strong Customer Regulation 2018/389 in Europe, which applies to financial institutions. Article 4.3 literally mandates that user accounts be blocked after five failed attempts. Not four, not ten, but five, regardless of the context, which is, of course, ridiculous and annoys customers more than it solves any security issue. Password complexity is exponential, so blocking the account after five attempts instead of ten won't complexify the attacker's life in any measurable way, but it will sure as hell complexify that of the customer. Opting for a different threshold, however, will likely get you a warning that gets reported to the authorities. Not to mention that vertical bruteforce is far from being the dominant threat anyway; horizontal bruteforce and credential stuffing are much more dangerous and prolific, as we saw a couple of weeks ago, but the law spectacularly fails to address those. What an epic failure!

Of course, any sound person who spent a few days in the attacker's shoes will be frustrated with such accumulation of nonsense, but the hard truth is that if you don't muster the courage to tackle this issue, either by doing it yourself or hiring someone to take care of it, it will inevitably escalate to the leadership team, who will be forced to hire a scribe expert that will make your life a living hell. Imagine having worked so hard to implement pragmatic security measures only to lose that freedom and be subject to new security policies written by some compliance officer who thinks that passwords should be renewed every 90 days[32].

Writing security policies does not create any quantifiable value. They are mostly there to justify and explain security measures to future reviewers and auditors. You cannot stop an attacker with a data classification policy nor force people to follow it, no matter how well worded it is.

But you can stop an auditor or the regulator from interfering with your work, which could be perceived as a form of legal attack. If we extend the metaphor, we can think of this threat as yet another scenario in our threat graph. How can we leverage our grounded experience to write short, pragmatic documentation that ticks all the boxes required by the law, negates absurd rules accepted as "common practices" and keeps nosy auditors at bay? Think of it as hacking the world of compliance.

So, what is the minimum set of documents required for a financial company like Mirage that has the ambition to grow to 1000 employees in the near future.

First and foremost, we need an information security policy. It's a document, usually 15 to 20 pages long, that describes the organization of the security team (to whom the security officer reports) and the commitments of Mirage in terms of security. What the company pledges to do to ensure the safety of its customers and their data: network isolation, encryption of sensitive data, threat modelling, password policy and so on.

We will keep it short, to the point, and cover as much ground as possible to get away with this single piece of document, at least for starters. A key point to keep in mind is that a security policy, like every other policy, is prescriptive. It uses language such as "should" and "must", but never describes how a given security measure is applied. That will be detailed in subsequent documents. *Example: "Sensitive data should be encrypted during transit and at rest using state-of-the-art algorithms."*

Our security policy will have five primary paragraphs:

---

[32] NIST 800-63B §5.1.1.2 : *Verifiers SHOULD NOT require memorized secrets to be changed arbitrarily (e.g., periodically)*

- Organization and governance describing the role of the head of security, their hierarchical attachment and any meeting rituals with key stakeholders, such as the compliance and internal control departments.
- Key security goals: these are your classic AICT criteria: availability, integrity, confidentiality and traceability and what they mean in the context of Mirage.
- Platform security explaining the least privilege principle and its application in various contexts.
- Application security with secure coding and references to the OWASP
- Detection and monitoring.

I put a template in the book's GitHub repo to help you get started. You are welcome to customize it to fit your needs. Some like to add sections about HR management, NDAs, legal frameworks, even fraud detection, but the points listed above are the bare minimum that every information security policy should cover.

Other important documents that we will start working on every now and then when we can spare an hour include:
- Data classification policy: A document that describes which type of data is sensitive. Customer data is…drum roll… confidential. The company's logo is…yes, public! GitLab has published a great classification policy that we can almost borrow as is: *https://bit.ly/3CzUKw2*.
- Incident response: A short two-pager that mandates all abnormal security events to be reported to a dedicated email: security@mirage.com, triaged and investigated.
- Access right management: A document that mandates all access be nominative, protected with two factors, principle of the least privilege and so on.

You will find a template for these documents in the book's GitHub repository that you can freely adapt to your context.

Many companies fall into the common trap of spending an agonizing amount of time on each and every word of these policies. Big banks pay consultants heavy fees to write these same documents, thinking it will magically solve all their issues. The hard part about data classification policy is not writing the document; that's a one-hour copy-paste at worst. Anything more is a waste of time. The challenge is enforcing its provisions in a clever and transparent way, without tying up two employees full time with manual checks and Excel spreadsheets.

A lot of our data is in S3 buckets, right? Say that the policy mandates that all customer data should be encrypted at rest to protect against unauthorized physical access to hard drives. We can, for instance, write a small routine that finds buckets used by applications, tag them as such and automatically call AWS API endpoints to enforce all sorts of security measures on these buckets: logging, versioning, encryption, deletion protections and so on. Any new bucket bearing that tag would inherit those same security properties, no matter what the creator of the bucket intended. Automatic and by-design protection that spares us the litany of processes and manual controls that typically follow the writing security procedures. That would be a great project that will assuredly bring to life this empty shell of a document.

We won't be doing that today, though, because the underlying threat scenario dwarfs those of employee authentication, excessive permission on production and even partner access, so we have to be content with the document to divert compliance for the time being. We log the task for the future when the time is right.

Some companies choose to have dedicated teams whose only job is to write these documents in their ivory tower, then spend the rest of their time ensuring that they are properly applied across the company. I strongly believe that security teams that build systems should oversee their policies and procedures. They may be audited by a third party (internal or external). Their policies may be questioned or even revised by these bodies, but they should retain their ownership. Otherwise, the company ends up with a weird disconnect between what is written and what is actually implemented or even technically possible, causing misalignment between teams and unnecessary headaches. You build it, you run it, you own it.

As we have just seen, policies are prescriptive. They mandate all sorts of security controls. On the other hand, procedures and standards describe how we implement such requirements. The tech document we published about the WAF implementation and partner access would count as procedures, for instance.

Given the heavy work we already performed on the Mirage application, we decide to start with a document called "application security". Its purpose is to highlight every security measure in place on the app, from requiring 2FA to partner authentication. Again, you'll find a template in the book's GitHub repository: https://github.com/sparcflow/Blitzscaling

We write these documents in plain and simple terms, cutting through the non-sense jargon found in many official documents. It takes us a couple of hours spread over a few weeks to finish this first body of documentation, but that should keep any auditor at bay. We send this collection of documents to Robert for approval and adjustments. It may take them weeks to review it all, but at least it should give us peace for the time being. His team will add the necessary regulatory references to make it look official.

The cavalry arrives

We start the week as we always do, by going over our threat graph. It's our little routine every Monday to keep that helicopter view over our entire security landscape.

It has moved quite a bit since its first inception. As it's meant to. We continuously audit small patches of the infrastructure and application code every Friday to find new vulnerabilities, novel exploitation paths, new entry paths... and following each discovery, we faithfully update the graph accordingly and reevaluate our upmost priorities.

We also take advantage of requests on the channel *#security-requests* to deep dive into obscure and often forgotten services. The more we know about the tech environment of the company, the stronger our asset inventory and therefore the more holistic our security posture will be.

As argued before, employee authentication is still a major issue. Most assuredly, the next big one. A single sign-on platform significantly reduces our exposure to many forms of credential theft on the various apps we currently have. But just how many of them do we have, and do all of them support an SSO integration or should we add some blending magic?

We drop a line to John in IT asking about an inventory of software apps. His team helps unlock accounts, configure computers and assist every employee in the company, so they must have the closest picture to a full inventory:

"We maintain an Excel file of all the apps on which we need to create an account for newcomers. I will share it with you. It's a nightmare to keep track of everything when there is a new app literally every month," complains John.

He almost falls off his chair when we confide in him about the start of our SSO project to automate 90% of account creation and manipulation. He eagerly offers his help to boost the project.

"We need to make a strong case for this SSO project to be fully endorsed by Henry," we explain. "Can you help me build a new Excel sheet, listing all applications you know of and whether or not they support an SSO integration?"

We take five minutes to set up a quick template composed of the following columns:

App name | Data | Sensitivity | SSO support | MFA support

The idea is to rate each app according to the data it holds. A HR tool that holds employee salaries is a confidential tool, so it has to be ideally protected with an SSO. Failing that, at least allow us to enforce two-factor authentication for everyone. *Oh, good heavens, are we quoting the data classification policy?*

In any event, once the inventory is over, we'll have a measurable ROI for the SSO project that we can easily sell to Henry, i.e., how many critical apps will be protected with SSO, along with the time we'll save on user management.

"We have a solid list of about 50 apps," says John, "I'll fill in the list according to the template we just did and send it your way. We need to reach out to the finance team to get the full list of SaaS tools used at Mirage. They see all the transactions on our expense accounts. I would not be surprised if some teams took it upon themselves to deploy tools and independently handle their users."

"Genius! Thank you. Will do that," we reply.

"Oh, by the way," John interjects, "I wanted your opinion on something. The risk team is asking us to prepare Windows computers for their department," says John casually.

Please don't say what I think you're going to say...

"I was thinking of setting an Active Directory on an AWS server to easily manage their workstations. Would you mind giving us a hand with the security settings?"

Oh, what fresh hell is this? Can't we just ban Windows workstations like GitLab did[33] ? We muster everything we can to reply in a calm tone: "Well, I have nothing against Windows, but why Active Directory when you can set up Azure AD and delegate all that maintenance pain to Microsoft? It's much easier and safer that way, don't you think?"

"My teammate and I used to administer Active Directory. We don't know Azure AD and levelling up on it will slow down the project by at least a couple of weeks. You don't like Active Directory?" he skeptically asks.

---

[33] *https://bit.ly/3WWaVMw.*

"My issue with Active Directory is that it's not set up to be secure by default. There are so many settings kept for historical reasons that it is objectively hard to secure an AD setup. Disabling NTLM, SMBv1, forcing SMB signing, LDAP signing, etc. It's a nightmare to continuously keep of track of everything. Any company would need a few experts dedicated to this task. We don't have that luxury. I strongly recommend you look into Azure AD. I'm ready to help you folks set it up rather than blindly go with the most familiar solution. What do you say?"

"Ok, let me look it into it and get back to you," says John hesitantly.

We know that we are likely asking for a big favor, but hopefully our previous help on the device management project will buy us the goodwill needed to see this through.

"Yes, let's book a few slots to go over it together and even lay down the first bricks together," we reassure John. "I'll inform the risk team that their computers will have to wait a bit. I am sure they will understand the trade-off involved. Speaking of Windows, I remember someone mentioning something about some servers we have. Does that ring a bell? Maybe I misunderstood."

"You mean the accounting servers? Yes, we have three standalone servers on AWS. They're only used by the three people in the finance team. I will share the admin credentials with you so you can take a look."

We briefly poke around the servers to understand our exposure: these are standalone servers, not part of any Active Directory. They are isolated in their own virtual private cloud on AWS, and the firewall only allows administrative port 3389 from the VPN. The machines are running the latest Windows build.

Should we stop everything we do to focus on them? Clearly not, but maybe we can take 30 minutes to tweak a couple of settings. We can enforce a better password policy, add a lockout threshold against bruteforce attacks, activate all audit policies and program an auto-update every week at 4 am. We drop a quick message to the finance team to make sure they don't have a critical batch running around that hour. We can do much more. We want to do much more: application whitelisting to prevent unwanted software from running, log centralization and system monitoring with Sysmon[34] to detect common attacks and suspicious behavior, but that will have to wait. We must not lose focus on the more urgent threats.

---

[34] *https://learn.microsoft.com/en-us/sysinternals/downloads/sysmon.*

While we were chatting with John and tweaking Windows settings, we received a cascade of emails from Gabrielle, the co-CEO and the rest of the leadership team. Everyone is freaking out about a phishing email that seemingly impersonated Nate in an attempt to fool our CFO into wiring a million dollars. The email exchange was going on for a while, with everyone from compliance to operations chiming in with various ideas to counter this new scam. To our horror, we notice that Robert seized the occasion to preach once more for employee training and phishing simulations. That's when Henry looped us into the exchange, either to counter the argument or to schedule a phishing simulation… we don't know.

We slowly inhale a breath of air and think calmly about the situation. The phishing email is coming from a random address where the alias was set to Nate's full name.

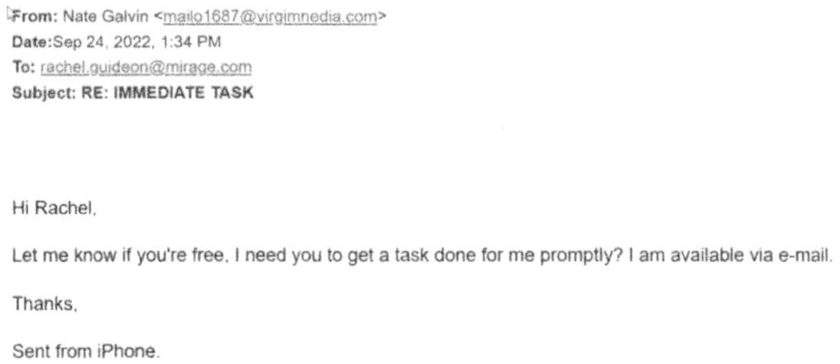

From: Nate Galvin <mailo1687@virgimnedia.com>
Date:Sep 24, 2022, 1:34 PM
To: rachel.guideon@mirage.com
Subject: RE: IMMEDIATE TASK

Hi Rachel,

Let me know if you're free, I need you to get a task done for me promptly? I am available via e-mail.

Thanks,

Sent from iPhone.

Figure 12-1: Phishing email

That should be easy to block. We hurry back to John and ask for temporary admin privileges on Google Workspace to check out the spam settings[35]. We enable all the security checks related to spoofing employee names and company domains and turn on other settings, such as attachment protections.

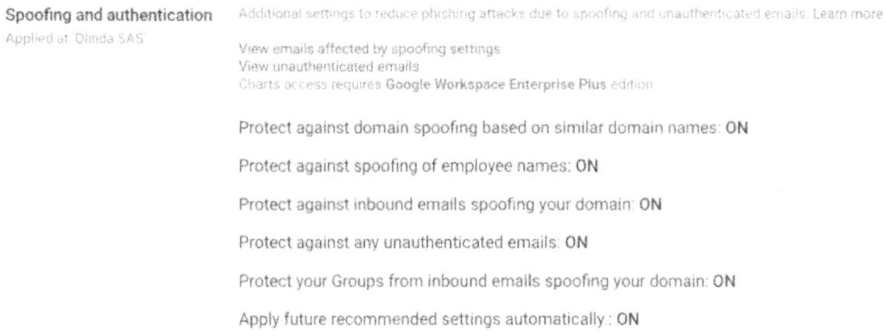

Spoofing and authentication
Applied at 'Olinda SAS

Additional settings to reduce phishing attacks due to spoofing and unauthenticated emails. Learn more

View emails affected by spoofing settings
View unauthenticated emails
Charts access requires **Google Workspace Enterprise Plus** edition.

Protect against domain spoofing based on similar domain names: ON

Protect against spoofing of employee names: ON

Protect against inbound emails spoofing your domain: ON

Protect against any unauthenticated emails: ON

Protect your Groups from inbound emails spoofing your domain: ON

Apply future recommended settings automatically : ON

---

[35] *http://bit.ly/3ZGa83x*

Figure 12-2: Google workspace spam settings

Now Google will easily flag `mailo1687@virginmedia.com` as masquerading for Nate's identity and reject their email or send it to spam with a huge red banner.

While we are on the admin console, we also enforce TLS encryption for all outbound emails and increase the reputation of our domain by enabling email authentication using DKIM and email origin verification using SPF[36]. This latter configuration requires some DNS tweaking, but we already have the inside knowledge thanks to our WAF sessions with Steve, so we quickly drop the infrastructure team a line about the necessary changes we're about to do. They promptly validate them.

We replay the offending email from our personal address and, lo and behold, now the email ends up in the spam folder with a huge red banner saying it's a phishing attempt.

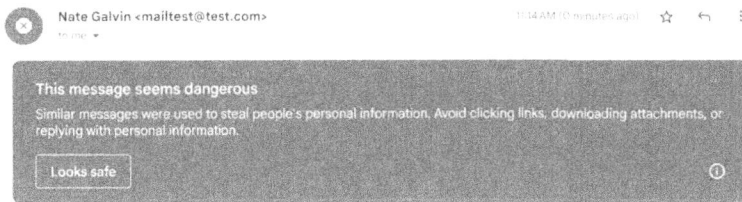

Figure 12-3: Phishing email is now detected

We respond to Nate and the rest of the leadership team, briefly explaining the upgrades we made and how it would prevent similar future attacks. We close the email with a single sentence that unapologetically removes phishing simulations from the table:

"Phishing simulations don't teach us anything new. People follow instructions and they click on links. Instead of praying that people won't fall for a scam that harms the company, we should strive to build an environment that cannot be brought down with a single person's mistake. Nobody should be able to initiate a million-dollar wire transfer. We must have a double validation scheme for such large amounts. I am sure Robert would agree that it makes sense from a compliance perspective as well."

---

[36] Summary of SPF, DKIM and DMARC: *http://bit.ly/3CPTiWx.*

Hopefully that will be the end of this charade. We message the finance team to learn more about their process to update the IBAN of vendors and reach out to operations to understand if their back-office application indeed allows people to just wire millions without any validation. We will help them beef up this setup if need be. We also loop in the risk team to review the delegation process for large amounts.

Just as we finish firing these messages, we get a new pop-up from Serena saying she found a potential recruit who could fit the persona.

This day is one frenzied event after the other.

We open up the resumé of the candidate, full of expectation. There is so much work to be done here that we need at least three people for a year just to catch up with everything.

Richard was a penetration tester for two years in a small consulting firm, primarily working on web and mobile apps. He does not have much knowledge on AWS, Golang and Ruby, but he dabbled with some Python and Java code to develop Burp extensions and automate some exploitation requests.

"I know he is very young and he does not have any certifications or fancy degree, but he was extremely enthusiastic on the phone, and he was eager to learn more about our technical stack," said Serena in almost an apologetic way.

"I love it! Set it up!" we respond.

If you have the luxury of finding candidates who tick all the boxes: great human skills, tech expertise in your current stack, relevant experience and good threat modelling, by all means, go for it. The reality, however, is that these unicorns are rarely available as-is on the market. It's too easy to sit in a corner complaining about the lack of talent just because you cannot find the polished set of skills you were hoping for.

Recruiters and managers have to keep in mind that great talent is more often made than found. Instead of waiting one or two years for that precious unicorn, it's much more rewarding and time efficient to invest in someone with the potential to develop the skills you're looking for. You get access to a significantly bigger share of the talent pool, unwavering loyalty and commitment, and a brighter future for your team and the company.

I call it "hiring for potential". We don't extend you an offer for what you currently know but for what you can achieve in the future once given mentorship and autonomy.

Of course, it's much easier to evaluate a set of established technical skills than something as elusive as potential and hunger for improvement. Richard is a text-book case. His consulting firm only works with big companies willing to pay for year-round penetration tests on their web applications. He never had the chance to work on Docker, Kubernetes or AWS. Our goal, therefore, is to evaluate his capacity to level-up on this. One way to proxy this insight is to explore his current level of mastery in the subjects he listed. If he took the time to break down SQL injections into their most fundamentals units, chances are, he will do the same with any other technology if given the opportunity. Let's dig into that:

"So, what can you tell me about SQL injections? How do you find them, how do you exploit them?" we ask him on the day of the interview.

"Hum, huh…SQL injections are SQL code inserted in parameters that finds its way to the database because of unchecked input. I simply use sqlmap (https://sqlmap.org/) and it takes care of everything," he tentatively responds.

We can tell he is nervous by the shakiness of his voice. Still, we push further. It is so easy to fully rely on tools and the abstractions they provide without ever dissecting what's happening under the hood. We don't need people who only operate tools. We need people who understand their limitations and can tweak and extend them to be more potent.

"Yes, but what happens underneath? Let's say you don't have sqlmap. How would you go about it? Phrased differently, how would you write your own version of sqlmap?"

Again, the goal is not to encourage people to roll off their own version of sqlmap—although, it could be a great learning experience—but to see if Richard can reason from first principles and is not simply content with whatever solution is available to him.

Thankfully, he went on to describe the various ways of detecting and exploiting SQL injections: induce errors by adding quotes or bad syntax, UNION statements, time-based queries and so on. We almost had to cut him off to make time for other questions.

Good so far. We continue exploring other types of vulnerabilities he is familiar with. About half an hour in, we decide to switch gears:

"You mentioned that you once came across Docker in a pentest. How does Docker work?" we ask.

"Huh? I mean, yes, I think I saw a Docker image in an assignment once, but I did not check it any further. It does packaging of some sort, right?" he responds.

Nice try, but we will drag him deeper.

"Yes, you can say that. But how does it work—at the system level?" we ask with a wide smile.

"Maybe some form of virtualization?" he tries once more.

"How exactly? Which kernel concepts are involved? How does it handle system calls?" we ask.

Of course, we're not expecting an answer here. Richard never got a chance to play with Docker or investigate its internals. We're looking for a simple "I don't know", which is the ultimate sign of humility and intellectual honesty. A person who never admits ignorance will never bother to research it in the first place. The first step to acquiring knowledge is a self-awareness of one's gaps.

Richard quickly capitulates feeling terrorized that he missed what he thinks is a critical question. We reassure him that the interview is not over and start explaining roughly how regular containers work on Linux: namespaces to isolate objects, cgroups to limit resources, layers mounted as directories and so on.

While explaining these advanced concepts, we're assessing a couple of things: how fast is this person absorbing new information? Do they stop us if something is unclear or contradicts previously acquired knowledge? Can they synthesize back and restructure the knowledge they've received? And, of course, does their ego accept such directional feedback or do we end up in a confrontation? This is the real evaluation part of the interview. The Docker question was just an excuse to get there. After all, a lot of mentoring will take the form of this rough exchange where we break down the big picture of a technology and send them off to level up on it, share their findings, challenge them some more and iterate our way to mastery. If our communication styles do not match, for whatever reason, we won't achieve maximum efficiency when working together.

We can take it a step further and revisit some of these questions again in a second interview to assess if the candidate was curious enough to research the subjects they missed. The goal is to measure improvement between that first interview and the second one—where we debrief the skill test. Even if it's only two datapoints, that gives a valuable indication to the potential of the candidate.

Everything can be learnt. Disqualifying a candidate because they don't know your favorite tool or don't follow your coding conventions is arbitrary and rash. When they don't know something or cannot recall a given factoid, the reflex should always be: "How much time they need to level up on this issue?" That's what we ultimately care about in the long run.

That's one way to interview for potential, and Richard shows great promise. His skill test submitted a couple of days later displays interesting creativity. When answering the famous "how would you hack Mirage?" question, he got the reconnaissance part quite right, showing a mastery of the basic components of the Internet: DNS, HTTP and so on. He also nailed the initial entry-point vulnerability, which is expected given his penetration testing background. He did stumble a little bit, however, in the lateral propagation and data exfiltration.

We grill him a bit during the debrief, again going from first principles to land on the common lateral propagation techniques.

"Say, you are local admin on a Windows machine. How would you pivot to other machines?" we quiz him

"Huh... I guess I would look for an unpatched vulnerability on some of the exposed ports," he replies

"That's definitely one way. What are other options? Just list them in bullet point formats. Whatever comes to your mind," we ask.

"Huh... Looking for passwords in scripts, dumping passwords of local accounts... I can always try to bruteforce or wait for the admin to connect on the machine and get their credentials using... huh...darn, I forgot the name of the tool but I know how to find it," he thinks out loud.

He has the correct intuition about getting the results, he just lacks a bit of structure to synthesize and deliver answers through a proper threat modelling framework. That's fine; it comes with experience and thinking in advance about such topics. What matters most is that he has a great foundation that we can build on, and he is willing to learn about new technologies.

We spend the rest of the interview talking about our day-to-day activities from hunting vulnerabilities in the web app to setting up infrastructure components to building secure gateways with our partners. His eyes light up at the opportunity to build the security practice of a financial company from the ground up, with such a wide scope of autonomy! He shares our excitement for hands-on involvement and breaking new topics. Toward the end of the interview, he openly says that he can't wait to join the team!

We extend him the offer the next day and he accepts it on the spot!

Our glorious security team just grew by 100%.

**

We go back to our list of active tasks: building the inventory of SaaS tools that may be compatible with an SSO. John's team did a great job investigating the options proposed by each app. They granted us temporary admin permissions on each app to help them configure the various parameters when the migration will kick off.

It is remarkable how many SaaS vendors only support SSO on the most expensive plan. The website *https://sso.tax* captures this phenomenon quite accurately. Everyone's go-to-market strategy seems to offer core features of the product for free, but push companies to pay for security. As if security is some sort of add-on or tax reserved for the elite, which is, of course, ridiculous. When there is a data leak on a given product, both the vendor and the company whose data leaked share the news headline! AWS learned this the hard way with the multiplication of scandals on S3. Now the default settings and warnings when creating S3 buckets are pretty restrictive and help avoid accidental mistakes.

As we explore the list of SaaS products currently used by Mirage, we realize what a disaster user management is across all tools. There are over 60 apps unearthed by IT. Some have six-digit password requirements. Others don't even offer the option of adjusting password policies. Several apps hosting customer data have more users than the current headcount of the company. Others feature everyone as admins, or worse, a single admin account shared by the whole team. If the weak authentication on the Mirage app is a match near a kerosene barrel, then this is a drunk president holding their finger over the nuclear launch button.

Single sign-on is one way to homogenize authentication settings and enforce adequate protection against identity theft and abuse of privilege, but the sad reality is that we won't extract the same benefit from each and every integration. It will heavily depend on the capabilities of the target app.

As we study the integrations proposed, we discover that some products delegate only the authentication to the SSO. Roles and permissions would still need to be handled manually within the app, defeating the purpose of a centralized source of truth. Others don't support automatically creating users, so IT would still need to create users manually on the app, then grant them access on the SSO before they can finally connect to the app. Some products, in a feat of brilliance, support the SSO, but always allow users to connect with their weak local passwords. Each tool has its own edge case and short comings. It's maddening.

This is to say that single sign-on—just as any security measure, for that matter—delivers a spectrum of protection that can vary by app and context. We can take it as is and live with the limitations and risks they introduce, or, if we have the will and the means, we can cover these shortcomings with our additional custom tooling. For instance, for those miscreant apps that don't support automatic user creation, we can automate it through their APIs as soon as users get granted SSO permission. For other apps that cannot disable password-authentication, we can routinely set random passwords, thereby forcing everyone through the SSO portal.

When the dust settles, we estimate that we could cover 66% of all Mirage apps without upgrading to more expensive plans. And more crucially, achieve a 90% coverage of apps holding critical data. That's a fair number that should seduce Henry. We'll negotiate higher pricing plans or a commercial gesture for the rest of the apps as the SSO gains traction and people realize how much time it saves them. We cannot let these critical apps go unmanaged and be protected with just a simple password authentication.

For the rest of the apps and for the time being, we will activate 2FA when possible as a first temporary measure to mitigate the risk. We'll revisit them in the next quarter to see how things have evolved. It's far from the ideal case but we have to kickstart the project to get that momentum going. Once SSO is prevalent throughout the company, we can easily push these last apps to cave.

Now that we have dissected the landscape, we can set up a meeting with John to discuss the features we absolutely need, security-wise, from this SSO provider: Support of multiple authentication protocols: SAML *(https://bit.ly/3FhnPhn)* and OpenID *(http://bit.ly/3T7mKhD)*. Integration with Google Workspace to avoid creating the same user multiple times, multi-factor authentication, specifically WebAuthn to protect against credential phishing, the ability to apply more restrictive security options on some apps and users: for instance, require WebAuthn for all employees but allow time-based OTP for shared service accounts. And, of course, we need logging and easy automation through APIs.

Together with IT, we draft a request for proposal and send it to a couple of known contenders. Same as for the WAF, we are looking to quickly PoC a solution on two or three apps, write down a specification that contrasts both tools, compare pricing and make our decision. We timebox the whole selection process to three weeks. The advantage in the scale-up world is the velocity of deals at every level, from the CEO to the finance and legal teams.

While IT is exploring each contender, we draft a quick email to Henry to validate the purchase. We start with the rationale derived from our threat model; the observation made on the poor user management in the apps and the estimated SSO coverage.

So far, Henry has kept his end of the deal. Each time we asked for resources, financial or otherwise, he barely blinked. As long as the rationale was clear, the project went ahead full steam. His unwavering support was a key success condition that we raised at the start of our collaboration—and rightly so as, hopefully, these pages have demonstrated. Without full sponsorship of a knowledgeable and credible person from the executive team, it is very hard to rock the boat and get over the defeatist response of *"well, it's always been this way."*

There was one particular instance where that promise of support came under heavy challenge. As part of our regular and ongoing snooping around the app and infrastructure to update the threat model, we found an interesting vulnerability.

On the Manager app, a customer who uploads invoices sends a classic POST HTTP request and receives back a URL pointing to the uploaded file:

```
# request
POST /api/invoices/create
Host: manager.mirage.com
...snip...

# response
HTTP 200 OK
Server: shieldsec
```

```
https://manager.mirage.com/api/user/63c24726-f50d-4c1d-86e7-
8305edde204c/invoice/01.pdf
```

Browsing this URL yields the file as expected. However, the curious thing is that this URL will stay valid forever, even if our session on the app expires. In fact, the only thing required to access the file is to know the user's ID (e.g., `63c24726-f50d-4c1d-86e7-8305edde204c`), a randomly generated string of characters... "Well, it's not that bad," one might say at a first glance, but curious things happen on the Internet. File URLs get cached by browser plugins or shared by threat intelligence websites. A simple search for similar URLs yields a hundred customer documents available on the Internet:

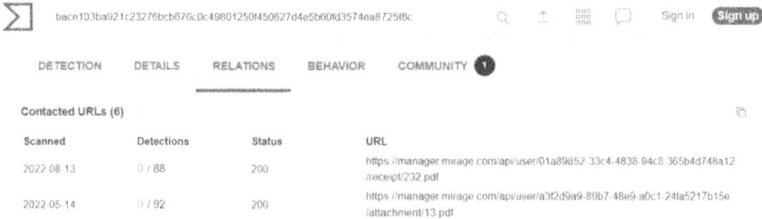

∑	bace103ba921c23276bcb87Gc0c49801250f450627d4e5b60fd3574ea8725f8c		Q ⬆ ⊞ ▭ Sign in **Sign up**

| DETECTION | DETAILS | RELATIONS | BEHAVIOR | COMMUNITY ① |

Contacted URLs (6)

Scanned	Detections	Status	URL
2022-08-13	0 / 88	200	https://manager.mirage.com/api/user/01a89852-33c4-4838-94c8-365b4d748a12/receipt/232.pdf
2022-05-14	0 / 92	200	https://manager.mirage.com/api/user/a3f2d9a9-89b7-48e9-a0c1-24fa5217b15e/attachment/13.pdf

Figure 12-4: virustotal.com holding a link in its database

That's not good. That's a poor design decision waiting to morph into a PR crisis... If the attacker gets a hold of the user ID, they can download their entire collection of documents: invoices, receipts, proof of identity and so on. User IDs are not actively advertised by Mirage, but they are not secret per se. Any information that is not encrypted or hashed should be considered public, because it's only a matter of time before it will be. Exhibit A: the user ID.

What's going on here? Why is it that this request should be exempt from the authorization flow? We dig into the code and find the following commented line of code:

```
...snip...

def download
    # TODO: put back authorization when the iOS app fixes the cookie
bug in the WebView (#Tech-12378)
    # authorize(user_id, object)
    send_file(get_file_s3(receipt_name, user_id),
            filename: receipt_name,
            type: "application/pdf")
...snip...
```

Damn you, mobile, again!

We clone the repo of the mobile iOS app and quickly zoom in on the WebView used to download files:

```
...snip...
let url = URL(string: file_download_url)!

webView.load(URLRequest(url: url))
webView.allowsBackForwardNavigationGestures = true
...snip...
```

Indeed, this code simply calls the target URL without including the user's session cookie, even though the iOS app receives it upon authentication. We reach out to Neil, the head of the mobile app team, for help:

"I am bit rusty in Swift. Could we please schedule a quick pairing session with a developer to solve this issue, maybe next week? We currently have files over the Internet holding customer data that can be downloaded by anyone because of this unresolved bug **#Tech-12378**."

He replied on Slack, rather coldly: "Do you have someone from product to lead the initiative and write the design specification? The team's agenda is booked until the end of the semester."

"We need a design specification for this?" we ask incredulously, "we're talking about adding a session cookie to a HTTP request sent by a WebView. There is zero impact on the customer since they're already authenticated on the app. It should be rather straightforward. All I am asking for is to pair with a developer who has a couple of free hours so I don't spend weeks struggling with Xcode[37] just to test the fix."

To no avail... The lead mobile reiterated that they did not have the bandwidth to prioritize this topic, which seemed outlandish. They did not even look into the code to evaluate the solutions, no matter how hard we tried to convince them. They dismissed our arguments and stopped responding over Slack. In hindsight, maybe text messaging was not the best format for this type of discussion.

We are not that proficient in mobile development that we could whip out a solution from scratch. Richard, who knows more about these development environments, is not due to come in for another two weeks...The only way to solve this stalemate was to escalate to Henry, who promptly jumped on the subject and set the record straight:

"If we cannot take two hours to put a cookie in a HTTP request, then we have some serious issues. Every team should have at least two pipelines: one for feature requests and another one for technical debt, bugs and security vulnerabilities. We cannot only deliver feature after feature, in the same way we cannot stop the world and only work on bugs. We must have the right mix of both. That's how we deliver continuous quality."

Fifteen minutes later, we had our slot scheduled for next week so we could quickly test and implement the fix.

Now that's sponsorship! And it reflects a deeper truth about the key ingredient for security to flourish in any company. You cannot have the right conditions of success as the lead or head of security if the tech environment itself is broken. A secure code is but one attribute of what constitutes quality code, in addition to performance, modularity, readability and so on. A tech team that does not strive for mastery and quality will inevitably end up producing garbage code, which in addition to being buggy and slow, is swarming with vulnerabilities.

---

[37] Xcode is Apple's development environment to write apps for all their operating systems: MacOS, iOS, etc.

Of course, it is much easier when the security team can just own 100% of the remediation process and implement fixes autonomously, but one cannot always enjoy this luxury across all the technical landscape of a company. In the case of Mirage, we were bound to come across a vulnerability that could not suffer waiting two or three weeks while we leveled up on the technology. On those rare occasions where an escalation is the only way to push things further, you sure as hell hope to have the sponsorship of someone capable and willing to changing things.

Like any trump card, one must wield it with care. Involving Henry in every conversation to fix a vulnerability is a sure sign of incompetence. After all, every escalation is a failure of communication. Richard's skills in mobile development would have probably helped mediate this case. He could have forged a solid relationship with the mobile team in anticipation of such an issue.

We will be looking for additional teammates with complimentary knowledge in other parts of the technical stack to reduce this form of dependency on other teams.

Where were we? Yes, the draft for the chosen SSO solution went to Henry and the finance department for validation. As soon as the deal is signed, we'll start working on the first apps. Knowing how fast Mirage moves, the first inventory we compiled will probably become obsolete in a couple of weeks. We agree with John to update it at least once a month until we fully migrate every app to the SSO.

The IT team will help us reign in many of the commercial apps behind the SSO. But there is another category of apps that unfortunately escapes their attention: internal apps put in production by developers and the infrastructure team. Remember Jenkins? Time to find out just how many other Jenkins-like apps there are in Mirage. They're not catalogued in any inventory or list we can find. We need to dig them up the hard way.

We pull out private DNS records in Route53 hoping to get a comprehensive list of registered apps, but we cannot find Jenkins on the list. Odd. We send a message to Steve, who quickly prompts back:

"You were close, yes. We setup wild card domains, such as *.production.mirage.co in Route53 to point every subdomain to our Kubernetes cluster. Requests coming in go through Traefik, which delivers them to the appropriate app according to their HTTP Host header. That way, we can add as many apps as we want without declaring a new DNS record every time," he explains.

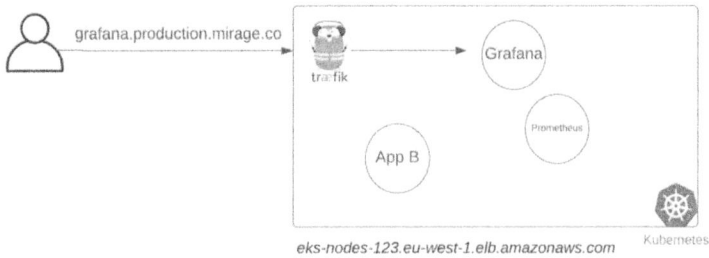

eks-nodes-123.eu-west-1.elb.amazonaws.com   Kubernetes

Figure 12-5: Traefik redirecting requests to the right app

As an example, Steve pulls up a real application currently running on the cluster called Grafana. It's a monitoring tool used to visualize metrics, such as latency, errors rate and so on. The domain name *grafana.production.mirage.co* is nowhere to be found on Route53. Instead, it is declared directly in the GitLab repository of the app:

```
# file prod.yaml
spec:
...snip...
  rules:
    - host: grafana.production.mirage.co
      http:
        paths:
          - path: /
```

When deployed to the Kubernetes cluster, a routing rule would be created that says, "route traffic for *grafana.production.mirage.co* to this app." Since the wildcard domain **.production.mirage.co* always sends traffic to the Kubernetes cluster, the request eventually finds its way to the app.

This means that in order to get a full inventory list of all internal applications currently running within Mirage, we need to search through all repos for routing rules that resemble that definition above[38].

We use the open-source tool ghorg to clone every available repository on Mirage's GitLab:

```
$ ghorg clone all-groups \
--base-url=https://gitlab.miage.co --scm=gitlab \
--token=XXXXXX --preserve-dir
```

---

[38] Alternatively, we could have also extracted the list of routes from Traefik's dashboard as well.

162

Then, we put together a simple grep command to dig out every internal domain available. We'll use the rust version of grep called ripgrep (*https://github.com/BurntSushi/ripgrep*), which is an order of magnitude faster than regular grep:

```
$ rg "mirage.co"-g "prod.yaml"

mirage/infra/grafana/deploy/prod.yaml
34: grafana.production.mirage.co

mirage/infra/elasticsearch/deploy/prod.yaml
23: logs.production.mirage.co
...snip...
```

Between these results and the private domains declared on Route53, we get close to 30 open-source apps available to anyone on the VPN or the production network: Jenkins for scheduling arbitrary tasks, Elasticsearch to sift through business data, Grafana with access to metrics and application logs, Kafka cruise control to manage Kafka partitions, which can be conceived of as databases holding critical customer data, Kowl, another Kafka tool that can read business data on these partitions, Airflow to schedule tasks manipulating huge volumes of data, etc.

None of these apps were configured to support any semblance of authentication. Zero, zilch, nothing. We don't even have to come up with a fancy exploit to take over the production environment. We can simply use these freely available management tools that are at our disposal. Elasticsearch contains the list of every payment and transaction made by every client, as well as their full banking information. Kafka partitions contain raw customer requests, including cookie sessions, password hash and the actual OTP as it's sent by SMS, so we can effectively impersonate any customer. Jenkins, as we already saw, is admin over AWS, of course.

We add these apps to our SSO inventory. The lack of authentication on internal apps is a scourge that plagues all companies, big and small, and they all stem from one fatal mistake: stubborn faith in perimetric defense, which is best illustrated by the case of GitLab.

We come across the last internal app on the list: GitLab, but thankfully, this one is at least protected with simple password authentication, which when compared with other tools seems like leaps ahead in terms of security. We've almost closed down the tab to start drafting the SSO integration when something catches our eye. For the first time, we notice a small little "globe" icon near the name of the repositories:

Your projects 330   Starred projects 0   Explore projects   Explore topics   Pending deletion   Filter by name...

All   Most stars   Trending

P   backend / swift-service 🌐
      Jsonnet POC to deploy an application with its configuration and make it reachable   ★ 0   ⑂ 0   ⌥ 0   ⎘ 0

T   mirage / acquisition-service 🌐
      Simple test to understand a bit how cuelang is working   ★ 0   ⑂ 0   ⌥ 0   ⎘ 0

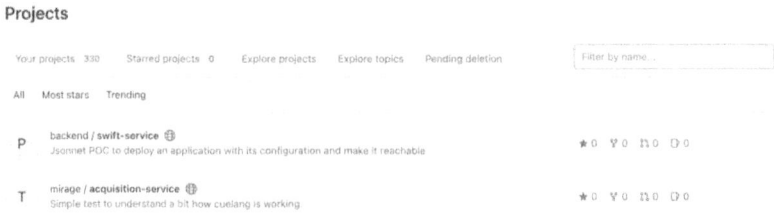

Figure 12-6: Public repositories on GitLab

We know that icon. We've seen that icon in other contexts. That can't be right. How the hell did we miss this? We hover over the icon only to see six letters forming the most dreaded word in security: "public".

All application repositories are public! That authentication page is as useless as a political campaign promise, and just as deceptive. Anyone with access to the VPN or production network can explore the code in GitLab and dig up hardcoded credentials, look for vulnerabilities, find secret keys leaked in job outputs and so on. Even GitLab was not spared by the safety illusion of the "internal" network.

"Hey, infra team! Me again," we prudently say. "As I was studying the configuration of our apps to put them behind the SSO, I noticed that all repos on GitLab are public, meaning we don't need authentication to explore the code and pipelines logs. I know the instance is hosted on AWS and only accessible through VPN, but that seems a tad excessive. How come all repos are public by default? Could we switch them to private?" There is an urgency in our tone that we cannot quite hide.

"It was easier to leave them public when we migrated from GitHub," responds someone on the chat. "Some apps fetch their package dependencies from other repositories on GitLab. We did not want to over complicate the migration. We put GitLab behind the VPN, which should be enough, no? It's a trusted component."

The notion of perimetric defense is so ingrained in in the psyche of network and system engineers that it is so very easy to fall prey to such misconceptions. Us humans, we like to reason in absolutist terms: it's either dangerous or safe. Good or bad. Trusted or untrusted.

But the reality is much more complex than that. The world is not a struggle between dualistic forces. It's full of nuances and subject to abounding perspectives. The Internet is not bad. It's just the path that many people follow to connect to systems around the world, and yes, occasionally perform attacks on companies. Similarly, the discussion should never revolve around whether a component is "trusted" or not. Might as well wonder about the color of abstraction. Not all grammatically sound sentences and questions are fruitful to pursue.

A more useful approach is to subject the VPN (or any technology) to different hypotheses—which, in our case, would amount to attack scenarios—and see how it holds up. It's no longer an absolute evaluation, but a conditional test resting on well-defined assumptions. Next, we weigh up the scenarios where that technology defaults and see if the risk is acceptable given the potential impact and probability of attack. Let's give it a go.

VPN is a technology to build encrypted network tunnels between systems. It does not protect individual apps, which are layer-seven components. It protects networks. So, unless we fragment the network into multiple risk zones, ideally one app per network, we end up in a situation where access to one app (and therefore its network) automatically opens access to all other apps on the same network, which inherently balloons up the blast radius of a single breach. Mirage has one VPN network, so pretty much all employees have automatic access to all of the above applications: Elasticsearch, Kowl, Jenkins and, of course, GitLab.

Beyond this architectural limitation, VPNs themselves are not immune to attacks. A number of zero days were published on many a VPN technology. A lot of them helped breach thousands of companies. Also, VPN credentials of our employees can be stolen through phishing. for instance.

When phrased as such, it becomes crystal clear that the current VPN setup does not shield us from as many attack scenarios as one would first think. It does a decent job encrypting a wireless connection in case of eavesdropping. It reduces the attack surface of applications by adding an extra hoop that attackers must jump through, but it's a very low hoop indeed...There are many more pathways that are left naked, and exploiting these pathways should not automatically seal the company's fate.

Knowing that, how can we protect against these eventualities? By stacking up additional protection and detection layers! Trust does not even factor into the equation. There is always a residual risk that our tooling will be shattered by an attacker. The ultimate question is and always will be: how many other layers still stand?

"Are you suggesting that we don't even trust the VPN?" replies an infrastructure teammate. "That's crazy; in that case, let's not trust IPSEC and SSH altogether!"

"That's not what I am saying," we respond. "A VPN can be bypassed with a single successful phishing email, an unprotected stolen laptop, a web vulnerability, a compromised dependency, such as an npm package and so many other scenarios that I probably cannot think of. It happens every week. Such events should not be game over for the company. We should never be one vulnerability away from closing doors. So, humor me, how would you revisit the current design of apps and systems based on the premise that each of them can be compromised. Much more interesting, right?"

That shook them off from their comfort zone, but it should not really. Computer science was founded on the notion of building reliable parts from unreliable components, from refreshing bits in memory to cache coherence algorithms to TCP's handshake model. What we suggest is simply to extend the definition of unreliability to cover malicious actions.

Each security measure neutralizes or complexifies a set of threat scenarios. The winning strategy is to stack enough of them on top of each other so that their gaping holes don't align with each other. We have to assume that one layer will give away to the imagination and curiosity of the attacker and prepare the second, third and, hopefully, the fourth layer in response.

While we are still discussing GitLab, we pull its inbound firewall rules and marvel at the list of IP addresses allowed through the gates. Even the current VPN restriction is a myth; there at least three external partners that can access the code base.

"Looking at the firewall rules applied to GitLab on AWS, we can see that other networks do have access: we have this integration with SonarQube to scan our code, another one with Prismic to help manage our corporate website and, finally, Sentry for error handling. I mean come on, folks! We allow the IP addresses of third-party companies to have full access to our code base with its secrets and vulnerabilities," we say.

To further prove our point, we do a quick search for keywords such as "password", "secret", "aws_secret_key", etc. To no surprise, we come up with a few dozen examples that we share with the team to prove our point. Exposing actual production secrets neglectingly committed to the code wins over Marc, who decides to step in and settle the discussion.

"You're right. We're past public repositories now. Let's discuss how to fix it!" concedes Marc.

I guess we should have started with that.

Fixing this GitLab issue is one of those projects that scares the bejesus out of infrastructure admins. It's a classic case of "press a button" and shit will break. It's easy to switch a repo from public to private. Doing so, however, will propagate failure to every app that tries to fetch some dependency without providing credentials. It will also block all developers who never bothered to set up their Git access through SSH or HTTP personal tokens. We're about to cause a cardiac arrest of every development environment within Mirage. It's not "customer-facing critical" but quite annoying at a very large scale.

Given how exposed GitLab is, we decide to lump this issue in with the SSO efforts and tackle it immediately. What good is plugging the SSO to an app that continues to allow anonymous access anyway?

We start by listing every usage of the git command across all repos:

```
$ rg "\bgit (clone|fetch|pull)"
mirage-manager/.gitlab-ci.yml
87: git clone https://gitlab.mirage.co/...

...snip...

$ rg "\bgit:"

mirage-manager/Gemfile
11:gem "codice-fiscale", git:
"https://gitlab.mirage.co/gems/logger.git"

mirage-manager/Gemfile
30:gem "mirage-monadic", git:
"https://gitlab.mirage.co/gems/mirage-monadic.git"
...snip...
```

The infrastructure team was right, indeed. Many development teams hosted their packages and libraries on GitLab and therefore call them when building their apps.

The good news is that only 30 of the two hundred repos seem to call the git command. So, right here, right now, we can theoretically switch all 170 other repos to "internal", making them only visible to authenticated users.

Visibility, project features, permissions

Choose visibility level, enable/disable project features and their permissions, disable email notifications, and show default award emoji.

Project visibility

Manage who can see the project in the public access directory. Learn more.

Internal	⌄

The project can be accessed by any user who is logged in.

Figure 12-7: Setting to control the visibility of a project on GitLab

As for the remaining 30 repos, GitLab provides a temporary token through an environment variable CI_JOB_TOKEN that we can inject into the script responsible for building apps. When this script is run on GitLab to compile an app, the CI_JOB_TOKEN will contain a special read-only token to authenticate and clone the required dependencies. The syntax changes according to each language, but it roughly resembles the following commands:

```
git config --global url."https://gitlab-ci-
token:${CI_JOB_TOKEN}@gitlab.qonto.co".insteadOf
"https://gitlab.qonto.co"
```

That's the line we need to add to all these 30 repos to keep the deployment process intact.

To keep the developer's local environment from blowing up with errors, we also write a quick article in our security FAQ on how to set up an SSH key to clone, pull and commit code to GitLab. We drop a message on the main dev channel to alert them of the change, should they encounter an error:

"Hey folks, we're switching GitLab repos to private, meaning you need to authenticate to GitLab before cloning repos or pushing new code. We'll start off with one team, protect a couple of apps, refine the doc and the process, making sure everything is okay before generalizing to all repos.

Here is a quick how-to. It's a one-time configuration. Let us know if anything unexpected happens."

We link the how-to for developers to help them set up their GitLab credentials. We'll pin it in our FAQ security page along with other articles. As a precautionary measure, we also send a message to the tech leads and the infrastructure team to request help to disperse this message:

"Can you please drop a line about this change during tomorrow's daily meeting? If developers miss it, they will encounter errors and suffer delays in shipping features," we tell Charles and the rest of the tech leads.

Good thing Richard is starting tomorrow. Lots of work to do!

**

Following his first couple of days of onboarding, we took Richard through the threat model, the various projects we worked on, from the MFA to the WAF to the SSO, and explain the current challenge:

"Henry signed off on the SSO provider. We have dozens of SaaS products and internals apps that need to be protected. How can we get it done in the fastest way possible?" we ask him.

He reflects for a few seconds, then replies back: "We can decentralize the work and ask every app or product owner to tweak their authentication settings. We then follow up with them every week to see how they advance on the topic."

"Okay, how long do you reckon that would take?" we ask him with a slight smile.

"I don't know. I guess it depends on their current tasks and how they prioritize them. Do we have some kind of leverage to make them go faster?"

That's the key question...No, we don't. We don't have strong enough leverage to do that. Their incentive is to ship features, close prospective customers, generate leads, and so on. The sheer will of Jira tickets and project management fu will not help us overcome this misalignment hurdle. We need to get our hands dirty.

We already dismantled this myth a couple of chapters earlier with the penetration test and 2FA, so we take the time to familiarize Richard with our hands-on approach.

"Internal control had a list of ten vulnerabilities that they dragged out for more than a year in Jira tickets without much success. Would you rather chase people adding chores to their jammed-up calendar or just...fix it?"

Richard's eyes widen in disbelief.

"You mean I could just log into the..." he picks up the first app in the list "Salesforce app and configure the SSO interconnection? That's it?"

"Well, I would start with something less high profile and with fewer people to first master the SSO configuration, warn the team in question, schedule a small proof of concept and set up a detailed plan that covers potential edge cases...but, yeah, essentially, that's what I am saying. Preaching is overrated. Let's get shit done."

"Better to ask for forgiveness than permission!" we conclude.

As we continue switching the last GitLab projects to private and testing that the deployment pipelines are still functional, Richard dives into the world of SAML, OpenID and other delicious SSO concepts. We both agree to start with a small SaaS tool used by the IT team to manage physical devices. It's by no means the top priority, but it's the perfect testing ground for our debut in SAML configuration. We can suffer a downtime of a few hours should we break authentication.

Somewhere in that busy day, we take a few minutes to configure the global security settings of the SSO.

We start with password complexity. That's an easy one. Ten characters, no automatic renewal, and no meaningless character restrictions. We enter a list of banned words, such as "mirage", birthday years, employee names and so on.

Multi-factor authentication? Yes, please! We'll start with only supporting WebAuthn. It's a tad restrictive, but every laptop provided by Mirage is modern enough and comes equipped with a Chromium-based browser that supports FIDO2. Perhaps we'll have to a create an exception list for a few people running Firefox, Android, and Linux, but these should be exceedingly rare. We'll put in a purchase request for a hundred YubiKeys for people wanting multi-device access. If 90% of the company is behind phishing-resistant authentication methods, we're already much *much* better off.

"So, how is it going?" we ask Richard after a couple of hours.

"I think I am almost done. As you can see, using my test account, I can successfully authenticate on the app. I think we're ready for our first trial. We just need to import the IT team's Google account into the SSO tool and send out invitations so they create their accounts."

We round up the IT team, explain the setup, and go through the invitation process together. We'll use this experiment to write down procedures that we'll later share with the rest of the company.

Everything goes as expected: authentication, MFA, connection to the test app. John even got a designer to come up with a beautifully branded home page for the SSO. It's the small details that make all the difference!

Having validated that everything worked properly, we set out to tackle the first big fish in the pond: Jenkins. Nobody knows how many people use Jenkins. The infrastructure team guesses that it's all of the 100 developers in the tech team, but no one can back that claim since we don't have any authentication in the first place.

"I will reach out to some developers to confirm their usage of the app. Can you please investigate how to set up SAML authentication on Jenkins?" We ask Richard.

We drop a quick message to Charles, Tony and some other developers. It turns out they only use Jenkins to run preconfigured jobs. Most of them don't even know how to update jobs on Jenkins. Everything is handled by the infrastructure team. If we translate this usage to Jenkins permissions, it means we can grant read-only access to all developers by default and keep the infrastructure admins over Jenkins. Developers will be able to run jobs and view their output but not read or update their configurations.

We'd be able to close access to the admin console script and protect existing jobs from tampering. We're bound to have some exceptions, maybe some test job created for some odd corner case, but we'll adjust along the way. Again, we're looking for the first quick win to neutralize 99% of the underlying risk. We'll iterate afterwards through small improvements.

Sold.

We help Richard get through the finish line with the SAML setup and configure the necessary roles on the SSO that we will map to Jenkins roles. Every developer will automatically inherit these permissions given their affiliation to the Tech department, sparing us the need to attribute them manually for every new joiner.

Like everything on Jenkins, we have to download and install additional plugins to handle SSO *(http://bit.ly/3T6rZv4)* and custom permissions *(http://bit.ly/4289v0m)*, but other than that, it is pretty smooth. We test out the new access rights and confirm that it indeed restricts access to the infamous admin console access.

While testing available jobs on Jenkins, we see some that interact with the production environment, allow deployment of untested code, dump production databases and so on. We make note to put them on our exploitation graph. We are about to make it slightly harder to abuse them by requiring two hops: the VPN and the right SSO profile, but it's still a viable attack path. Once we're done fixing one-step vulnerabilities, they'll probably be right next on the list.

Before disabling anonymous access on Jenkins, we send out invitations to all of the tech team to activate their accounts on the new SSO portal and post a short communication on the *#dev-all* channel.

"Hey, folks, we're setting up a single identity provider to authenticate every app at Mirage. No more manual account creation, maintenance or hundreds of passwords to manage. You'll have one platform to access everything. We're migrating apps one by one. We'll start with Jenkins. Other than the first one-time setup, it should be transparent for you.

Please activate your account through the link you've received by email."

A brief message. It's to the point and it stresses the benefit to the users, not some obscure security paradigm. They will have less friction, less authentication screens to go through and less user management chores. The security aspect of it all? That's not their problem. That's ours to get right.

We monitor user activation on the SSO. Once we got a few hits confirming that people could indeed enroll on the platform, we switch on authentication on Jenkins. We hurry to ask some developers to test their access. Everything seems to be working OK.

We monitor possible complaints on the channels dedicated to IT and infrastructure. As expected, a couple of people complain about losing access to the configuration of some jobs. We jump on a call together, but we quickly realize that the job was last run six months ago. They had to concede that it was not really needed in the end.

Developers at Mirage have the habit of complaining on IT and infrastructure channels when something does not work out. That's their first reflex. The first reflex of the IT and Infrastructure when they get spammed by these complaints is to blame the source of these sudden requests: us. After all, we're the ones making deep structural changes to the way things currently work. We're the ones breaking the apps, sending swarms of angry users to disrupt their current projects, adding delays and increasing toil.

So, a critical aspect of every change we perform is to own its consequences and inconveniences. It's too easy to update a setting and walk away from the blowback, letting other teams deal with it. That's how frustration builds up into future blockades that hinder security projects altogether. When other teams shy away from ambitious security changes, they most often shy away from the consequences of these changes. If we can demonstrate that we own the process, from implementation to maintenance, we can earn almost a free pass to every wild idea we want to implement. They know that we will be there to shoulder the toil and own our mistakes should we make one. It's a very important psychological consideration that is worth keeping in mind. It can make or break the relationship with other teams.

This also gives us our hard reality check: does the chosen solution reduce the identified risk as expected or is it so hard to use that people inevitably forage their way around it to perform their duties. This sort of customer support service keeps us grounded in the realities of the corporate world and will help us design more and more pragmatic solutions that eliminate the risk but also fit the context of our employees and customers.

Together with Richard, we start going through the rest of the critical apps, replicating the same strategy. Reaching out for admin access, figuring out what access roles are actually required, testing the configuration, sending a brief communication and forcing everyone to move on the SSO platform. We're literally shoving this SSO thing down the throat of everyone at the company, yet almost no one is raising an eyebrow. People are so focused on their work and level of productivity that as long as what we're proposing works properly and does not add tasks to their day, they don't object much. Flexibility is certainly one of best features of startups and scale-ups!

More often than not, meticulous and detailed planning is not the answer to getting things done, rather the answer to one's own insecurity, to the fear of failing. Teams with excellent security profiles often fail miserably in the field because the challenge seems so insurmountable and they won't settle for anything less than perfect. But that's unrealistic. How can one reduce the immense risk of credential theft? There are thousands of cracks that can be abused by attackers.

The secret is to start small and iterate. First, experiment with the change in a controlled environment, validate the hypothesis, discard what does not work and then progressively generalize at scale. A bias towards action is the single greatest trait of an individual, not just in security, but in any industry. If there are thousands of attack scenarios, then we'll bloody chop them one at a time.

A couple of weeks pass by and we're down a dozen apps already. By now, everyone in the company has an account on the SSO portal. The IT team hooked it to the Google workspace and every new joiner has their new SSO account automatically created. John is almost in tears for no longer having to create accounts manually on each SaaS apps.

"I owe you big time! Let us know if you need anything," says John one morning.

While Richard is busy integrating SaaS tools—he clearly prefers it to creating tickets in the end—we look back at the internal apps in our inventory. We've already taken care of tools such as Grafana, GitLab and Jenkins. They support an SSO integration and they are now well protected from prying eyes. However, many other simpler tools don't provide any authentication means in the first place: Prometheus, Cerebro, Flower, etc. They just sit there, simple web pages with an open window to our production network.

It's just maddening how even open-source software, from the big to small names, treat security as an afterthought. Authentication and authorization are not hard problems in computer science. If you've taken the time to solve high-scale metrics and alerting, you can surely conjure up a simple RBAC model in a couple of hours to protect that web page of yours...

So, what can we do to protect these apps? Enforce network isolation? Maybe, but a first look at the VPN configuration quickly disparages any hope. Everyone in the company lands in the same network segment. We cannot isolate developers from the infrastructure team, for instance, to grant some teams more access than others. Of course, we'll have to rework our VPN strategy at some point, but that's a heavy project that can easily take months. Maybe we can find a trick with a better effort/reward ratio.

We spend a couple of hours researching possible solutions for this conundrum. Maybe we can set up a sort of authentication proxy that can plug into the SSO, authenticate users before letting them access some web apps. It does not solve the authorization problem, but it's a huge leap forward from open bar access.

As we're pondering these questions, Marc drops us a quick message:

"Hey, do you have time to talk? We'd like your opinion on this new architecture we're working on."

"Sure," we respond, then hop on the call.

"As you probably know, we currently only have one AWS account holding everything from production servers, staging databases and other miscellaneous resources. We're actively working on splitting these components into different AWS accounts to ease management and have a better isolation between environments. We don't want people to accidently delete a production database just because it's sitting right next to a staging one. Do you have any security constraints or requirements we should take into account?"

The question is heavily geared toward AWS because of Mirage's current context, but it can be easily extrapolated to a much broader one: how should we design a system architecture that complicates the life of an attacker, yet is still manageable by a team of four or five people in the infrastructure team?

It's easy to blindly scream for hardware isolation, separate admin laptops, three-tier models and other hardcore measures that seem to completely ignore the extra maintenance cost, the inability to scale and the incredible waste it generates for developers to quickly iterate on their features. If developers waste two hours a day switching environments and suffer long delays to debug their code in life-like conditions, that's a huge loss of time to market that can make or break a company.

Developers are incentivized to bypass anything that complicates their development lifecycle...including pesky security controls, hence all the exceptions, generic accounts and shadow access one commonly finds in many companies.

Before diving into the target architecture, we first need to answer the following question: what is our security boundary? What's the frontier line that cannot be easily crossed by an attacker should they compromise a first component?

In a classical on-premises architecture, network is king. That's the primary ingredient to enforcing a first level of segregation and isolation. You can be root on every server in a DMZ, but that should not help you change the firewall rules unless you compromise the firewall itself. You may find a server that can escape such rules, but in a well-protected network, you should stay confined to your DMZ.

In an Active Directory environment, the frontier is the Forest, the highest logical element that can be subdivided into multiple domains, each containing computers, users and other objects. If you pwn a domain within a Forest, you can automatically and by design connect to any other domain within the Forest, but your credentials won't carry over to another Forest. Unless, of course, admins establish a trust between these two Forests, which is another issue. But by design, the frontier is the Forest.

In the Cloud, however, network routes and firewall rules can be changed at will with a single API to the right service. These permissions are even granted to apps and tooling to automatically configure the infrastructure. They are within the attacker's reach. Therefore, the network is no longer the frontier. It's a valid protection but not a security boundary. In AWS, the security boundary is the AWS account in its entirety! Unless you've configured trust between two AWS accounts, they are considered distinct and separate with their own set of permissions, encryption keys and so on. Any real segregation we plan must therefore involve separate AWS accounts.

Now that we've got that cleared up, as usual, let's think of this from first principles. What are we protecting and what are we fighting against? We can almost see the threat graph materializing in front of our eyes.

On the left, an attacker who managed to achieve some form of access: developer credentials or a shell on a compromised app.

Let's start with the typical use case of a developer. They need to test features, debug, rapidly iterate over their code. They should be able to do it with complete autonomy in a test environment fully isolated from the production. So long as we can guarantee full isolation between the two environments, they can have root access on the staging account for all we care. The production environment will still be protected. Guaranteeing this isolation is much harder in practice, so take this last interjection with a grain of salt.

Ergo, we must have at least two isolated environments: production and staging. Developers have access to staging resources to iterate over their features. They can pull secrets, create databases, deploy apps without review and so on. Production, however, is off limits, and their access is restricted to read-only on some non-sensitive resources to debug new features and manage incidents.

Next up are attackers that compromise an app and suddenly land inside the production environment itself. Ideally, we want to limit the blast of such a breach. Hacking a form uploader or an internal tech tool should not grant unfettered access to the SWIFT service. In that sense, we must have different production environments; let's say, a first AWS account for banking operations, a second for tech tools such as Grafana and Jenkins and maybe a third one for non-critical public apps such as the corporate website, blog and other resources. These environments will inevitably interact with one another, but these flows will be heavily restricted, checked and kept to a minimum. Grafana can pull metrics from the banking AWS account through dedicated APIs but it cannot get access to S3 buckets holding customer information, for instance. Should the Grafana or any similar app be compromised, and the attacker find a way to achieve admin access on that platform, they would still be confined to that tooling AWS account. The impact is not negligible, obviously, but they still have all their work ahead of them to bypass our protections and compromise banking apps. They have to deploy significant resources to bounce from one account to another, giving us plenty of room to detect them.

It is tempting to be even more granular; after all, the card payment service should be isolated from the SWIFT service to limit the blast radius to a single payment type. Currently, they all run in the same Kubernetes cluster in the same AWS account. Breaking such inter-connected components, however, is a major migration that requires moving around critical production resources, migrating data across accounts and coordinating the move with the operations teams. It would be foolish to shoot for such a big change on the first iteration of this project. Complex solutions are not built as a spontaneous first draft but are usually the fruit of multiple iterations and smaller improvements.

We can live a couple of years with all banking apps in the same AWS account. We'll bolster this account with proper network segregation, inter-service authentication, container hardening and tight detection measures specifically targeting these propagation scenarios. We still have to implement all these things, but it's much easier than exploding these critical apps across multiple AWS accounts from the get-go. That may come in later iterations.

Finally, an important aspect of any good system is the integrity of logging and traceability. An attacker that takes hold of the production account and everything in it should not be able to destroy the audit trail they generated. These should be exported and safely stored in a different environment, another AWS account.

"Alright, so to recap, from a security standpoint, you'd recommend at least four separate AWS accounts: three for production workloads hosting different types of applications, one for staging and another one for audit purposes," summarizes Marc.

"At a minimum, yes, that's right," we reply.

"Alright, that sounds close to what we have in mind. We want to make sure that every production environment has its own staging one, so that means banking production, banking staging, tooling production, tooling staging and so on. But I guess that's a minor detail for you."

"Great initiative. Actually, I don't mind having a dedicated AWS account for the security team so we can automate some controls such as permission check and so on. We don't want those running in regular production environments."

"You got it. The data team asked for their own account as well, which makes sense since they run intensive workloads and batches."

When the argument is made this way, isolation of resources sounds ridiculously obvious, yet it is a common point of failure. Sure, companies apply basic network filtering, maybe even have a dedicated out of bound admin access, but this segregation does not extend to the logical infrastructure. Servers and workstations are usually all tied to the same Active Directory, the same one hosting users in the HR department. Compromising one silly workstation tied to Active Directory suddenly leads to critical production workloads running on servers in the same AD. One of Microsoft's most remarkable achievements (and most harmful decision) was tricking admins into tying the corporate directory (users, emails, printers) to production servers.

Some companies tackle that by blindly multiplying Active Directory domains, but they're hammering the nail into the wrong coffin: the security boundary in Active Directory is the Forest, not the domain. All domains trust each other by default within the same Forest, so multiplying them does not overly complicate the attacker's hopping spree from one domain to another.

This is to show that the same reasoning about separation and limiting the blast radius applies whatever the technology or environment we're in. We could make the same argument for LPARs on Mainframes. There is a name for the line of reasoning we applied in the last few paragraphs; it's commonly referred to as "assume breach". We constantly assume that a piece of infrastructure is compromised and measure the impact and blast radius on other resources.

Strive to find the best balance that reduces the risk and limits friction. We'll cover any residual risk through complementary protection and detection soon enough.

"By the way, Marc, do you mind if I run something by you, I am kind of stuck here. We'd like to put some apps that don't support any authentication behind the SSO. Do you know if we have any recommendation on how to elegantly do that?"

"Let me look up something quickly. There may be something we can use," he responds before resurfacing five minutes later.

"So, as you know we route traffic through ShieldSec, the WAF, then to an AWS load balancer that distributes traffic to a number of servers that are part of the Kubernetes cluster. Each machine hosts a HTTP router called Traefik that delivers the request to the corresponding app."

"Yeah, we leveraged Traefik to add IP whitelisting for the apps that receive webhooks from partners."

"Exactly, well, you can also plug Traefik into the SSO and require authentication before accessing certain apps. You'll need to use an open-source middleware for that, but it seems feasible."

"Wow, amazing. Thanks, I will look into it."

We spend the next few days playing with Traefik middleware and testing an open-source SSO integration *https://github.com/thomseddon/traefik-forward-auth.* This piece of code deploys a container that proxies all requests destined for an app. On the first connection, it redirects the user to our SSO portal using the OpenID protocol. If the SSO portal grants access, it then attaches a cookie to the browser and allows the user through. The end application is none the wiser. We go through the now familiar flow: proof of concept, tech document, implementation, then documentation, and have it up and running in a few days in front of Prometheus, a monitoring solution.

It won't solve the granular authorization problem, but most of the apps we're protecting are just read-only interfaces that give out too much data. You can't do much damage on Prometheus, Sidekiq, Flower and the like. However, they do divulge unnecessary information that can be leveraged to further an attacker's agenda. Or they can simply present exploitable vulnerabilities. Adding authentication on top will go a long way already!

With the IT team and the precious help of Richard, in just a few short weeks, we managed to transition all the company to the new SSO system and integrate almost all apps that support it. Sure, some teams were a bit cautious at first, but many were happy to get rid of the pain of user management, especially in a scale-up that recruits 30 people every two weeks.

There still dozens of apps not part of our SSO landscape. We can't go around cancelling their contracts, as some are actively used by many teams, however, we can set up some ground rules for future vendors. If an app holds critical information or interacts with our infrastructure, then it should have support SSO. A non-negotiable term that we will try to enforce with the help of legal and IT.

It makes little sense to enforce this rule on a SaaS product that the marketing team wants to test out for video editing, for instance, so we still have some flexibility going on. We reach out to the legal team to help set up such rules. All contracts flow through their approval process, we simply ask to add a security check to that process.

Now you see me

As weeks went by, the SSO portal slowly took over the bookmark of every employee and contractor at Mirage. Operations people wrote procedures around this new form of user provisioning and the IT team systematically introduced it as the first tool in their onboarding sessions. Some derelict apps are still fiercely resisting the SSO wave, but it's coming for them sooner or later.

Having the SSO as a unique source of truth for active user accounts, we added a few automated rules to deal with employee churn: every user account that is inactive for more than 45 days is automatically suspended. Every employee whose HR contract has come to an end is automatically disabled on the SSO.

During a lunch with Steve and Richard, we discussed the recent improvements to the infrastructure:

"Splitting AWS accounts was a killer improvement for security. I am so glad you folks went full steam with the project," we remark.

"It's not so much security that sparked the initial discussion, to be honest," he responds, "but maintainability and ease of exploitation. The migration is still far from done, but the bulk of the resources are separate now," he follows up in a matter-of-fact tone.

"So, what's the latest findings in security?"

"Richard found a way to poison the cache of some parameter in the app to retrieve the payment information of almost every customer. We patched it that day by adding an authorization check on the faulty request. On the corporate side, the SSO is almost done, as you know. We're also working with IT on workstation security. They're rolling out two device management solutions: one for Apple devices and another for the dozen or so Windows computers," we reply.

"Oh boy...are we going to have a shitty antivirus that will hog so much memory that the computer will crash? We already have a web browser for that you know," he replies almost to the beat.

Ha...who can argue with that? When John reached out to configure the Apple-specific device management, most of the settings were pretty straightforward: enable the local firewall, disk encryption through File vault, automatic updates, minimum password length and session lock out. We pushed the button a bit further with Gatekeeper to only allow applications with identified developers to run on the machines. The IT team was a bit dubious about this last setting since it would generate a lot of tickets asking for exceptions and workarounds, but they agreed to test it on some critical populations first (business operations that mostly rely on their browser to perform their duties) before possibly extending it to the rest of the company.

Just like many one-stop-shop solutions, one critical aspect of device management is the risk induced by centralization. If all devices have a common agent and are controlled through a single platform, how do you prevent an attacker from taking over that platform to achieve lateral propagation across workstations? Sadly, this risk is seldom accounted for by device management vendors. There is no double approval or some sort of multi-signature process for deploying scripts or remotely controlling a machine, which is maddening. All we can do for now is forward logs and alert on suspicious activity (more on that later).

The antivirus question did come up in the discussions. Will a third-party antivirus really contribute to the security of Mirage? And is it enough to justify the cost—from $10 to $20 per endpoint? It might almost seem like heresy, but if it is so elemental, shouldn't it be settled fairly quickly?

Let's see, despite all their marketing propaganda, almost every antivirus relies on two mechanisms to spot malicious programs: hardcoded signatures and some form of heuristic analysis of the file's structure. These may be effective mechanisms against already known attacks or simple adware that plague the Internet, but they spectacularly fail to address more complex attacks. Even your run-of-the-mill ransomware changes forms so often that many antivirus signature databases fail to keep up. In reading different hacking accounts and pentest reports[39], no attacker ever came across an antivirus protected machine and threw up their hands in despair. It does not happen. A simple modification to an already flagged payload, in-memory execution, staged payloads, a different packing method, encryption, encoding...all these techniques can successfully evade the most advanced antivirus on the market.

---

[39] *The account of Phineas Fisher breaching Hacking Team is such a classic tale* http://bit.ly/3iWGZAY. *Also, check out and Bill Dermikapi's Twitter thread about the Uber hack* https://bit.ly/3QWdRqc

It seems like the antivirus is more suited to protecting against threats targeting the individual user, such as adware and crypto miners, rather than the more complex threats targeting corporate assets.

This lack of efficiency is aggravated by the horrible performance of these software. In order to perform their analysis, they often scan every file that touches the disk. Constantly. It's a nightmare for developers who run heavy I/O commands, such as "npm install" or "docker", which frequently download thousands of files.

We could also argue the counterpoint and adopt the same stance we took on the WAF: even though we know that determined attackers can bypass it with enough skill and resources, their attempts will trigger enough alerts and warnings to warrant an investigation, which should betray their presence. But the stark difference is that a lot of antivirus solutions share the same bypass techniques. In-memory execution is efficient against Symantec, McAfee, Defender, Avast...pretty much every antivirus. So, an attacker can get away with scarcely any alerts.

In the end, as you can see, the question is far from being straightforward. It all boils down to a solid threat analysis and ROI calculation.

On MacOS, there is objectively less adware and other shenanigans. I know many that people cringe when they read that.

"MacOS is not safer than Windows," they will vociferously shout back. *"It's just as broken and subject to many malware, look at this study,"* they exclaim before sharing a link to a paper put forth by a totally "unbiased" antivirus solution.

First, no. MacOS does not store reversible passwords or weakly hashed credentials in memory. That alone makes it inherently less shitty than Windows. It's a harsh take, but a reasonable one. And second, no one is claiming that MacOS is safer or better designed or even more secure for that matter... just that the type of malware addressed by an Antivirus is numerically inferior on MacOS than on Windows. Which, again, is factually true, at least for the time being.

So, if the core threat addressed by a regular antivirus is not that proliferate on the platform, and the technology itself can be easily bypassed by new strains of malware and a myriad of techniques that are one Google search away, and it heavily impairs developers and costs $20 an endpoint…then maybe, just maybe, it's not the best investment right now. Perhaps it's enough to rely entirely on the free, lightweight and native XProtect[40] antivirus built into MacOS to counter these threats. It does not hog much CPU and memory. It has a hundred or so signatures that are maintained by Apple, much less than the tens of thousands of rules usually shipped by third-party antivirus products, but it may just be good enough against your run-of-the-mill adware.

To compensate for this lack of coverage, we'll use the device management tool to push for an aggressive update policy. These two actions should take care of the bulk of the threat at the workstation level.

Furthermore, to contain any potential threat and avoid viral propagation within the company, we rely on other protection and detection measures: strict network isolation between workstations, WebAuthn as a second authentication factor on the SSO, no shared admin account on workstations and eventually, down the road, log forwarding to our SIEM.

We follow a similar approach on Windows, though their default antivirus, Windows Defender, is arguably much better than any other third-party product out there. In any case, these Windows computers will be used by the risk department who don't need that much performance, so by all means, let's keep that one, forward the logs to our SIEM and have some meaningful detection alerts.

Once we're done with the device management for MacOs, we switch to Microsoft Intune, the device management chosen by IT to handle Windows computers. Intune's interface can be a real maze of menus, policies and profiles to configure. Luckily, Microsoft provides a security baseline—a group of settings that pretty much covers all the basics: enabling device guard, blocking inbound traffic via the firewall, activating the antivirus, blocking Internet macros, and so on. Now that's what one would expect from a mature vendor.

---

[40] http://bit.ly/3koDnbk.

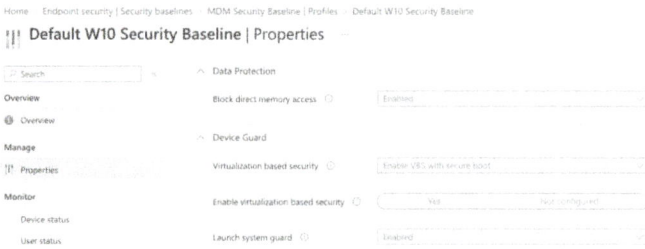

Figure 13-1: Intune security baseline

That ought to be enough for 12 endpoints.

"What do you think of an EDR? Should we get one?" asks Richard while we're configuring the two device management tools, almost echoing our own train of thought.

EDR for endpoint detection response or XDR for extended detection response, or is it MDR now for managed detection and response? Whatever is the latest, the goal is to surreptitiously monitor all system and network activities on an endpoint to identify suspicious patterns. Whereas an antivirus would almost exclusively rely on string matching, an EDR would primarily rely on behavioral analysis of the process' activity, network connection and files opened to report any anomaly. There is always some form of string matching going on, but it's often just one feature of a more holistic approach involving machine learning and threat intelligence that can make classic evasion a little bit noisier, even cumbersome.

…Or so goes the tale.

Not all EDRs are created equal, of course, many deceptively tout their rugged signature engine as the latest development in AI, whereas others swim in user land completely oblivious to simple rootkits that change the underlying kernel[41]. Weeding out the good from the bad and the ugly requires extensive PoC and analysis, but before we even go there, we need to put it back in context of our threat map. Do we have threat scenarios that exclusively rely on workstation compromise to wreak havoc in the company?

---

[41] Windows sysinternals is still the reference in terms of a deep dive into Windows' behavior: *https://bit.ly/3HopNy0.*

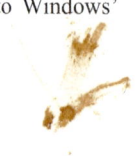

"If we go back to our threat map," we reply to Richard, "yes, we can get some workstations compromised through phishing that bypasses our email security settings, or through physical access or even attacks that leverage advanced malware distributed through trusted websites. While there won't be a massive propagation given our strict network settings that ban inter-workstation communication, an attacker could target some admin workstations, steal credentials and perform changes to AWS, Kubernetes and other core infrastructure components. In this last particular case, the entry point is rather narrow, a dozen or so workstations, but the impact can be quite high. That being said, I think we're better off focusing on reducing that potential impact by tweaking our infrastructure settings, thus making AWS, GitLab, Kubernetes and other core components more resilient to such attacks before blindly throwing money at the problem in the form of an EDR."

We know that a developer or an admin may have extended rights on AWS. Let's first trim down those accesses, setup detection on AWS that specifically targets potential abuses and close any obvious loopholes before installing an EDR on every workstation to deal with unknown and elusive threats. Let's first manage our known knowns before chasing the wild geese that are the unknown unknowns. The former is a precise, scoped and straightforward way to remediate, while the latter is so broad that it almost distracts us from every other practical problem we may have.

A lot of security teams get so obsessed with workstation security that it becomes their only playing ground. Sorry to break it to you but workstations are not that important. At least, they should not be. This becomes crystal clear when one follows a rigorous threat modelling approach, as we've covered in this book. Workstations are a means to an end. That end is accessing critical information on servers, databases, warehouses, SaaS tools and so on. That's where the data lives. That's where we should start our protection and remediation efforts. The most important thing to get right when dealing with workstations is containment. We can almost never protect every single workstation from compromise, but we must be able to contain the infection to that single host and forbid it from propagating to all other workstations, servers and databases. Workstation security is often a numbers game. No company will pay a ransom for a single poor workstation. But get a thousand of them down and now an attacker has decent leverage over the company.

If you achieve this containment—through network filtering, a rigorous update policy, and protection at the data level—you instantly lower the value of the workstation from the attacker's perspective. These simple actions reduce major risks to residual ones that we can accept while we work on more important threats targeting other parts of the platform. Accepting the risk means accepting the fact that the workstation can be compromised. Now let's design an architecture around that assumption and make sure it does not endanger the rest of the company. That's a much healthier approach that allows us to stack many security layers rather than throwing all our eggs into that workstation security basket.

As we were prepared to close this device management chapter, Richard excitedly shows up at our desk to share his latest findings:

"You won't believe what I found when poking around the MacOS device management...They're opening the SSH port by default on every computer."

"No way... Why? They already have an agent on the host, so why do they need an SSH port for incoming traffic?" we ask inquisitively.

"I don't think it's actually used, but that's not even the worst part," says Richard excitedly. "The IT team needs to run some post-install scripts in admin mode and the vendor's documentation encourages them to create a user on the machine during installation. It's the same user...with the same password on all machines."

And that's how two small misconfigurations unleash the torment of the afterlife on a company. This is a reputable MacOS device management tool...supposedly the best one, yet they seemingly push customers to build a house of cards that can be brought down with the slightest push...

They offer no easy way to disable SSH so Richard had to come up with a bash one liner for the SSH service on all machines. He also helped John change the provisioning script to create a temporary admin unique to each machine to carry those post-install instructions.

This incident does, however, raise a bigger point.

We did a decent job hunting down existing critical one-hop vulnerabilities, but we're still in the state where one flaw can be unknowingly introduced in the system, putting us almost automatically back in the danger zone.

What many infosec discussions fail to take into account is that a company is a living organism. Every day, hundreds of people are interacting with code, infrastructure, data, printers and computers, sometimes in completely unexpected ways. Any little change can potentially open new security holes. How can we tame this ever-changing environment without defaulting to obviously nonsense constraints, such as *"every change must be approved by the security team."*

Some companies choose to take such a heavy-handed approach, but when you look closer, it is often at the expense of innovation and feature delivery. A team of two, three, even a dozen people that is flooded by various requests generated by more than 300 people is not a sound strategy. It's a floodgate that slows down business, one that people will eventually bypass out of sheer desperation. People are most innovative when they want to avoid a traffic jam.

"Well, you want decentralize as many decisions as you can," says Henry while talking about this same structural and organizational issue. "I agree that you should not position your team as the gatekeepers of tech changes. Nobody likes bouncers. Plus, the math does not hold. At its core, this question is really about quality. How do we continue to deliver quality as we scale?

In my opinion, there are three measures that you should look into: First, you need a set of standards that codifies good practices and can help other teams make the right decision without knocking on your doors. Had you told John that one essential security measure is the uniqueness of the password across workstations, he might have set things differently.

Second, whether we like it or not, mistakes happen. How can you design an environment where people cannot easily make mistakes? Or at the very least, one that greatly minimizes the impact of their mistakes or quickly bubbles them up to the surface so you can take the appropriate action. We need more resiliency.

Finally, you need a framework where people can raise their hands when they're stuck on a security question. They should know when to reach out to you and Richard."

Well phrased.

If one perceives the production of various features as separate flows advancing in parallel before reaching their final release stage, then it indeed does not make sense to force these flows to converge and patiently wait at the door for our review. We want to keep these flows separate, independent and running as fast as possible. Rather than concentrate them all at the same congested entry point, we can give them material to be independent in their journey, and like Henry suggested, guidelines on when to ping us ahead of time, so we can shape their flow one way or the other to help them get to their destination in a faster and more secure way.

As for the second point about resilience, he basically rephrased the holy concept of defense in depth, where many security layers reinforce each other to form this impenetrable wall of protection and detection. We're still in the early phase of our security program, but that's clearly the direction we're taking. We'll circle back to this point in a few paragraphs when talking about detection.

Together with Richard, we re-organize our FAQ page to make it more reader friendly. We organize it by stack and by type of request. We add keywords so people can quickly search for information. We cannot be exhaustive, but that's a good start that will allow other teams to be autonomous in their journey. We'll complement these docs along the way as we work on upcoming issues.

To help people be more proactive, we also set up a few sessions with teams to share our threat model, explain the different attack scenarios and how we think about security, especially the infrastructure and IT teams since they often help other teams implement changes on their apps. We setup a dedicated session for newly joined people to imprint this view of security right from the start. Henry is right. Had John known that one of our best defenses is the uniqueness of the admin password, he may have intuitively implemented the right solution.

It's important to stress that these sessions are not the classic user awareness training delivered in regular companies, where people with dark robes loudly chant "don't open emails from unknown people", "don't plug in USB keys", etc. None of that horse shit. In our sessions, we start by explaining our threat model: types of attacker and critical assets. We explain our vision of security: pragmatic, by design and multi-layered. And finally, we share the tooling and standards that can help them be autonomous to secure their features. It's a radically different approach, a more empowering one, custom to each team's needs... and people freaking love it!

Then, we reflected on broad situations where we should be consulted by the product, legal, IT and infrastructure teams. We can sum it up in two key points:
- Any project that manipulates confidential data (customer information, strategic docs, etc.)
- Any project that touches our infrastructure and our product

We set up a point with several directors of the company that run projects at Mirage: product, legal, IT, etc. The goal is not to be a road blocker in the lifecycle of these projects, but to point people to the set of security standards we wrote, have them include a consultation with the security team given certain criteria and communicate our willingness to help them reach success faster. We're creating alignment around security and helping teams be more and more autonomous.

I have to stress this once more. We're not asking project managers to knock on our door for each project to validate this or that setup. Rather, we're pointing them to a set of standards and requirements, such as partner authentication, SSO integration with SaaS, workstation security and so on. Most will pick and choose the right documents when they need them and be fully autonomous. Some will have specific questions that will require a slack response or a 20-minute meeting, e.g., *"we want to authenticate emails using a secret code, how do we do that?"* A few though might request more assistance and may give rise to two or three workshops, e.g., *"we want to redesign the authentication flow, what should we have in mind?"* That's a vastly different paradigm from forcing every project to invariably be reviewed by the security team.

The success of the system depends on the goodwill of team leads who follow and interpret these questions, but we will complement it with continuous active monitoring and auditing of modifications to the system, just like we have been doing for the past couple of months.

Now that we have a good grasp on inter-team ground rules, let's shift gears a bit to highlight another important problem.

The dynamic and changing nature of a company can bite us in the face in another insidious way: when thinking of solutions to security issues.

Take Gatekeeper in our earlier configuration. It's easy to dial up that protection to refuse any non-notarized app (i.e., an app that was not approved by Apple). It's a great security measure, but deploy it on thousands of workstations and you'll get flooded with user complaints to exceptionally accept this or that app they absolutely need to close a sale. This is especially exacerbated in a scale-up environment that welcomes dozens of new people every week. Everyone is working hard on shipping new features, probably using new tools and components. So, while the security measure is objectively good, its maintenance cost is so huge that it can sink the productivity of the whole security team. Suddenly, you cannot even secure those AWS permissions because you are constantly interrupted to validate new apps for users.

Everyone can spit out a half-baked solution that oversimplifies complex problems: *"whitelist executables and DLLs"*, *"filter all outbound traffic"*, *"remove admin rights on workstations"*. All these solutions may be great on paper or in an isolated and controlled lab environment, but their lifecycle cost exponentially balloons up in a dynamic scale-up environment and can eat up the capacity of the team to deliver other important security features. We managed this complexity for Gatekeeper by first testing the setting on a smaller population. We reduced the scope to keep complexity at bay. Similarly, maybe whitelisting executables is too much of a pain on workstations and we can simply have audit rules, which can feed our detection algorithms. Or maybe we can start with servers, which are much more static than workstations.

The point is that the lifecycle of a security solution is just as important as the threat it addresses and should be part of the discussion when weighing options. No security solution should be conceived in a vacuum.

**

Following the recent projects, ranging from the WAF to the SSO to device management, it's time to put the threat graph back in the spotlight once more and take a more holistic view of our current situation and strategy.

So far, we have managed to implement several protection measures, mainly targeting one-hop vulnerabilities. We have been strengthening that first layer of defense presented to attackers: WAF, authentication of customers, employees, partners and so on. But this first layer is solely composed of protection measures. What happens if they get bypassed? Do we even know when they get bypassed? One glaring deficiency that jumps out is our overall lack of detection measures. Our SIEM, as put together by Nina, only aggregates customer authentication events, yet we have so many more sources we can leverage: AWS, Kubernetes, SSO, device management, etc., all of which can help us greatly lower the probability and impact of many of the attack paths that we countered or that are still out there.

Also, we still did not manage to take a deeper look to the permissions issues on AWS and other production components. They used to be one-hop vulnerabilities, but thanks to the SSO project and the separation of AWS accounts, we narrowed down what used to be untethered access to some apps, such as Jenkins, to only a few people. Still, we need to assess current permissions and trim excessive access. The only way to reliably perform such critical changes is by checking logs and making sure that every permission was at least used once in the last couple of weeks or months. As you can see, this goes very much hand in hand with the centralization of logs and therefore the detection project. This gives us our next two big ticket items: log centralization and permission reviews.

This is no longer our first rodeo; we now have the necessary operating system within Mirage to efficiently bring home these projects: a quick proof of concept to assess potential solutions. A technical document that details the approach. Share the approach with key stakeholders of the tech team and then work on the implementation.

"I fear I don't know much about AWS to be reviewing its permission system. How does it all work?" questions Richard, full of doubt.

It's an understandable feeling. As stated previously, it's ludicrous to expect a transverse security team to fully master every technology within the company. Therefore, one fundamental characteristic of such a team is its ability to acquire the necessary knowledge on any given topic. In the same way that a pentester is expected to level up on that SAP system the week before the assignment, security teams should have the willpower, curiosity and management support to dig into any subject.

"I happen to know a bit of AWS. Let's review some of the core concepts behind the identity and access management service. I'll then point you to some papers and conference talks to explore more on your own," we reply[42].

This almost feels like the fun R&D part of the job. We have our own AWS accounts courtesy of the infrastructure team. We can easily test faulty configurations, replicate attack patterns and attempt fixes in quick iterative cycles.

Access rights on AWS deserve a book on their own. Each of the dozen AWS services used by Mirage has at least a few hundred permissions, allowing everything from reading tags to starting servers. Each of these thousand permissions can be further scoped to one or many resources and subject to one or many conditions. Permissions can be attached to users, roles, inherited from groups, directly placed on the resource itself or a combination of it all. AWS sure built a convoluted system to cover as many possibilities as one can dream of, yet in doing so, they—wittingly or not—traded exhaustivity for increased complexity.

Sadly, complexity is often the garroter of security as it yields unintended and poorly understood edge cases. Admins frustrated by the 400 distinct permissions on a single service often hurry up to slap a wildcard "*" access on the user's access rights and call it a day…

This is further exacerbated by an infrastructure team stacking multiple AWS accounts and the many cross-account permissions such a configuration entails. The sheer complexity of tightening permissions in this case can easily lead to paralysis through analysis, i.e., we spend so much time investigating and refining each and every permission that we never reach the implementation phase.

"The key to succeeding in such complex projects is slicing. We cannot and will not address every tiny bit of permissive access in our first pass. We have to slice this project into two or three parts. In this first iteration, we want to solely focus on the most dangerous permissions. Permissions that directly grant admin access, or grant modification on all resources.

---

[42] A collection of AWS privilege escalations by Rhino Security Labs http://bit.ly/3Xrlqllll.

A policy that grants unlimited access to all S3 resources? Let's scope it to one or two objects and/or limit the actions to non-destructive ones. A policy that allows us to describe all machine configurations? It's not great, but let's not bother with it now since it cannot be used to gain meaningful access to the machines. At least not in a direct way. Let's weed out all the critical permissions first, those that can be directly leveraged by attacker to break into the service or damage the business, then we'll do a second and third iteration in the coming months to refine the permissions further," we explain to Richard.

While he is getting acquainted with the quandary that is the AWS IAM service and its permission system, we start looking into CloudWatch and CloudTrail, the native logging solutions on AWS, so we can send back all traces to the SIEM. As stated previously, we agreed with the infrastructure team to set up a dedicated AWS account to safely aggregate all kinds of security logs.

To our surprise, they already configured all accounts to forward logs to an S3 bucket on that dedicated account, where they will be forever stored as unstructured objects.

mirage-root-cloudtrail-organization-global

General details

Trail logging	Trail log location	Log file validation	SNS notification delivery
Logging	mirage-root-cloudtrail-global/AWSLogs/o-192c5dXqmE/702860712345	Enabled	Disabled
Trail name		Last file validation delivered	Last SNS notification
mirage-root-cloudtrail-organization-global	Last log file delivered	September 17, 2022, 14:57:13	-
Multi-region trail	September 17, 2022, 15:18:59		
Yes	Log file SSE-KMS encryption		
Apply trail to my organization	Enabled		
Enabled for all accounts			

Figure 13-2: CloudTrail settings

In an on-premises infrastructure, the simple action of centralizing logs can be a year-long project, yet a good cloud provider makes it possible through a simple series of clicks. That's why I cannot help but smile when I read yet another tweet warning of the glaring dangers of the infrastructure cloud setup...Have these people tried an on-premises architecture?

We cannot forward everything to the SIEM as the storage and indexation cost would be prohibitive. We only want to keep the last three to six months of activity in the SIEM to investigate curious cases and set up our detection alerts. If we want more data, we can always selectively load it from S3 on demand.

This is probably as good a time as any to pause a bit to talk about the current SIEM setup. Nina went ahead and set up a managed Elasticsearch to aggregate security logs. Should we continue using this tool or switch to other solutions, such as Splunk, QRadar or Graylog? There is no one-size-fits-all, and those who claim that Splunk is expensive have clearly not spent days tuning Elasticsearch mappings and lifecycle policies.

Ultimately, an SIEM should accept and parse several log formats, from JSON to simple text, provide a fast and easy searchable interface and, most importantly, allow detection alerts to be set up that give us enough context to act on them. Threat hunting or searching for patterns is meaningless without a strong alerting system, which is a feature severely underdeveloped in many log solutions.
Teams may have a soft spot for the flexibility of Elasticsearch or Splunk's ecosystem of apps, but in its most basic form, a SIEM should allow the security team to search and alert on suspicious behavior.

So, should we prepare a request for papers and go tool-hunting to replace our Elasticsearch with another tool? Maybe, some day if we hit a hard limitation with our current tooling, but for now, after digging a bit in Elasticsearch's security module, we find pretty much everything we need.

Chasing the next shiny tool just because of hype or to conform to market trends does not usually reflect good decision-making. AWS, Kubernetes and other log formats we need are based on JSON, which is well supported by Elasticsearch. The tool has several open-source log collectors. And we can configure alerts based on threshold, aggregations, even unusual events using machine learning. It's as good a tool as any to lay down the foundation of detection.

Ingesting data won't be the trivial operation it could have been on Sumo Logic, Splunk or other commercial products, but we have a full AWS account at our disposal. We can whip out some Golang magic combined with an AWS Lambda[43] to automatically move every new audit log created on S3 to Elasticsearch.

---

[43] Think of AWS Lambda as a service that takes a binary or zip file and executes it when a given event triggers: a cron expression, a new file created in a bucket, a HTTP request, etc. It's the archetype of serverless computing.

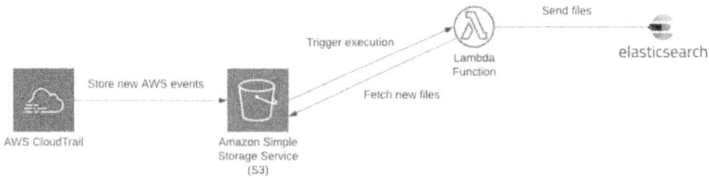

Figure 13-3: Diagram to export logs to Elasticsearch

Every time a new file is deposited on S3 by CloudTrail, our code gets triggered in the AWS Lambda service. It fetches the new file, parses the JSON event, and sends it to our SIEM. Thankfully, the code is not awfully complicated and is low maintenance since we won't be performing much processing on these events. Maybe one filter or two to drop some noisy events that pollute our logs, but that's it.

Let's quickly review the skeleton of the code to get a sense of it all. The program kicks off in the main function, prepares connectors to the S3 service and calls the start of the lambda:

```
func main() {

    s3Client := s3.New(session.New())

    // HandleRequest is our entry method of the lambda
    lambda.Start(HandleRequest)
}
```

Next, in the HandleRequest method, the entry point of the lambda, we extract the list of new files placed on S3. They have been sent as parameters of the trigger event by CloudTrail. We download each of them and then push them through the custom method pushDataToES to Elasticsearch.

```
func HandleRequest (ctx context.Context, s3Event events.S3Event) {

  for _, record := range s3Event.Records {
     key := record.S3.Object.Key
     bucket := record.S3.Bucket.Name

    // we skip non-log files
    if strings.Contains(key, "/CloudTrail-Digest") {
        continue
    }
    data, _ := s3Client.DownloadObject(bucket, key)
    pushDataToES(data)
}
```

pushDataToEs is simply a wrapper around a HTTP POST request to Elasticsearch's API to ingest new documents.

That's roughly the skeleton of the code running as a lambda. We need to add error handling, fetching the secret token to communicate with Elasticsearch, maybe some processing to enrich or filter logs, but you get the general idea. You will find the full version of the GitHub repository of this book[44].

Even a platform as flexible as AWS requires some custom tweaking to fully fit into our environment. Today, it was a simple Lambda connector to pick up logs from S3 and send them to Elasticsearch; tomorrow, it may be automatic controls of the WAF rules. A security team composed of builders empowered to deliver products and tooling will naturally thrive and won't be dependent on the availability of other teams who may not be incentivized to deliver security projects.

Now that AWS logs are flowing to our SIEM, we join Richard to start writing the skeleton of the code that will pull all permissions assigned to users and roles on AWS. We want to extract all policies in a nice CSV file to easily search and automate flagging overly permissive access.

We start with listing all users currently defined on AWS in a Python script:

```
client = boto3.client('iam')
users = client.list_users()['Users']
```

...then iterate over each one of them to pull their policies.

There are two types of policies that can be tied to a user: an attached policy and an inline policy. The difference is historical and has no practical incidence, but we need two different API calls to retrieve both:

```
for user in users:
  uname = user["UserName"]

  attached_policies = client.list_attached_user_policies(UserName=
uname)

  attached_policies = attached_policies["AttachedPolicies"]

  inline_policies = client.list_user_policies(UserName=uname)
```

The variables for both attached_policies and inline_policies contain a list of all the permissions granted to a given user. We go through each policy, retrieve its latest version and then its list of unitary permissions recorded in the Statement field:

---

[44] Serverless framework is a common tool to deploy lambdas. Here is a quick tutorial http://bit.ly/3JxsyxL

```
for pol in attached_policies:
  pol_arn = pol["PolicyArn"]
  pol_version = client.get_policy(PolicyArn=arn)
["Policy"]["DefaultVersionId"]
  statement = client.get_policy_version(PolicyArn= pol_arn,
VersionId=pol_version)["PolicyVersion"]["Document"]["Statement"]
```

For each permission in the statement field, we extract the actions—that is, the list of privileges targeted by this statement—the resources they apply to and the effect (allow or deny).

```
for elt in statement:
  actions = elt["Action"]
  resources = elt["Resource"]
  effect = elt["Effect"]

print(f"user,{username},{effect},{actions},{resources},{pol_name}"
)
```

We start by printing them in a nice CSV format to manually explore the resources:

```
user,prometheus_service,Allow,ec2:Describe*,*, prom_ec2_read
user,prometheus_service,Allow,ec2:List*,*, prom_ec2_read
user,jenkins,Allow,iam:*,*,iam-admin
...snip...
```

The goal is not to manually review the resulting 800 lines, but to derive rules to spot permissive access that we can inject back into the code and automate analysis. For instance, we notice that policy names are a good proxy for what the policy actually does. They usually contain the name of the service and type of access: prometheus_**ec2_read, iam-admin**, etc.

So, we go back to the code and automatically flag policy names that include "admin" or "write".

```
keywords = ["admin", "write", "fullaccess"]
if any(key in pol_name for key in keywords):
  dangerous = True
```

We also know from the AWS documentation that the "action" field in permission will contain keywords such as put, update, add or insert when it alters the resource. We therefore add a rule to automatically flag these keywords if they apply to wildcard resources "*".

```
keywords = [":put", ":update", ":insert", ":add"]
if any(key in action for key in keywords) and resource == "*":
  dangerous = True
```

Some services are clearly more important than others. A user or role with write access to the IAM service can easily alter permissions and therefore gain significant privileges. A user or role that can read secrets stored in the SecretsManager or ParameterStore services can glean database passwords and other secrets, so we add a rule to specifically flag these services.

We continue skimming through the first output to codify every rule that our brain flags as an easy abuse to gain privileges on AWS. Whenever we have doubts over a permission, we go back to our AWS account playground and test it out, or Google potential existing hacks leveraging it.

We rerun the script and reprint the CSV with an additional column reflecting this analysis:

```
prometheus_service,Allow,ec2:Describe*,*, prom_ec2_read,
prometheus_service,Allow,ec2:List*,*,prom_ec2_read, dangerous
jenkins,Allow,iam:*,*,iam-admin,dangerous
...snip...
```

This small investment in automation will help us reiterate this extraction and analysis as often as we'd like with little to no overhead.

The above export focused solely on user access. We must do the same for roles and groups. It's roughly the same pattern so we won't detail it here. You can find the full script ready and loaded in the book's GitHub repository[45].

Armed with this solid foundation of dangerous permissions, together with Richard, we spend the next couple of days planning and testing ways to strip down the many unused and overly permissive IAM policies we find.

Logs are paramount to the success of this exercise. Jenkins, for instance, has an admin policy attached to its account. The only way to replace this policy with finer and more granular access is to study access logs, enumerate commonly used permissions and explode that wide admin access into a smaller collection of privileges.

This is by all accounts a dangerous operation. One wrong or forgotten permission and we can break a production service or paralyze a development team. We will move very carefully, schedule changes with the infrastructure team, and develop a robust QA plan for each change to make sure we don't cause any regressions:

```
Jenkins user:
Access key: AKIA564BVDQONPMVDCQX
Query to search for activity on the SIEM:
    userIdentity.accessKeyId: "AKIA564BVDQONPMVDCQX"

List the individual actions it needs and the target resources.

QA before release:
    Execute randomly selected 10% of jobs on Jenkins
```

---

[45] https://github.com/sparcflow/Blitzscaling

```
    Communicate the change to the teams

monitoring after release:
    Monitor Slack and Sentry for errors reported on Jenkins user
    Monitor the SIEM for access denied requests
```

In another instance, we find that all developers have write-access to production buckets that contain payment files, an access that one developer used once in two years during an incident. Clearly, they don't need it anymore. What about that service account that could administer every SQS queue on AWS? When looking closely at its activity and its codebase, we realize that it only really needs occasional read operations on a single queue.

This analysis is 100% fully fueled by the event history of AWS on CloudTrail and CloudWatch. If an action is not listed in the logs, either it's not used or it's not an action currently supported by CloudTrail. AWS documented these short comings in the following link *http://bit.ly/3XLt27Y*. We can therefore quickly eliminate this latter hypothesis, which gives us an iron-clad argument about the safety of the permission reduction operation.

This is a very crucial part of the operation because many security teams hit a steadfast wall when it comes to permission reduction. Most arguments against it roughly fall into two categories. It's either a fear of breaking some deeply mysterious yet critical job that runs once in a blue moon or some manifestation of personal offense, as if people are no longer trusted to have those privileges.

We can address the first argument with the event history argument. A privilege that is not used is probably safe to remove and tends to reflect an error during that service's setup or an evolution of its usage. A privilege that is historically only executed on object A should not extend to object B, C and D. This can be further verified by looking at the code. That's the easy part.

Removing privileges historically granted to developers or admins is much tougher to sell because ego quickly steps into the mix.

"I am the director of engineering, as such I find it only reasonable to retain my admin access over the components of our service," replies one unhappy director.

"Look, Dave, I understand," we reply, "of course, you should, but we're just removing unused permissions. You have not created IAM users or deleted databases in over 12 months. That probably means you don't need them. Anyway, the process to handle these resources has drastically changed. Since we setup SSO, users are handled automatically, and service accounts are described in this GitLab repository and managed by the infrastructure team."

"But what if we're in an incident and I need to react fast by reconfiguring our databases, for example?" he asks.

That's the favorite argument of everyone looking to retain extra permissions. What if there is an exceptional situation that requires exceptional privileges? How can we debug or recover the production environment?

I understand this line of thinking, but this argument could be used to justify anything. Let's just make everyone admin all the time in case there is an incident and we can only reach employee 51 on the list. Exceptional circumstances should not be used to justify nominal behavior. Exceptional circumstances should have exceptional procedures.

"We have a process for that. Every incident involves the infrastructure team, and they're pretty much admin over everything. If your team needs any extra permissions for the duration of the incident, of course they can easily get it. My point is to remove extra permissions that are not used in our day-to-day operations, not to block you folks from working. That would not be serving anyone. If you ever feel it to be the case, let me know and we'll adjust. Ideally, any developer should be able to test and change whatever they want in the staging environment, but the production machines? That's off limits. Every intervention on this environment should be automated and well tested. Forget about security; it's paramount for resiliency and availability."

Make no mistake. We're not swaying Dave here with our sweet words. We're simply reminding him that we are on his side and ready to step in to resolve any unpleasant situation. We're collecting the fruit of a relationship that we've been building with everyone on the tech team over the past few months of collaboration and mutual help. They know that we're not some security nuts living in an isolated castle, answering only to the holy ISO 27K1, throwing absurd commandments with no consideration. We've proven in the past that we stand by teams and help them navigate new process and development practices. From GitLab authentication to the SSO. We even assist them during incidents caused directly or indirectly by our changes. We did not leave anyone hanging, unable to complete their tasks or deliver their features because of some holy security principle. If they need special permissions to investigate a bug, we'll promptly unlock them. If it's a recurrent need, we'll help them build the tooling, so they would not need this permission anymore. If they're stuck because of a change we made, we'll investigate, rollback, learn and then try again together. We're all in this together and they know it; that's how we can move the needle on such an important topic.

Reworking permissions on a shared platform such as AWS requires tremendous alignment. Don't put it on your first month's task list or you'll face an unmovable mountain. First, build trust and teamwork, then leverage those to tackle difficult topics such as permissions.

Back to the technical part of restricting permissions. Everyone agrees that a pure whitelist that explicitly states what an actor can perform on a system is the golden standard. There are fewer surprises that way and one has a lesser chance of falling prey to some unknown edge case. There is one exception to this rule, however, and that concerns what can be referred to as permission boundaries.

Most security teams in organizations fight a hard battle to reduce permissions and implement a maker-checker system for very sensitive actions, but the fact of the matter is that, at the end of the day, there is, somewhere, someplace, an admin service account that can cut the throat of a company. It may have the power to delete databases, delete the Kubernetes cluster, delete the GitLab instance and so on. After all, someone has to retain administrative rights on the platform to make it work, whether it's a break the glass account, some infrastructure component, the CTO or the whole infrastructure team.

The idea of permission boundaries is to cap the maximum level of permissions that can be granted to administrators. Nobody should have the privilege to delete production databases. Even admins. It's a major migration that is carefully orchestrated and probably only happens once every two or three years. No admin or service account will need this privilege in their day-to-day operations. The idea of boundary permissions is not to simply remove this permission from the set of privileges granted to the admin, but to deny the action even if the permission were to be granted somehow. Picture this: an attacker or a ransomware takes hold of an admin service account and chains vulnerabilities to upgrade its permissions to the following:

```
{
  "Version": "2012-10-17",
  "Statement": [
    {
      "Effect": "Allow",
      "Action": ["s3:*", "iam:*", "rds:*"],
      "Resource": ["*"]
    }
  ]
}
```

Even then, with these all-powerful privileges that control several powerful AWS services, they cannot delete the S3 bucket that holds backups and logs and other critical resources. The right permission boundary would exclude these actions from the list of possible actions on this AWS account.

Now that's defense in depth! There is, of course, a way to remove the permission boundary, but that should involve pwning one or several other components outside the initial security boundary, i.e., outside the compromised AWS account.

Sadly, the concept of permission boundaries has not yet conquered the heart of every cloud provider and vendor. AWS and Google Cloud implement different versions of this concept under the names Service Control Policies and Credential Boundaries, respectively, so we can leverage it at Mirage.

In defending against a ransomware threat, for instance, we list all the resources that should never be deleted, except for a major migration: various S3 buckets holding production data, customer records and logs, production databases and their snapshots, Kubernetes clusters, database, critical service accounts, and so on. We then set up a Service Control Policy in the AWS master account[46]:

```
{
  "Version": "2012-10-17",
  "Statement": [
    {
      "Sid": "DenyDeletionResources",
      "Effect": "Deny",
      "Action": [
        "s3:Delete*",
        "rds:Delete*",
        "eks:Delete*",
      ],
      "Resource": [
        "arn:aws:s3:::mirage-manager",
        "arn:aws:s3:::mirage-ps-*",
        "arn:aws:s3:::mirage-root-cloudtrail*",
        "arn:aws:eks:eu-west-3:123456789:cluster/prod*",
        "arn:aws:rds:eu-west-3:123456789:db:pg-prod*",
      ]
    }
  ]
}
```

It's by no means exhaustive, but it's a very strong protection against an all-powerful malicious admin account. The neat thing about this feature is that the implementation cost is, at best, a couple of hours of reflection to validate the list of resources to be protected. Deployment is safe since we're forbidding actions that never happen anyway.

Back to our AWS access analysis. When looking at permissions, we noticed many instances of service accounts displaying no sign of activity on AWS. It often happens that users are requested and created because of an initial use case that ceases to exist, or following a migration. An infrastructure lives its own life. The faster the growth cycle, the more frequently the platform changes. We need to add this dynamic flavor to our security controls as well. They cannot be frozen in time, conducted simply once a quarter or once a year.

---

[46] The master account should contain no infrastructure components, only management settings such as SCPs. More information about AWS Organization http://bit.ly/3l82akQ

We research a way to automate disabling accounts following a long period of inactivity, but AWS does not provide any built-in way to do it. We can, however, use the Lambda service to execute a piece of code every week, list user accounts without activity during the last six months, for instance, and disable their access keys. We share the idea with Marc from the infrastructure team, but he is a bit doubtful:

"That could be a bit dangerous, no? What if you wrongfully disable an account used in production? What if we have a batch that only runs once a year that uses that account?"

"The LastUsedDate[47] date of user credentials are made available by AWS in a simple API call; we're not manually deriving this info from past activity. So, it should be as reliable as we can hope for. I understand your concerns but, frankly, if we have a job that runs once a year, then it may suffer a one-hour delay while we reenable the account. We're not deleting accounts; we're just disabling them. It's easy to revert the change back."

We can feel he is not entirely thrilled by the idea. We decide to tone it down a notch, hoping for consensus:

"How about a compromise?" we ask, "Let's just flag these unused accounts for now, maybe send the list on a Slack channel. We'll disable them manually following a check with the tech team. After three or four weeks of good behavior, we can turn on automation all the way. What do you think?"

If we have to compromise to quickly reach the production line and get our first feedback loop from the real world, then so be it. There is nothing worse than procrastination disguised as perfectionism.

Our work on AWS permissions closes some gaping loopholes in our systems. Sure, there are still some permissions that need to be better scoped and refined. The five people on the transfer team do not always need to upload those raw banking files on S3. However, they occasionally need to fix bugs and replay faulty files sent by the partner. We can't just clamp down these privileges without providing a credible alternative to help them correct mistakes. That will require some thought and testing and will have its place in future iterations of permission reviews.

---

[47] *http://bit.ly/3FitlQD*

Following the same approach, Richard takes on Kubernetes, the second most important production environment. Same ramp-up period to identify everything that can be abused on Kubernetes, same reliance on logs to gain confidence in our proposed changes and same strategy of going after the great whales: admin service accounts, tooling accounts that can read all secrets and so on. The first instance of this project will probably take him a couple of weeks, but just like with AWS, the goal is to end up with scripts and written knowledge to accelerate the next iterations by tenfold[48].

While he is working on Kubernetes, we start thinking about our detection strategy.

So many companies simply externalize this whole endeavor to a third-party security operation center (SOC) and fully rely on their much-advertised expertise. These services can easily cost north of €200k a year, depending on the volume of logs analyzed. We cannot shake the feeling that it's a steep price to pay for what will probably be, at best, off the shelf detection patterns. Our past experience as pentesters does not exactly comfort us in this choice either. We have seen so many SOC teams dutifully reporting every frivolous nmap scan on Internet-facing assets yet failing to notice a password spraying attack across workstations, disabled antivirus, and other obvious attack patterns.

When people think of an SOC, their imagination goes straight to rows of human analysts and experts manually combing through gigabytes of logs looking for that small needle in a gigantic haystack. It's the gargantuan task projected by this visualization that likely pushes them to simply externalize the service. Where can they even find such specialists?

Yes, we will probably end up with huge amounts of logs and traces, but we know Mirage's environment better than some third-party analysts. If we design our detection efficiently, we may not even need a single full-time analyst. What if we try to automate our way out of the question?

Once again, let's go back to first principles. What's the purpose of a detection system and why do we need it?

---

[48] Overview of Kubernetes' RBAC model: *https://learnk8s.io/rbac-kubernetes*

Our threat graph details many possible exploitation scenarios, each taking advantage of known vulnerabilities and misconfigurations. We fully mitigated some of these scenarios such as the RCE on the form upload by fixing the code and slamming a WAF in front of the app, but an attacker has the luxury of time and resources. What if they find a way to bypass our protections? What if they find new ways of exploiting the app that we simply could not foresee? Our protection measures, however solid, always leave a small crack in the window whether we realize it or not. We often refer to this crack as residual risk. One of the first goals of a detection system is to cover these residual risks.

Another poignant example is the Jenkins AWS policy. We stripped down its admin access and replaced it with read-only access to a handful of S3 buckets holding customer information, among other things. It's a great step forward, but Jenkins can still be abused to download every file from those S3 buckets. The access is legit. The two or three teams with access to this job need to retrieve invoice file for debugging purposes. The requested files change every time so naturally Jenkins needs read access to the whole subfolder of the bucket. Therefore, a single vulnerability on Jenkins could leak the entirety of customer invoices. How can we cover this risk given that we already tightened access as much as we could on Jenkins and AWS? The answer is: we cannot easily do that, for the time being. But we can detect early signs of abuse!

A Jenkins service account usually downloads three to five files a day. If it suddenly starts to download 100 files an hour, we raise an alert that will prompt an immediate investigation. That's a behavior that, barring an incident or some unusual bug, is never supposed to happen. We effectively covered our residual risk through this detection mechanism.

A common trap to avoid with detection is to substitute it for protection. The two activities serve very different purposes. Protection is the essential first layer that withstands the hardest blow of the attack. We have to tighten access, configuration and so on to reduce that threat level by 80 or 90%. Once we can't advance any further, then we complement that approach with detection to scrape additional basis points of risk reduction. Starting with or focusing solely on detection can be a smart short-term approach when you're in a hurry or when your hands are tied, but it's a losing strategy in the long term. First, shut the doors and the windows, then set up the alarm.

Given our recent work on AWS to tighten permissions across all services, it's the perfect training ground to start experimenting with detection rules. We will set up our alerts on Elasticsearch Security using simple threshold queries that we can refine over time. If a certain event or pattern goes over the threshold, it will send an alert on Slack.

Forget about machine learning algorithms, that's icing on the cake in our current security landscape. We're not there yet. Let's start nice and slow and target specific scenarios we know are critical—for instance, that Jenkins abuse we discussed earlier. Below is the count of objects downloaded over the past few days:

Figure 13-4: Count of objects downloaded by Jenkins every day

Our intuition was correct, the service rarely exceeds a dozen files a day.

Based on this insight, we create a simple threshold rule to cover the residual risk of someone abusing this service to download hundreds of customer files.

Figure 13-5: Threshold rule that fires when the number of downloads goes over 100

Once it's running, we put it to the test: we steal the Jenkins credentials, download 100 files and lo and behold, we receive a Slack notification a few minutes later:

```
--
Rule: "Unusual Jenkins S3 access"
jenkins called GetObject eventName over 100 times
--
```

Our first detection rule is live and running!

We follow the same logic for the access granted to the transfer team. Remember how they can download and overwrite raw banking files? This access is supposed to be only for debugging. If they abuse it, we should receive an alert.

The two detection rules above share a common trait. We accept to let go of single occurrences and focus on larger scale attacks. Losing one file is deemed acceptable. Losing a hundred or a thousand, however, is not. This risk appetite may vary per service, file type, etc. but the arbitrage is the same. We don't want to flood our system with meaningless alerts that will eventually mask real attacks. We want each alert to be pertinent and capture our attention.

For other AWS permissions, we may follow a different approach. For instance, the service account used by GitLab to push Docker containers to the AWS ECR service[49] is always coming from the same pool of IP addresses attributed to the GitLab machines. An attacker that grabs these credentials might try them on from their VPN or private server yielding a very different IP…. Let's alert on that shall we? According to the logs over the last couple of months, this should never happen as these credentials are always tied to the 10.87.0.0/16 network, so we write a simple rule that fires if there is an event that violates this assumption.

We continue to diligently work through the list of permissions assigned to a given user or role, already slashed down to a minimum through our access review project. Each time we define what is considered "normal" behavior and, by extension, how it can be abused. It's almost like planting canary tokens, and in a sense it is. It's just much more insidious. Instead of creating dummy accounts and spreading them all over the infrastructure, hoping for an attacker to stumble on them, we make assumptions about our current traffic. And as soon as we observe new or inconsistent behavior, we flag it! The canary is the deviation itself.

As we comb through the access logs of the different teams, we notice something interesting. The infrastructure team rarely, if ever, use their privileged access to create service accounts, change permissions of even interact with the IAM service. We ask Steve about it, who, as usual, gives us the missing context:

"Yeah, we don't like performing manual actions on AWS," he says, "we're in the process of automating many of our admin tasks through tools like Terraform and Ansible[50]."

---

[49] Amazon Elastic Container Registry (ECR) stores and shares containers https://aws.amazon.com/ecr/.

[50] Terraform https://www.terraform.io/ and Ansible https://www.ansible.com/ are tools that describe infrastructure components in code to allow automatic management of resources.

That's very interesting information. Basically, we can put up a detection rule that flags every interaction with the IAM service not performed through these tools. It's such a powerful rule.

Say an attacker finds a way to elevate their privileges on the platform and is looking for a way to achieve persistence by creating access keys, changing trust relationships, updating permissions and policies and so on. An attacker unaware of Mirage's process won't go through our standard tooling to do that. There is a good to fair chance that they'd rather do them manually through a script or direct calls to the AWS API. As soon as they modify any of these objects in IAM, we would receive an alert!

What if they find a way to hack our tooling and perform their changes through a Terraform or Ansible user? Terrific question! Then we'll setup other detection rules to cover this blind spot. For instance, changes performed through the Terraform user always come from the same pool of IP addresses and use a known user agent. An attacker who steals the credentials of the Terraform user won't likely bother to replicate these properties, therefore allowing room for detection.

What if they are very careful and mimic these properties from the first request? Well then, they win...this round. We will make sure to have another hundred detection rules ready for them to make one single mistake!

In the alerts we've showcased so far, we always projected some hypothesis on the attacker: they're going to leverage Jenkins to download files, they're abusing the permissions of the transfer team and so on. It's a good start and we need these types of rules, but this approach contains an important fallacy: we project our way of thinking onto the attacker, which can be treacherous. The attacker may be more imaginative than us. What if they find a way to download the data without going through Jenkins?

We need to further broaden our detection mindset. We know where our data is located. We have logs of systems accessing or allowing access to this data. If we're able to clearly distinguish the regular pattern to access the data, we could easily alert on any deviation from that baseline. In essence, instead of starting from permissions and thinking of ways to misuse them, let's now start from the sensitive data and work our way to detection rules that cover suspicious access. This brings us to the second use case of detection: detecting the unknown unknowns!

To counter this type of unknown and unforeseeable scenario, we concentrate our detection efforts on the data itself. How many requests per day does the S3 bucket mirage-proof-identity receive? From which IP addresses? Countries? Service accounts?

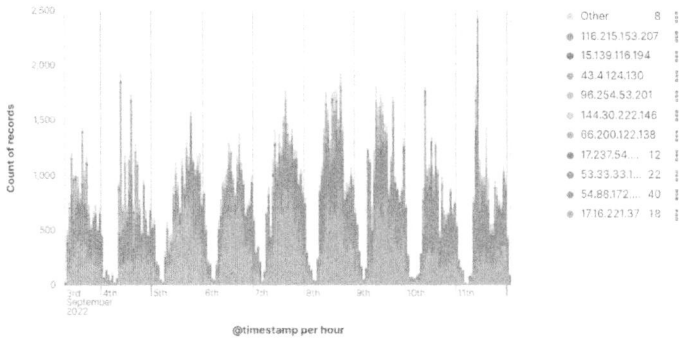

Figure 13-6: Distribution of IP addresses accessing an S3 bucket

We know that in any given hour, an IP address downloads between 500 and 1000 customer documents. An attacker who tries to empty the bucket, as they often do, will surely shatter this number. So, a very powerful alert we can set up is: "if the number of downloads per IP address goes over three standard deviations, send an alert." We don't know under which conditions this alert would pop: maybe the attacker bribed a user, hacked the web app or retrieved some form of credentials. We don't care. We just know that no single IP address should ever download this much data.

Such rules will necessarily make assumptions about some attributes of the requests. Above, we aggregated the requests per IP address. But what if the attacker has a large pool of IP addresses at their disposal so as to mask any suspicious activity? No matter, we'll add a second rule to cover that blind spot. This time, by aggregating on the service account name. We run the same analysis and discover that no single service account downloads more than 1000 different files an hour...Alright, let's set it up!

Let's do another one for fun. For instance, we know that all Mirage tech employees are located in ten countries. There should be no reason whatsoever to have new AWS API calls coming from, say, Japan. One rule we could implement is to detect an alert if more than 20 calls are issued from a previously unseen country.

```
not geoip.country_iso_code:("US" or "DE" or "IE" or "ES"…)

Group by: all results, threshold: 50
Time period: 1h
```

The list of countries is hardcoded, so this rule will require some maintenance, maybe an update every month or so, but it is a powerful rule. An attacker that gets sloppy for a minute will jump out like a sore thumb.

Following the same logic, we can easily come up with dozens of rules that trigger low false positives yet yield actional alerts that only trigger when something highly unusual happens: a nasty bug, an incident or an attacker[51].

So far, we've leveraged detection to cover known exploitation scenarios and unknown attack patterns. The last notable use case of detection is to maintain the level of security steady in time.

Every remediation or protection action we take operates on a snapshot of the environment at a given point in time. Today, we put a WAF in front of the app, but we have no guarantee that it will still be standing firmly tomorrow. Today, we reviewed security permissions and chased down broad access, but tomorrow, someone could attach a new admin policy to a service account, which might be justified…or not. We can't wait until the next chance assessment to dig out all these malpractices, and we cannot stand as gatekeepers of every change. The pace of security checks must match the pace of the infrastructure changes. That's when detection comes into play.

We have a near real-time report of everything that happens on AWS and other components through our continuous log stream to Elasticsearch. We can make sure that the protections we put in place were not violated by subsequent changes. For instance, we spent a couple of days migrating all apps behind a WAF, so let's make sure that developers and infrastructure folks follow the procedure and continue to put every new app behind the WAF.

To do that, we will monitor all new public records created on Route53. If their CNAME does not point to our WAF, we will raise an alert:

```
eventName: "ChangeResourceRecordSets"

and
requestParameters.changeBatch.changes.resourceRecordSet.type:("AAA
A" or "A" or "CNAME")

and not
requestParameters.changeBatch.changes.resourceRecordSet.resourceRe
cords.value:*shieldsec*

Group by: all results, threshold: 1
Time period: 15 min
```

---

[51] AWS allows users to limit permissions by IP addresses or network interfaces, which can upgrade many of these detections to the protection realm, but it's a very cumbersome and complex setup for this first iteration.

Remember that this detection complements the work we did to deny direct traffic from the Internet unless it came through the WAF. Theoretically then, this detection rule should never fire. It's a watchdog that will indeed spot new, unprotected domains, but will most importantly signal a faulty process. Somewhere, a developer submitted a change to create an unprotected public DNS record that was approved by the infrastructure team, despite our current standard that mandates that all incoming traffic goes through the WAF. In which case, a reminder of the standard may be needed.

The work we did on the AWS permission was a complex and intricate one. We'll probably need to go through these permissions every quarter, but as stated previously, we cannot wait until the next quarter to discover a new "iam:*" permission that grants unlimited access over the identity service, for instance. We want to deploy watchdogs that recapture the essence of our protection philosophy and run it in real time.

When assessing permissions we hunted for policies with wildcard actions "<service>:*", or containing a "put" or "update" or "insert" over a wildcard resources. Let's set up detection rules for these types of policies. Basically, every time a new policy is created (`eventName: PutPolicy`), we will inspect its body for these tell-tale signs of permissive access. If there is a match, we'll send an alert.

Following the same logic, we want to be alerted when sensitive privileges are granted, such as read objects in Secrets Manager *http://bit.ly/3TbUR8r*, Parameter Store *https://go.aws/3l8BC2Q* and so on. We can leverage the list of sensitive permissions that we crafted previously.

We can get as creative as we want with these detection alerts. The only golden rule to observe is to limit the number of false positives. There is such a thing as alert fatigue, and if we get too many alerts on a given day, the important ones will slip through the noise. The detection alerts we described so far all respect this important criterion. We make assumptions about some properties of an event, exclude the most common ones based on reliable properties and focus on the abnormality we want to alert on. This means that every detection rule inherently has blind spots. A rule that detects data exfiltration on S3 will probably whitelist a couple of common service accounts to maximize precision (less false positives) but will have poor recall (will catch less attackers). The way around this conundrum is to create additional rules that cover the previous blind spots. In this case, an additional S3 rule that detects data exfiltration but excludes known IP addresses or known user agents rather than usernames.

If we follow this approach of high precision and target around half a dozen alerts triggered a day, we can challenge the conventional need for a dedicated SOC center often touted by auditors and consultants. If we build a team of security engineers that continuously audit the platform, fix vulnerabilities and set up and curate high-precision detection alerts, we can genuinely wonder what benefit an externalized SOC would bring. Generic off-the-shelf detection rules that can hardly be customized? Shallow investigation by an analyst unaware of Mirage's specificities and context? We're much better served by automation in this case.

It's not a question of scale, either. It's easy to jump to the conclusion that a company with 200,000 employees and 34 offices would have no choice but to accept the dreaded loss in precision alerts and therefore externalize the detection function altogether. The argument is fallacious because externalizing noisy alerts won't make up for the loss in precision. If a team cannot engineer their detection alerts in such a way to reduce false positives, then there is serious work to be done at the protection level to first standardize, homogenize and cut unnecessary noise. Detection only makes sense once we define and agree on what is normal and expected within an environment so we can go hunting for abnormal activity. Using detection rules as a substitute to actually fixing vulnerabilities will yield a sea of positives, rendering the effort moot.

A commonly repeated mantra in many security circles is that the attacker always has the edge. They only need to find one vulnerability. They only need to get it right once to checkmate the company. Yes, in a poorly protected environment, that's entirely true. One vulnerability is all it takes. But that's not the environment we're designing now, is it? Since we have joined Mirage, we've been stacking layer upon layer of security, each one requiring a set of skills to bypass. Sure, we're just getting started, but ideally, an attacker who finds a path traversal should fight the WAF to go through. In doing so, they trigger enough alerts to rouse the whole team, who hurriedly block them. Should they stealthily bypass the WAF and land a shell on the container, then our second alerting system should fire up. A shell spawned by the web server is an unusual event, after all, that we can alert on by monitoring system calls. The hardened container should heavily complicate their maneuvering: absence of regular Linux commands, AWS metadata endpoint unreachable from the container, read-only folders and so on. Each of these measures is an additional hurdle they have to jump through without tripping any additional wires along the way. This is predicated on having a functioning protection and detection at the system level, but bear with me. It's all coming soon at Mirage.

Suppose the attacker artfully navigates their way through these landmines of hardening and detection to gain root privileges. There is another unusual event, ergo, an alert that should scream bloody murder! Suppose they still land valid AWS credentials. As soon as they test these credentials from an unusual IP address, a new country or simply with the wrong user agent, then we'll snag them right away. If they start leveraging these credentials for reconnaissance or data gathering, flooding our system with unusual API calls, that's another opportunity to haul them. As soon as they start manually testing for persistence in IAM, our alerts fire up once more, and finally, every file download on S3 floods the system with another round of alerts.

Now, let me ask you who has to get it right every time?

A security team that continuously studies their environment and manages to stack up layers of protection and detection based on known and expected behavior will destroy any semblance of advantage the attacker is having. It's their turf. It's their rules.

Since we're on a roll centralizing log activity from AWS and Kubernetes, we jump on the occasion to also grab user activity on the SSO, VPN and GitLab. We will subject them to the same scrutiny as AWS logs. Understand common patterns, make a hypothesis about the attacker's choice of weapon and add rules to detect them. There is no reason for someone to connect to the VPN from two different locations, create public repositories on GitLab, manually assign critical roles on the SSO and so on.

The potential of log analysis is truly mind blowing. We started by focusing on the key components of our cloud infrastructure, but we can drill much deeper than that. Falco *(https://sysdig.com/opensource/falco/)* is an open-source tool that gathers Linux system calls and offers the ability to apply interesting rules to spot tell-tale signs of compromise. When deployed on machines, we can use it to flag a root shell on a container, a bash spawned by the web server, a curl to the AWS metadata endpoint[52], a binary modified on the container, and so on.

Below is an example of a rule that flags any root shell spawned within a container:

```
- rule: root_exec_post_exploitation
  desc: Process executed as root or root group
  condition: spawned_process
    and container
    and root
    and proc.name in (shell_binaries)
```

---

[52] AWS metadata exposes temporary credentials that can be abused through SSRF vulnerabilities: *http://bit.ly/3GZVT1r.*

```
output: Process executed as root (user=%user.name
container_name=%container.name)
```

We will not deploy Falco right now as it's a project on its own that requires a bit of preparation and tech alignment, but we add it right up there on our to-do list once the threat graph makes it clear it's the next piece to pull. It's almost like a Sysmon[53] running on Linux.

Speaking of which, what about all those Windows servers and workstations that we recently deployed with IT? We can configure them to forward their logs to our Elasticsearch: Defender logs, authentication results, firewall configuration changes, AppLocker results and so on.

First, we install Winlogbeat[54], Elastic's agent to capture Windows logs and send them to our cluster. We don't care about most of the noisy events produced by Windows; below are some of the security events we really want to capture to have decent detection:

```
winlogbeat.event_logs:

- name: Security

  processors:

    - drop_event.when.not.or:
      - equals.winlog.event_id: 4720 # User was created
      - equals.winlog.event_id: 4740 # User account was locked
      - equals.winlog.event_id: 4723 # password change on an account
      - equals.winlog.event_id: 1102 # Audit log was cleared
      - equals.winlog.event_id: 4624 # Successful login
      - equals.winlog.event_id: 4625 # Failed login
      - equals.winlog.event_id: 4732 # Member added to security group
      - equals.winlog.event_id: 4735 # Security group was changed
      - equals.winlog.event_id: 4697 # Service installed
      - equals.winlog.event_id: 4698 # Scheduled task was created
      - equals.winlog.event_id: 4741 # Computer account was created
      - equals.winlog.event_id: 4674 # privileged access
```

You can find the full configuration file in the book's GitHub repository with the complete list of events to watch out for, PowerShell logs, Defender logs, AppLocker logs and so on.

The main issue is that most of these events are not enabled by default on Windows—*really, Microsoft?*—so we need to activate them in the local security settings.

[53] http://bit.ly/3ZNllzX.
[54] http://bit.ly/3ZVxt1S.

File Action View Help		
Security Settings	Policy	Security Setting
Account Policies	Audit account logon events	No auditing
Local Policies	Audit account management	No auditing
Audit Policy	Audit directory service access	No auditing
User Rights Assignment	Audit logon events	No auditing
Security Options	Audit object access	No auditing
Windows Defender Firewall with Adva	Audit policy change	No auditing
Network List Manager Policies	Audit privilege use	No auditing
Public Key Policies	Audit process tracking	No auditing
Software Restriction Policies	Audit system events	No auditing
Application Control Policies		

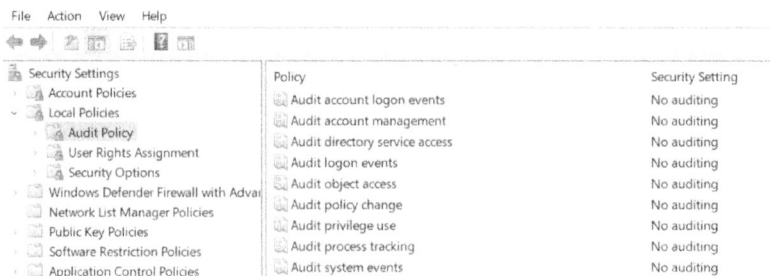

Figure 13-7: Enabling audit system events on Windows servers

If everything is set up properly, we should start receiving events on our SIEM.

Following our detection principles, we get to go through the logs and focus on specific attack scenarios: antivirus alerts, disabling the antivirus, changing firewall configurations, AppLocker violations, many unsuccessful authentications, an admin added to the machine, and so on.

We can even enhance monitoring using Sysmon to capture process activity, network and file events. SwiftOnSecurity is famous for its baseline Sysmon configuration[55] that we can tweak to fit our needs. Here is a link to a customized version[56].

Winlogbeat natively processes Sysmon outputs, so we quickly end up with the logs in the SIEM. Now to the fun part: we can download Empire *http://bit.ly/3Y6dvjl*, Mimikatz[57]...all the goodies in the attackers' arsenal and replay common hacking scenarios, study what logs they generate and write detection rules based on them. Think of the most basic commands executed by attackers: Mimikatz, reconnaissance commands, Reflective DLL[58] and so on. You don't need an EDR to detect classic credential dumping using Mimikatz and its variants. You can achieve a pretty decent coverage with the following simple rule that monitors any wide read access to the LSASS process hosting credentials.

```
winlog.event_data.TargetImage :"C:\Windows\system32\lsass.exe"
and winlog.event_data.GrantedAccess: "0x1010"
and not (process.name: "MsMpEng.exe" and
process.executable:*Windows*Defender*)
```

---

[55] *http://bit.ly/3ZFLX5v*
[56] *https://github.com/sparcflow/Blitzscaling*

[57] Mimikatz by gentilkiwi *https://blog.gentilkiwi.com/mimikatz* is a tool to extract Windows credentials, replay Kerberos tickets, dump DPAPI vaults and so much more. It's the Swiss army knife of Windows credentials.

[58] *http://bit.ly/3cwuTcp.*

```
Group by: all results, threshold: 1
Time period: 10 min
```

That's it. Except for a few exceptions, such as Windows Defender, no process should ever access the lsass.exe process, which is responsible for authenticating users. Can it be bypassed? Sure! Faking the process name, duplicating the handle to the LSASS process, killing Sysmon or Winlogbeat, along with many other techniques. But again, this first rule will probably catch 90% of threat actors. We will deal with the last 10% in the near future, when our threat level justifies it.

No matter how hard they try, attackers do leave distinctive breadcrumbs. Almost nobody executes the whoami command on their machines, certainly not on many machines at once. Almost nobody installs Windows services, dumps the SAM registry hive[59] or runs 1000-character-long PowerShell commands. All these oddities will end up feeding our detection engine in the SIEM. We may not be able to implement all these detection rules from the get-go, but we will slowly ramp up as the project matures and as we get new insights.

We rinse and repeat for MacOs workstations.

We start toying with the idea of getting database logs but quickly give up on that idea. PostgreSQL requires installing the pg_audit extension, which slightly hits performance and requires a reboot to activate. These are very impactful changes that require a deeper analysis and coordination with the entire tech team. One does not simply restart a production database in a bank without first going through a thorough approval system. We shelve the idea for now as the effort/gain ratio is not quite there. We still have some low- and medium-hanging fruit we can go after in other areas.

---

[59] http://bit.ly/3GToEge.

Git-fucking-ops

The work on detection is far from over. We've gathered logs of the main components of our infrastructure and put up at least 50 rules in this first iteration to cover the most obvious attack scenarios. When we look at the threat graph, all our first entry points have detection associated with them, which is good enough for now. We'll continue going deeper in the infrastructure stack and improve our position in future iterations.

"Hey, I noticed something interesting when working with the dev team on a new invoicing feature," says Richard in our daily meeting. "Developers have their code in GitLab repositories and, as you know, every new change proposal, AKA a merge request, triggers tasks executed on GitLab: non-regression tests and container building. So far, so good. But the thing is, the code that performs all these tasks lives within the repository itself! So basically, anyone with the ability to create a merge request can change the content of the tasks that will be running on GitLab machines!"

Hum...he may be onto something! What if we can dump credentials living on GitLab machines through this type of code execution?

We open a draft merge request on a random repo to look more closely at the usual development flow. We notice multiple jobs being executed: "lint", "rspec", etc.

Figure 14-1: GitLab pipeline

We are familiar with these jobs given our involvement in the development of features, but we never really investigated how nor where they were defined. A little probing in the code reveals that these jobs are defined in the `.gitlab-ci.yml` file included in the same repo:

```
#.gitlab-ci.yml
...snip...
lint:
  stage: test
  image: 789754624623.dkr.ecr.eu-west-1.amazonaws.com/mirage-ruby:3.1.0
  script:
    - make lint

rspec:
...snip...
```

That's interesting! Since we can open a merge request, we can make any changes we'd like to this testing job. Let's cheat a bit and inject an env command in the .gitlab-ci.yml file to display all environment variables in the lint job:

```
lint:
  stage: test
  image: 789754624623.dkr.ecr.eu-west-1.amazonaws.com/mirage-
ruby:3.1.0
  script:
    - make lint
    - env
```

We submit the merge request and inspect the output of the lint job we just altered:

```
Running with gitlab-runner 14.10.1
  On gitlab-docker-runner-default WjRAHAz-

...snip...

$ make lint
..................................
330 files inspected, no offenses detected
$ env
LANG=C.UTF-8
AWS_ACCESS_KEY_ID=ASIAQVCEA7PPIEIEJXMAZ
AWS_SECRET_ACCESS_KEY=mtnaKsjeKapirqCyeaWSqaz578atry
AWS_SESSION_TOKEN= IQoJb3ceaacetezyrutrjhre///…
...snip...
```

Hello, AWS access keys! We fetch their corresponding role name:

```
$ export AWS_ACCESS_KEY_ID=ASIAQVCEA7PPIEIEJXMAZ
$ export AWS_SECRET_ACCESS_KEY=mtnaKsjeKapirqCyeaWSqaz578atry
$ export AWS_SESSION_TOKEN= IQoJb3ceaacetezyrutrjhre///…

$ aws sts get-caller-identity
{
  "UserId": "AROA56XRQ6WDXOK8ZDZET:6787adcee98c1357e ",
  "Account": "789754624623",
  "Arn": "arn:aws:sts::789754624623:assumed-role/gitlab-
runner.ec2/i-6787adcee98c1357e"
}
```

We seem to have impersonated the gitlab-runner.ec2 IAM role. We switch back to our own user and inspect the policies attached to this role:

```
$ unset AWS_ACCESS_KEY_ID AWS_SECRET_ACCESS_KEY
$ aws iam list-attached-role-policies \
  --role-name gitlab-runner.cc2

"PolicyArn":
"arn:aws:iam::aws:policy/AmazonEC2ContainerRegistryFullAccess",
```

The default AWS policy `AmazonEC2ContainerRegistryFullAccess` grants unfettered access to ECR, the container registry of AWS. We can effectively change applications in production to run our custom code, and do many more shenanigans on the infrastructure. We can replace any running app with our own version containing a trap door that wires 10 cents from every transaction to our bank account. How frightening (or exciting) is that?

And that's just one random repository. We have 300 of them now...imagine the number of credentials we can dump if we weaponized this attack *en masse*.

We visualize the attack path in our mind. An attacker needs access to the VPN or the production network, then they must go through the SSO or a GitLab API key to reach the repositories. That's a two-step vulnerability path that could do quite some damage. We quickly review all other existing threat scenarios and, clearly, no other comes even close...for now. Should we spot a new one-hop vulnerability scenario, we'll swiftly shuffle our priorities.

The crux of the issue is the journey of the code from development to production. It's a thorny path fraught with risks of takeover and unauthorized modifications. Mirage's setup is a textbook example of how many tech companies handle their code base. Let's dissect it a bit to better evaluate our exposure and remediating actions.

Each app has a GitLab repository where the code is stored and versioned. A developer works on their separate Git branch[60]. When their code is ready to be shipped, they create a merge request, which, upon approval, applies the modifications to the master branch.

Each commit pushed to GitLab on any branch triggers a job composed of a series of tasks: unit tests, linter—soon a vulnerability scan when we get the chance to add it—and so on. Some of these jobs only run on the master branch, such as the job in charge of deploying the code to production.

As we saw earlier, each task is a collection of bash commands embedded in the repository itself within the `.gitlab-ci.yml` file. In the spirit of transparency and since developers often move across teams and can work on various micro services, they have been granted access to practically all repos. Anyone can submit code change proposals (merge requests) to any app.

---

[60] If you are fuzzy about Git concepts, check out this nice article that thoroughly explores its core tenets: *https://phoenixnap.com/kb/how-git-works.*

One recurring and crucial job executed in the pipeline builds the container that will be running the application. Containers built on regular branches are pushed to the staging Kubernetes cluster on the staging AWS account, while containers built in the master branch are pushed to the production AWS account where they'll be deployed on the production Kubernetes. We're effectively considering every regular branch as a staging environment, where anyone can push arbitrary code and build any container they want. But the master branch, since it requires human review and approval is deemed safe enough to be shipped to production.

This setup is roughly similar across all Mirage application repositories on GitLab. But it goes way beyond that. It also applies to repositories holding infrastructure code! When Steve mentioned earlier that they no longer perform manual actions and were using tools like Terraform and Ansible, he was referring to the transition to an infrastructure as code through a GitOps-based model.

GitOps is a process of automating infrastructure changes, app deployment and operations through Git. Instead of manually changing components via a UI console or uploading Jar files on a server, one describes, in code, the desired infrastructure or deployment strategy. Then, a special tool will interact with the production environment to make it true. Ansible, Terraform, Chef, ArgoCD...all offer these capabilities.

Goodbye fat finger syndrome and hidden changes to the infrastructure! I remember a day when people used to exude fives kinds of sweat before releasing changes on a server. Now, you submit a merge request that runs tests on your changes, displays what's going to change and applies those changes following human review. Safe, repeatable and easy to roll back. These properties are key for teams like us who routinely flirt with breaking changes in an attempt to secure a component. They encourage us to iterate and experiment with different settings without fear of breaking everything with one push of a button.

Enabling encryption on all S3 buckets using Terraform, for instance, would be as simple as adding this block of code to a repository[61]:

```
resource "aws_s3_bucket" "mirage-docs" {
  bucket = "mirage-docs"
  ...snip...
  server_side_encryption_configuration {
    rule {
      apply_server_side_encryption_by_default {
        sse_algorithm      = " AES256"
      }
    }
```

---

[61] Terraform documentation regarding AWS S3 buckets: *http://bit.ly/3XthDKh.*

```
        }
}
```

How hard is that using a proper IDE or a smart combination of Linux commands?

All of this is great, but there is a critical assumption that can make or break this whole setup: That it's okay for GitLab to harness so much power over the infrastructure! Indeed, to have proper infrastructure described as code, one needs to commit the code to a Git-like repository and trigger jobs that will alter the current configuration. There is no way around it. These CI/CD tools need admin accounts on AWS, Kubernetes, databases and so on to perform these changes.

Let's pause for a second and reframe this common setup from an attacker's perspective.

If we grab a GitLab personal token and can reach the instance from a network perspective, we can append Bash code to the `.gitlab-ci.yml` file located in the same repository and trigger code execution on any of GitLab's machines running these jobs. When we do that on repositories holding infrastructure code, we successfully dump **admin credentials** used to interact with the infrastructure. When done on repositories holding application code, we dump credentials allowing us to deploy any container, similar to what we demonstrated earlier.

We pour through GitLab's documentation to understand how to mitigate this attack pattern and stumble upon the notion of protected branches. A protected branch is a designated branch that can be configured to only accept merge requests. No one can directly push code without going through a merge request that might enforce a human review. Production environment variables injected in the pipeline can be restricted to these protected branches. So, in our earlier example, the attacker would not be able to dump production AWS access using a simple GitLab API token. They'd need to collude with one or more developers to smuggle their changes in a merge request. Much more difficult to pull off.

Clearly, we don't have this protection at Mirage, given our earlier extraction of AWS access keys, but maybe it was just a bad fluke. We have over 300 repos, so let's run a quick script to list all their branch protections. We initialize the GitLab client in Python:

```
gl = gitlab.Gitlab("https://gitlab.mirage.co",
                private_token=os.environ["GITLAB_TOKEN"]
    )
```

Then, we retrieve all repositories and iterate over their branch protection settings. We focus on the default branch, often called "master" or "main":

```
projects = gl.projects.list(all=True)
```

```
for p in projects:
  branches = project.protectedbranches.list()
  try:
   push_level = branches[0].push_access_levels[0]["access_level"]
   merge_level =branches[0].merge_access_levels[0]["access_level"]

  except:
    push_level = "N/A"
    merge_level = "N/A"
```

We also retrieve a couple of other approval settings that might facilitate malicious code injection:

```
p.approvals_before_merge
p.disable_overriding_approvers_per_merge_request
p.merge_requests_author_approval
p.merge_requests_disable_committers_approval
```

We organize all this information in a nice CSV. You can find the full code at the following link [script]:

```
Repo, merge_level, push_level, approvals, override_approvals…
mirage-manager, 40, 40, 1, true,…
...snip...
```

The repo Mirage manager, for instance, allows developers to directly push code into protected branches (push level 40), requires one approval, but allows people opening merge requests to change the number of approvals to zero, for instance. Catastrophic. Any developer can mess with this critical application.

Going through the rest of the list, we notice that the security settings vary greatly. Some repos don't have protected branches. Others have protected branches but none of the variables are marked as "protected". Even the few repos with this setting allow everyone to push code to these branches as if they were regular branches, bypassing any approval or review. Additional security settings are also lacking in many repos. People can auto-approve merge requests, change the number of approvals to zero, etc. It's a mess!

We make a note to address these shortcomings later and continue following the breadcrumbs of the code's life until it reaches production servers. Let's focus on the environment hosting these jobs. These jobs are not running in the ether; they're running somewhere on EC2 virtual machines within Mirage's infrastructure. How many EC2 machines are dedicated to GitLab? How many jobs are running per machine?

Everything is defined as code, so we track down the configuration of GitLab runners defined in the gitlab-settings repository:

```
[[runners]]
  name = "ruby-2.7-docker"
  url = "https://CI/"
```

```
token = "TOKEN"
limit = 10
executor = "docker"
[runners.custom_build_dir]
[runners.cache]
  [runners.cache.s3]
[runners.docker]
  tls_verify = false
  image = "alpine"
  privileged = true
```

Our eyes widen. Every job is running as a Docker container in privileged mode! That means that every job can directly access the machine's underlying disk storage and effectively take over the entire machine.

"You are right. This is the default setup on GitLab," replies Steve when we quiz him about these values. "We heavily rely on it to run Docker in Docker commands when building containers. We need to reach the Docker socket from within jobs so we need to run in privileged mode."

Ultimately, if every machine hosted one container, and one container *only*, that would not be an issue, but Mirage increased the level of parallelism allowed on its runners to boost performance and save costs:

```
[[runners]]
  name = "ruby-2.7-docker"
  url = "https://CI/"
  token = "TOKEN"
  limit = 10
  executor = "docker"
```

Every machine can, therefore, simultaneously run up to ten jobs, each one capable of snooping on the other nine. Even if we solve the branch protection issue and restrict secrets and credentials to jobs running on the master branch, an attacker would still be able to access them through tainted jobs running on non-protected branches. All they have to do is leverage the porous Docker configuration by mounting the underlying machine's file system and going through all the */proc/xx/environ* files of every running process[62].

Another flaw to remediate. They're literally popping up like mushrooms.

Moving on to the last step of app's lifecycle. Every app deployment is performed through a job launched at the end of the GitLab pipeline. It parses the app settings and creates the required resources in Kubernetes. The infrastructure team did not duplicate this code across all repos. Instead, they defined it in a central repo and leveraged the include directive in GitLab to inject it in every gitlab-ci.yml file.

---

[62] For detailed attacks on Docker, check out my book *How to Hack Like a Ghost* https://www.amazon.com/dp/B08FH9SQNG.

```
include:
  - project: global/gitlab-ci-files
    ref: v3.1.2
    file: deploy-prod.yml
```

We clone the repo global/gitlab-ci-files and explore the
deploy-prod.yml file:

```
...snip...

script: |
  aws eks update-kubeconfig --name prod
  kubectl apply -f
...snip...
```

Notice that kubectl deploys in the middle? That command requires
credentials. Credentials with extended rights, for that matter. We desperately
hope for these credentials to be defined as protected variables:

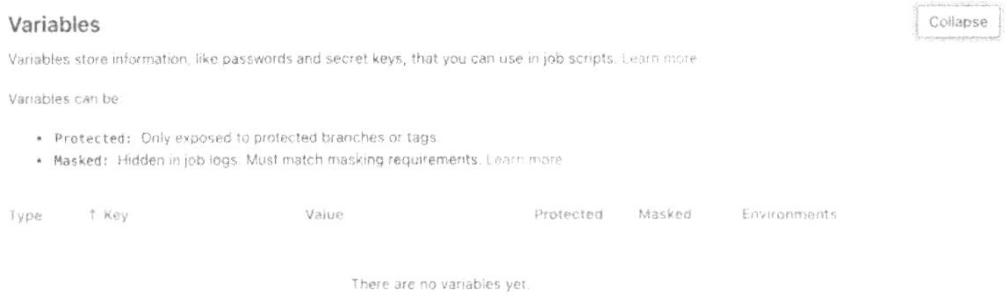

Variables   Collapse

Variables store information, like passwords and secret keys, that you can use in job scripts. Learn more

Variables can be

  • Protected: Only exposed to protected branches or tags
  • Masked: Hidden in job logs. Must match masking requirements. Learn more

Type   ↑ Key   Value   Protected   Masked   Environments

                             There are no variables yet

Figure 14-2: CI/CD variable defined at the project level

Wait, where are they? They're not at the repo level...We explore the
interface a bit and finally find them defined at the group level.

Group variables (inherited)
These variables are inherited from the parent group

Key   Environments   Group

TOOLING_PROD_DEPLOY_TOKEN   *   mirage

AWS_ACCESS_KEY_ID_PROD   *   mirage

KUBECONFIG_PRODUCTION   *   mirage

GITHUB_COM_TOKEN   *   mirage

Figure 14-3: CI/CD variables defined at the group level

So, that means anyone who creates a repo in this GitLab group, be it a test
repo or a real app, will inherit these production AWS access keys that later get
translated to a Kubernetes role. Let's check their access:

```
$ aws sts get-caller-identity
  {
```

```
    "UserId": " AIDA64CQXD7PJN48SSSV8",
    "Account": "789754624623",
    "Arn": " arn:aws:iam::886477354405:user/deploy-cicd-prod"
}
```

```
$ aws iam list-attached-user-policies \
  -- user-name=deploy-cicd-prod

"PolicyArn": "arn:aws:iam:: 789754624623:policy/decrypt-secrets",
"PolicyArn": "arn:aws:iam:: 789754624623:policy/eks-write",
...snip...
```

Oh, interesting, they can access the AWS Key Management Service to decrypt secrets. We go back to the deployment code and find the command that decrypts secrets. That's what Charles was referring to when talking about secrets weeks ago. Not only that, but these credentials can deploy and alter applications in Kubernetes. They're akin to admin...yet they're a free-for-all right now.

So, to sum up, with one merge request on the right repo, we can leak powerful credentials every day until Sunday, as well as abuse weak approvals, unprotected secrets, porous Docker configurations and so on.

It may seem like these flaws are specific to GitLab, but they are not. It's not the tool that is at fault, as we can find the same flaws in a many other Git-based vendors.

We start to glimpse the major threats that plague the GitOps and DevOps movements in general. Continuous improvement (CI) and continuous deployment (CD) get lumped up in a single acronym, but the CI part has a radically different risk profile from the CD part. CI means tests, fake data, staging environment. CD, on the other hand, represents deployment, often to production environments. One small misstep, one wrong optimization, one puny collision and the veil separating the two is punctured, leaking production and sometimes admin access to everyone: untested code pushed by a developer on their branch is running alongside a job that has the power to deploy containers to production. Test code is running on the same machine as the job changing components of the infrastructure and so on.

This risk is further exacerbated by the DevOps culture where the line between developers and operations are blurred and where everyone is supposed to chime into the infrastructure and handle the full lifecycle of their app.

In practice, we often accept that a developer can, if they really want to, ship malicious code into the app. Usually, this risk is mitigated by peer review, constraining the impact to a single business domain. Often times, this is further watered down with detection at the business level with methods such as financial consolidation reports. However, DevOps encourages developers to also handle the infrastructure used by their app. An infrastructure that is often times mutualized between multiple apps. Suddenly, the blast radius of one malicious change is no longer the app, but the whole infrastructure supporting it, and that's a radical shift in the risk profile that many teams readily accept without thinking of second-order effects, namely on security.

GitOps and DevOps are absolute revolutions. The decentralization and ease of management they provide are real game-changers, both in terms of maintainability and security. They solve one of security's hardest problems: how to escape the inevitable progression of chaos and slow death of hardened security settings—AKA: the second law of thermodynamics. Well, if the setting is hard-coded in a repo, you can easily track changes through Git and its review process. Should anyone bypass Git and manually switch that setting back to live on the system without changing the code, it will automatically revert to the old setting. That's precious and guarantees a stable level of security in time.

But there is an undeniable shift in the risk profile that one should absolutely be aware of when embracing these methodologies. The CI/CD platform will end up holding the keys to the kingdom, and one better make sure those keys are not carelessly scattered around the castle.

We've touched upon some remediation actions along the way, but let's quickly review the major and obvious threats we've covered so far to agree on prioritization:
* An attacker who opens a merge request on any repo can list unprotected secrets. These secrets sometimes have admin access, allowing them untethered access to the infrastructure and the app.
* An attacker who runs CI/CD jobs can take over the underlying machine to fetch production credentials from neighboring jobs.
* An attacker can sneak through, bypass or alter the approval settings and merge code in production, which will allow them to achieve admin access to the app and infrastructure.

We plot these threats in our graph, as usual, and think it over. The goal is not to forcefully destroy every threat scenario right this second. That will take time. Dealing with container isolation by replacing the privileged Docker runtime with something less porous like Sysbox[63] will take more than a snap of our fingers. It's much more efficient to throw money at the problem for now by reducing the job parallelism to one while we work on a long-term solution. Can we find other quick wins in this mess to at least reduce the risk to a more tolerable threshold?

As a first milestone, let's agree that a tolerable risk is any scenario that needs collusion of two or more people. So, essentially, every scenario involving a lone attacker playing with the CI/CD and wreaking havoc on their own is one we should fix. We accept that peer review is good enough to stop the most obvious attacks...at least for now. Once we deal with the current risk, we can question that assumption and address more complicated scenarios.

Branch protection seems like the quickest win. Every repo has a default protected branch set to *main* or *master*. Most interactions with the production environment happen on these branches by design. So, necessarily, most secrets can easily be restricted to this branch without any side effects. There will be some edge cases of some repo that needs read access to production data but, worst case, we can just limit these repositories to the few people needing them.

Richard jumps on the opportunity to deploy his Python scripting capabilities to list all secrets and all repos and start automating their branch protection setting.

"Just remember to test your changes beforehand and trigger the pipeline after your changes to make sure nothing breaks. Oh, and drop a message to each team before you start messing around with their pipelines." He knows the drill by now but better to be safe than sorry. Transparency and accountability are crucial for trust and good teamwork.

Branch protections are not much use if anybody can push code into the protected branches, which is the default setting on GitLab, mind you... We need to update that. This change should not pose many issues since developers are used to the merge request flow. We also take advantage of this opportunity to standardize the approval process: at least one approval everywhere. The person approving must be different from the author of the code or the merge request. These settings will upset one or two very small teams, but we can't have exceptions on any app that ends up being deployed to the production cluster. Repos that contain simple scripts and non-critical datasets can be spared for convenience, as long as they don't inherit powerful production credentials from their groups.

---

[63] http://bit.ly/3D4XYYR.

All these changes might seem radical, but in 99% of the cases, developers will not even notice them. These knobs were badly set, not because of some deliberate misconfiguration, but because the defaults are not good enough or following a one-time exception that lingered in time. The repository creation process is manual, so everybody ticked whatever boxes they saw. That's an important point that we need to take into consideration. It's always good to address the problem or the vulnerability, but that's only the symptom. We also need to fix the system, the structural thinking, and the way of doing that introduced that vulnerability in the first place. In this case, we must standardize the way we create and configure repositories in GitLab. We have to share with the infrastructure team the risk of running CI/CD pipelines and agree on a common set of good practices so we do not fall into the same traps.

These can be simple documents that we write and share, that maybe later we can translate into tooling and automation. GitOps applied to GitLab's own configuration in an interesting inception exercise. It will not happen overnight, but these are baby steps in the right direction.

Most developers don't need highly privileged roles on their repositories; they just need to push code. Occasionally, however, they need to set up environment variables for their CI/CD...which requires the maintainer role. This role also grants the possibility to remove every protection we just put in place... thank you, GitLab! If we're going to strip developers of their rights, we need to provide an easy way for them to set up these environment variables. Maybe a job on Jenkins that can set them up?

We'll cook something up in the near future, then downgrade everybody. The key is communication and timing. There is nothing worse than using security to block users from getting their work done. Let's offer them an alternative path, maybe even an easier one, see how they respond to that, adjust it to their feedback, and then cut the old access.

As we list these changes to perform across all our repositories, we can't help but appreciate our complete autonomy to make so many profound changes to our app and infrastructure landscape. No vendor can help us enforce these changes. No Jira ticket will help us get this done. Only our relentless capability to build, run and own security changes from the ground up will help us make a dent in the company.

We can go through the implementation phase of these various improvements to our CI/CD pipeline, but you already know the drill by now: proof of concept, technical document, review, delivery and monitoring!

So, let's just wrap up this chapter and move to the conclusion.

Next up

Just like every Monday for the past few months since we joined Mirage, we hold our weekly security meeting with Richard to go through our threat graph. Sometimes it's a five-minute meeting to confirm that our current priorities are still justified. Other times it's a fifteen-minute meeting that leads to an hour of follow-up by chat to discuss this or that attack scenario exploiting some new feature recently put in production.

When compliance comes probing around, we refer them to this graph or its nicer Excel version. When Henry asks about our roadmap, we send him this graph. When auditors come sticking their nose in our business, we slap that graph on their desk—along with the half-dozen policies we wrote. It's our most fundamental framework to make sure we deliver quality to our customers, and by quality, we mean relevant features and improvements to counter real-life attacks.

So many companies start the exercise backwards. They begin with a list of common practices and justify them *ex-post facto* in a meeting or in a risk analysis. They mind numbingly go down that ISO 27001 list, gleefully ticking meaningless boxes of wishy-washy security platitudes, thinking that they contributed to the security of the platform. The goal of security is not compliance. It's thwarting attackers while helping the business to thrive! The threat graph is a great way to always keep that in sight.

Around this decision framework, we're building a team of engineers that can deliver code, infrastructure components, policies and other tangible assets to improve security. We're currently two in the team but we're actively recruiting and looking for new potential. It's challenging. It requires constant learning and sometimes frustrating flexibility, but all that is quickly washed away by the thrill of fixing something that would otherwise stay broken for ages. If you learn to get high from solving problems, you'll likely do good in life.

And finally, we built a symbiosis with other teams: product managers, developers, infrastructure, even compliance, really. We are here to help them get shit done fast and securely. That's a competitive advantage. Sure, sometimes we blow up an app because of an edge case we did not anticipate, but everyone eventually does. That's the price of learning. We responsibly pick up the pieces, learn from what went wrong, improve our methodology, QA plans, testing phase and development practices and reiterate. This virtuous cycle is fueled by the strong sponsorship of a pragmatic executive who wants to see things move forward.

All in all, over the past few months, we seeded the ground that will allow us to scale efficiently. We need more people like Richard with the same spirit and hunger to learn. Of course, if we can find very experienced people who are willing to work in such high velocity teams, then all the better. But, we will have access to a much larger pool of talent if we also bet on potential.

As we iterate over the threat graph, going after each threat scenario and their underlying vulnerabilities by order of priority, we will inevitably start stacking up security layers one after the other. Take the app exploitation threat. An attacker might find a remote code execution on the app, spawn a shell, connect to the database and start siphoning data. We've already greatly reduced the probability of that first hop by adding a WAF in front of each app exposed on the Internet. Once we've rounded up all such one-vulnerability hops, we're bound to come back to this scenario and reprioritize it. Now, we consider that the WAF is no longer robust enough and readily assume that attackers with enough resources will find a neat way to bypass it. This assumption is critical. We must have the courage to postulate it even though we, ourselves, could not bypass it. The worst mistake defenders make is project their limitations onto the attacker. Leave your ego aside. Just because you could not figure it out, does not mean a kid in Sweden won't.

The WAF is breached. How can we stop an attacker after that? Let's see, we can harden containers by removing frivolous utilities: `curl`, `bash`, `git`, `whoami`, `vim`, `hostname` and so on. A container that runs a web server does not need all these tools, yet they are so important for an attacker to easily navigate an unknown environment. Hell, even remote code execution payloads are tested with `curl`, `cat` and `whoami` commands. On top of that, let's make every folder read-only, except for */tmp* and some local cache folders.

That's our second layer right there. Say they bypass this hardening and find a way to leverage rudimentary tools to interact with this restricted environment. In that case, we stop them from easily breaking out of the container by running the apps as non-root users. Combined with the hostile environment we set up, that should make it a bit harder for them.

What if they still manage to land a viable shell? Okay, let's add on top some system call monitoring with tools such as Auditd or Falco to detect suspicious behavior and quickly shut it down. When you think about it, a Rails or Python server rarely spits out a child "/bin/sh" process. Let's make a rule that detects that. A Rails server almost never queries the AWS metadata endpoint 169.254.169.254, or reads "/etc/passwd" or has a child root shell.

By following the attacker's route as they break every layer of security we put in place, we can stack just the right layer to make their life a tad more uncomfortable. We will take them down with a thousand paper cuts rather than a massive hammer blow.

We can flip the scenario and go after the root cause of the vulnerability instead. Let's make sure we detect potential remote code executions when the code is pushed to production. For instance, let's add simple vulnerability and dependency scans to the merge-request cycle. Every developer who pushes code triggers these scans. They would run in parallel to the classic unit tests so as not to incur any delays. Full open-source solutions that cost literally zero dollars and can bring tremendous value. Now, developers are forced to upgrade their dependencies every now and then. We decentralize an otherwise burdensome task and improve velocity[64].

We can adopt the same approach for patching systems and applications. Open-source tools like *dependabot* or *renovatebot* or even custom-made ones can automatically fetch the latest dependencies, propose upgrades that people can validate and apply with a simple click of a button. Unit tests and ideally integration tests are there to guarantee the safety of these changes. That's how a team of two or three people can manage an up-to-date inventory of over a hundred apps. Automation and decentralization.

Running down the threat graph, we naturally land on all these best security practices that one may find hidden in any evangelized security standard. The difference is the path through which we reach them. On the one hand, we reach a current practice because it deals with the next natural progression of a given attack. The choice inevitable. The timing is just right. On the other hand, we somehow must deduce the next action from the generically phrased control number 125 in a pre-defined list because it's the next item on the list. That's a vastly different paradigm.

Using the same drill-down technique, we will eventually land on VPN network isolation to separate each population according to their required access, whitelisting apps on servers, reviewing network filtering rules, restricting production access, cleaning exposed credentials from logs, centralizing application secrets in a vault, reviewing database access and so many other projects that will continuously pop in and out of existence as the company keeps growing and we keep unearthing new attack scenarios.

---

[64] Examples of open source static vulnerability scanners: *https://github.com/google/osv-scanner*, *https://brakemanscanner.org*

Every single one of these aforementioned projects is an opportunity for the security team to level up on a technology. Hardening containers is easier said than done. It implies going over every app, making an inventory of what binaries are needed, updating the Docker file to use multi-stage containers—that is, a first base image to build the app and a second minimalist one to run the actual binary. An incredibly delicate process that can blow up midflight if a customer calls an HTTP endpoint that triggers an image conversion for which we forgot the binary. No developer or infrastructure team will take the responsibility of implementing such a radical change. It won't happen, period. Even if it does, the process will hardly consistently repeat itself across the 10 different teams required to cover all the micro services.

It is up to us to lead the change, learn about the business, the app, the environment, the QA process and make it happen! And frankly, that's way more exciting than desperately tracking Jira tickets that keep piling up like dirty dishes on a lazy Sunday.

Anyone can rant on a ticket. A precious few can create value. Strive to be the latter.

Printed in Great Britain
by Amazon